RAILWAY ARCHITECTURE

RAILWAY ARCHITECTURE

Written by members and associates of
SAVE Britain's Heritage

Edited by MARCUS BINNEY
and DAVID PEARCE

BLOOMSBURY BOOKS
LONDON

© 1979 by SAVE Britain's Heritage
Library of Congress Catalog Card Number 79-23203

Printed in Great Britain

First published 1979 by Orbis Publishing Limited, London.
This edition published in 1985 by Bloomsbury Books, an
imprint of Godfrey Cave Associates Limited, 42 Bloomsbury Street,
London WC1B 3QJ by arrangement with Orbis Publishing
and Save Britain's Heritage (Association).

Frontispiece: Thorpe Station, Norwich

16 15 14 13 12 11 10 9 8 7 6 5 4 3 2 1

Library of Congress Cataloging in Publication Data
Main entry under title:

Railway architecture.

  Bibliography: p.
  Includes index.
  1. Railroads – Great Britain – Buildings and
Structures. 2. Architecture – Great Britain – History.
I. Binney, Marcus. II. Pearce, David.
III. Save Britain's Heritage (Association)
TF270.R34   725'.3   79-23203
ISBN 0 906223 62 8

CONTENTS

INTRODUCTION · MARCUS BINNEY 6

MAJOR CITY STATIONS · DAVID ATWELL 24

LARGE TOWN STATIONS · DAVID LLOYD 48

SMALL TOWN STATIONS · PETER BURMAN 68

COUNTRY AND SUBURBAN STATIONS · ALAN YOUNG 88

RAILWAY HOTELS · CHRISTOPHER MONKHOUSE 118

BRIDGES AND VIADUCTS · RICHARD HUGHES 140

ENGINE SHEDS · CHRIS HAWKINS AND GEORGE REEVE 160

RAILWAY TOWNS · SOPHIE ANDREAE 176

HALF STEAM AHEAD · DAVID PEARCE 190
British Rail's Attitude Today

REUSING RAILWAY BUILDINGS · MARCUS BINNEY 206

APPENDIX · MATTHEW SAUNDERS 230
Notes on Selected Stations and Associated Buildings

BIBLIOGRAPHY 248
BIOGRAPHICAL NOTES ON CONTRIBUTORS 249
PICTURE ACKNOWLEDGMENTS 250   INDEX 251

INTRODUCTION
MARCUS BINNEY

T HE PURPOSE of this book is to champion the cause of railway architecture, not just the railway stations, whether great termini or small yet delightful country halts, but the whole range of railway buildings, hotels, goods warehouses, engine sheds, train sheds, locomotive carriage and rolling stock works, bridges and viaducts, signal boxes, stationmasters' houses, railway workers' cottages and model villages. The railway companies were among the greatest patrons of architecture the nineteenth century produced. They were able to call upon the best architects available, both great names and new talents. The roll-call includes Sir Robert Rowand Anderson, George Townsend Andrews, W. N. Ashbee, Isambard Kingdom Brunel, Lewis Cubitt, John Dobson, Sir John Fowler, the elder and the younger Hardwick, J. W. Livock, David Mocatta, Sir Joseph Paxton, Sir George Gilbert Scott, both Stephensons, Francis Thompson, Sir William Tite, Charles Trubshaw, Sancton Wood and Sir Matthew Digby Wyatt.

Railway architecture ranges across the entire spectrum of nineteenth-century styles: classical, Gothic, Tudor, Jacobean, Wrenaissance, Deuxième Empire, Arts and Crafts, *cottage orné* and vernacular revival. No less impressive and remarkable are the more purely functional structures, many of which are landmarks in engineering development – the vast iron-arched roofs of the termini, the cast iron bridges over roads and canals, and above all the great viaducts.

The railway companies built to last. Their buildings remain among the most massive and enduring structures of the nineteenth century, and only the most complete, and short-sighted, neglect of standard day-to-day maintenance has brought about their deterioration.

The importance of the London termini in Britain's architectural history, indeed in architectural development all over the world, is now recognized – less so that of the great train sheds of other cities. Glasgow St Enoch, unforgivably destroyed in European Architectural Heritage Year, Manchester Central, slowly rotting away, and the great curved sheds at York and Newcastle, where to alight from an inter-city express is still a thrilling architectural experience. In numerous provincial cities and towns the railway station stands out as one of the best and the most significant public buildings. Huddersfield's great classical station, as handsome as any Victorian town hall, is the only building in the town listed as Grade 1; in Stoke-on-Trent, Winton Square, with the station, the railway offices on either side and the North Stafford Hotel opposite, forms, in Pevsner's words, the 'finest piece of Victorian axial planning in the country'.

Numerous smaller provincial towns – county towns and market towns – also boast a proud station; some of the best are to be found in spas, as at Malvern and Ashby-de-la-Zouch. Then come numerous interesting and delightful suburban stations, round not only London but also a number of provincial cities, notably Liverpool and Newcastle.

Finally there are the country stations, the still un-

discovered gems of railway architecture, many beautifully looked after, many transformed into houses, but, alas, too many still empty or derelict. Sometimes a whole series of small stations on a country line will be built in a single style, like Livock's gabled stations in the Midlands or Mocatta's stations in Surrey and Sussex. Good country stations, many of course closed, also abound in Northumberland. Enchanting too are buildings like the black and white bargeboarded station at Fenny Stratford, Buckinghamshire, the appropriately Gothic station at Battle, Sussex,

resort in Europe in late Victorian and Edwardian times. All too few, alas, remain in use to remind us of their splendour – the best, at St Pancras, is now part unused and part offices – but a visit to the Great Eastern or the Charing Cross is still a marvellous experience, and British Transport Hotels is now restoring the Grosvenor Hotel in Victoria to its former glory, though tragically a fire gutted the twin pavilion roofs at one end during cleaning. In Liverpool the Adelphi still conveys Edwardian opulence while the Caledonian and the North British are still the two best hotels in Edinburgh.

looking like the best of village schools, and the neo-Norman station at Glendon and Rushton, Northamptonshire.

The railway companies were also crucial in the development of the nineteenth-century grand hotel, of the type that sprang up in every spa and

Above *Middlesbrough, Cleveland; iron bridge with guilloche panels*
Right *London Euston; wrought ironwork gate at the old station*
Previous page *Glasgow St Enoch; the outer arch of the train shed, destroyed in 1975, European Architectural Heritage Year*

Among the railway's industrial buildings the great circular engine sheds, notably Robert Stephenson's noble Roundhouse in Camden, have long had a place in histories of functional architecture. However, the huge locomotive carriage and rolling stock works were also the most extensive industrial complexes of their time, larger than the greatest textile mills and rivalling the biggest iron foundries. The best, at Crewe, have recently been ignominiously destroyed after years of abandonment. However, the great locomotive works at Swindon survive, laid out to view before every passenger on the new high speed trains – a magnificant and superbly constructed series of enormous sheds, some of brick, some of stone.

The other principal industrial landmarks left by the railways are the warehouses, principally in the industrial towns of the Midlands and the north. At the best these huge, austere buildings, still very much in the Georgian tradition, are not far behind the greatest of contemporary dock buildings, such as St Katherine's Dock in London or the Albert Dock in Liverpool. Burton-upon-Trent, for example, besides its great series of breweries and maltings has two memorable railway warehouses, the Midland Railway bonded warehouse in Derby Road and the Great Northern Railway grain warehouse off Wetmore Road. Neither of these, it is worth noting, is mentioned in Pevsner's volume on Staffordshire. Almost all the Pennine mill towns in addition to their numerous impressive mills have good railway warehouses worth seeking out.

The railway's greatest contribution to the townscape of the industrial north, however, is the spectacular series of viaducts carrying the railways to the Pennine mill towns. Deservedly the most famous is the vast double red brick viaduct at Stockport, so deep that it seems almost like a tunnel as one passes under it, so massive that each pier seems to have consumed a million bricks. 'As I make up [my paintings],' Lowry wrote, 'I suddenly *know* I must bring in the Stockport viaduct ... I love it ... it is a part of my life, my dream.'

On the Yorkshire side of the Pennines, the viaducts, like the mills, change from brick to stone: the most breathtaking are the stately curving

Above *Glasgow Queen Street; capital in cast iron. The railway companies were fond of varying the detail of the classical orders*
Below, right *Glasgow; tenements framing the railway*

viaduct entering Huddersfield across the Colne, the enormous viaduct striding diagonally across the Calder Valley between Sowerby Bridge and Halifax and the awe-inspiring viaduct at Saddleworth, with a huge skew arch over the canal in the centre. Many of these northern cities and towns have marvellous iron railway bridges as well as viaducts; one of the best series, complete with battlemented turrets, is on the approach of the Liverpool line into Manchester as it passes the abandoned Liverpool Road and Central stations. They are certainly worth a visit, but soon, for cast iron bridges all over the country, because of their uncertain compression, are scheduled for replacement.

The best railway bridges in Britain, like Brunel's great Royal Albert Bridge at Saltash or the Forth Railway Bridge, hold a high place among the engineering marvels of the world: but we should never forget how vulnerable they are. Stephenson's tubular bridge over the Menai Straits was, in terms of progress in the history of construction, as important as Brunelleschi's dome for Florence Cathedral. Yet when it was gutted British Rail renewed it with supporting arches beneath, the very thing Stephenson, with his box girder construction, had eliminated – a case of so-called progress in engineering working exactly in reverse. Many of the railway tunnels are magnificent engineering achievements. None perhaps is more moving than the twin three mile tunnels built to take the Leeds–Manchester line through the Pennines. They were replaced within a few years of completion by a double tunnel nearby which is still in use today: yet though they have been abandoned for more than a century, so sure was their construction that even today one can see a speck of light at the far end.

Above *Rothley, Leicestershire; ornamental framing to station signs*
Right *London Blackfriars Bridge; ironwork of superb quality*

Finally come the railway towns and villages. Brunel's marvellous railway village at Swindon, only a decade ago threatened with complete obliteration, has now been restored in exemplary fashion by the District Council. By contrast, in the railway village at Wolverton, Buckinghamshire, where every house was listed, some 300 were nevertheless completely destroyed in 1975, the largest single massacre of listed buildings that has ever taken place.

In surveying this uniquely rich legacy of architectural, industrial, engineering and social history, it emerges that the present-day British Rail's board is probably the providential if unwilling steward of one of the greatest physical inheritances from the nineteenth century to be found anywhere in Western Europe. Yet since nationalization in 1947 British Rail's record as trustee of this unique legacy of usable, lettable real estate has been quite appalling. For while stations and other buildings are technically written into the annual accounts as assets, the attitude of railway management has been to regard every inherited building as a liability. The most elementary maintenance has been neglected, and as buildings have deteriorated in condition they have attracted vandalism. This has created a downward spiral of dirt and dereliction which has dented the whole image of the railways themselves, for as stations become shabby, untidy places, people are inevitably discouraged from travelling by rail.

Since its establishment in 1947 British Rail has acquired for itself an all too deserved reputation as the biggest corporate vandal and iconoclast Britain has seen since the Tudor dissolution of the monasteries. No single act of destruction quite ranks with the demolition of Penn Central station in New York, probably the greatest preventable architectural loss since 1945 in the West; yet the destruction of the Euston Arch, and the station and hotel behind; the demolition of the great train sheds at Glasgow St Enoch and Birmingham New Street; the total write-off of Birkenhead Woodside and Bradford Exchange; the loss of the Crewe works and of the great viaduct at Crumlin; the sale *for scrap* of the Cornish beam engines at Sudbrook, the finest and most dramatic group of engines in the

12

GONG WARNING
IN AND OUTSIDE LEEDS GOOD SHED
INSTRUCTIONS TO SHUNTERS POINT HOLDERS
WAREHOUSE STAFF HORSEMEN & OTHERS
THE POINT HOLDER BEFORE TURNING ANY
WAGON INTO THE WAREHOUSE ROAD MUST
SOUND GONG IN WAREHOUSE THREE TIMES
HE MUST ALSO GIVE NOTICE TO STAFF
OUTSIDE BY SOUNDING GONG FIXED ON WALL
AS FOLLOWS VIZ SOUND GONG AT SIDINGS
BEFORE SENDING WAGONS DOWN NO I ONCE
2   TWICE
3   THREE TIMES
4   FOUR TIMES
5   FIVE TIMES
6   SIX TIMES

Left *Halifax, West Yorkshire; gong warning*
Right *Saddleworth, Greater Manchester; viaduct. Note the skew arch as the railway crosses the canal above this Pennine milltown*
Below *Fort William, Highland; scenic grandeur*
Below left *Betchworth, Surrey; twisted column lamp standard*

INTRODUCTION

Far left *Hove, Sussex ; tunnel – note the rubbed brick voussoirs of the arch*
Left *Glasgow St Enoch ; demolished. Acanthus ornament to column base*
Below *Stratford East, London ; fine* porte-cochère *on square iron columns*

Above *Bristol Temple Meads; castellated door with dated scroll*

Left *Bramhope Tunnel, West Yorkshire; elaborate example of a tunnel entrance built as an ornamental landscape feature*

world; the dismantling of untold numbers of fine bridges, the destruction of hundreds of good small stations and the barbarous mutilation of thousands continuing in use, both large and small, put British Rail in a category of vandal all of its own.

All over Britain delightful country stations are left abandoned, as the photographs in this book show in all too graphic detail.

Yet the last two years (beginning in 1977) have seen a remarkable change in British Rail's approach to its great legacy. Millstones have been transformed into opportunities. Credit, as the final chapters show, must go to the new Chairman of British Rail, Sir Peter Parker. Launching a railway exhibition train in August 1977 he told the audience:

> British Rail are the keepers of a great national heritage.... We do our best, but we know it can't be good enough. But let me make it plain, we have a creative concern and for two reasons. First the heritage justifies itself, and, secondly, if we can do it justice, it's an added attraction to our customer service. Our paramount concern is our customer, and his or her confidence in us. That means the look of the railways matters.

Since then a major programme of station rehabilitation has been set in motion. In the summer of 1978 British Rail launched a series of advertisements stating unequivocally, 'Preserving the nation's architectural heritage has to be British Rail's concern.' Two years earlier such a statement would have been unthinkable. This is the measure of the progress that has been made.

This book is a first attempt at surveying the full diversity and significance of railway buildings. Though it has benefited hugely from the recent work of railway historians, notably Gordon Biddle, Professor Dyos and David Lloyd (who is a contributor), it cannot, of course, claim to be a comprehensive study. Nevertheless we hope that it will be of lasting value. In particular the collection of photographs taken specially by Christopher Dalton provides a unique record of our railway heritage.

Above *Corbridge, Northumberland; detail of the ironbridge*
Left *St Neots, Cambridgeshire; delightful wooden signal box with gothic detail*

22

SAVE's principal concern is to prevent the destruction of worthwhile buildings, but we also wish to stress the vital need to record, to document and to investigate railway architecture. The kind of systematic recording that is carried out on domestic, ecclesiastical and vernacular architecture needs to be developed for railway architecture. This is a contribution that can be made, indeed, must be made, largely from outside British Rail, by architectural schools, by polytechnics, by museums, by voluntary groups. The more we understand the unique achievements of the builders of the railways, the more we will interest people in the conservation, the continued use, not just of historic engines and rolling stock, but of all the diverse structures with which the railway pioneers endowed us.

Above *Roxburgh & Melrose, Roxburghshire; Grecian gentleman's lavatory with acroteria motif on the vents*
Left *Toddington, Gloucestershire; though little more than a halt, buildings were provided on both sides*

MAJOR CITY STATIONS

DAVID ATWELL

THE BUILDING of the great city termini railway stations was one of the most striking architectural developments of the mid-nineteenth century. It was a direct product of the Industrial Revolution. Not only was the building type innovative, the resultant structures were monumental in scale and unparalleled in their impact upon the city scene. No such significant addition to the townscape had occurred since the cathedrals of the Middle Ages.

The colossal train sheds and terminus hotels, made necessary by the numbers of passengers able to travel rapidly for the first time between large towns and cities, are an extraordinary social phenomenon. Another feature is of particular architectural and historical significance. This is the actual structure of the iron-arched train shed, perhaps the most remarkable structural development of the early Victorian period. The use of this type of great arched truss enabled, for the first time, very wide spaces to be spanned without any intermediate support. The first railway station to introduce this form of roof construction was Newcastle Central, begun in 1848 to the designs of John Dobson. Brunel's train shed at Paddington, begun in 1850, was the next, and between 1850 and 1890 there followed a notable series of celebrated stations ranging from the modest statement of Bath Green Park to the airy grace of York or to the massiveness of sheer scale of enclosed space at St Pancras. Sadly, this great series of monuments has been depleted by the incursions of both war and developers. Middlesbrough, designed by William Peachey in 1877, had a fine pointed-arch roof which was destroyed by bombing in the last war. Birkenhead Woodside, built in 1878 to the designs of R. E. Johnston and demolished in 1969, had an iron-arched train shed matched by a magnificent Gothic booking hall with an open timber truss roof of truly baronial proportions. Birmingham New Street, where the iron roof, built in 1854 to the design of E. A. Cowper, had a vast maximum span of 211 feet, was destroyed in the mid-1960s, to be replaced by the present coldly efficient airport-like terminal. At Glasgow St Enoch the colossal iron train shed was neglected for so long following the closure of the station in the mid-1960s that the structure became dangerous; its demolition during 1975 was an ignominious tribute to European Architectural Heritage Year.

The destruction of St Enoch is probably the most important desecration by British Rail since the infamous days of the demolition of Hardwick's Euston Arch in 1962. Built in 1875–9 to the design of engineers Sir John Fowler and James Blair, the superb iron arches of St Enoch had a span of 198 feet, and together with the huge contemporary Gothic station hotel (the third largest in Europe when it was built) formed the Midland Railway's complementary city terminus to London St Pancras. Having removed the train shed, the iconoclastic British Rail commenced demolition of the hotel and its cast iron *porte-cochère* late in 1977.

Any definition of the point at which a major city station becomes merely a large town station must necessarily be subjective: Hull Paragon, Chester, Stoke-on-Trent, Carlisle, Monkwearmouth and Huddersfield, for example, have terminal buildings

York; 1874. The curving train shed by William Peachey

or train sheds on a scale to rival any city, but when they were built they were not the termini of major railway lines, more the pompous achievements of local railway magnates. London Clapham Junction covers a greater acreage than any other station, and carries more through trains per day than any other; but few actually stop there, and, in spite of the elegant detailing of the long platform canopies, the station is really no more than a series of disconnected architectural incidents loosely linked either by bridge or subway and without any major polarizing force by way of a terminal building.

Above *London Euston; train sheds by Stephenson. Demolished 1962*
Right *London Euston; the Great Hall 1846–9. Philip and P. C. Hardwick. Replaced 1962–6*

Much the same can be said of Crewe, a station destined for greater fame in railway literary folklore than in architectural appraisal.

Any selective survey of the major city stations must begin with London, and, discounting certain lesser inner-city stations, fourteen large station termini remain in central London. Several of these can be more briefly discussed: Euston dates entirely now from 1962–6, and was designed by R. L. Moorcroft, architect to the Midland Region. However, it must not be forgotten that before the present unwelcoming edifice was constructed, there stood on the site the first railway station to be built in a capital city, the terminus to the London and Birmingham line, opened in 1837, the first long-distance railway out of London. The vast triumphal Greek arch by Philip Hardwick senior, the Roman Great Hall of 1846–9 by him and his son, and the utilitarian and simple iron roofs of the train sheds by Robert Stephenson all stood witness until the early 1960s of a complex of buildings that was of national, historic and architectural importance. Broad Street station, the terminus of the North London Railway, dates originally from 1865–6 and was designed by William Baker. It was considered good enough in 1868 for the *Building News* to remark that the 'exterior is superior to that of any other London station'. The once splendid terminus building in the Lombardic style is now all but submerged under later accretions of 1913 by the London and North-Western Railway associated with the Central Line link. The platform canopies were truncated in 1968, and only the stub ends of the 100 foot span twin iron roofs survive. Used now only by the few passengers on the dying North London route to Richmond, this great decaying station seems more of a ghost from the past even than Marylebone, and it is hard to imagine that it once was second only to Liverpool Street in the number of trains arriving daily. Blackfriars began as St Paul's station in May 1886 and was designed by J. Wolfe Barry, H. M. Brunel and Mills. It was the terminus of the London, Chatham and Dover Railway; an extension of this line penetrates further into the City to the now rebuilt Holborn Viaduct station. Blackfriars itself has been

rebuilt, but fortunately the traveller is still regaled by the rusticated pilasters that flanked the original entrance listing the names of the principal foreign stations that could be reached direct: St Petersburg, Leipzig, Brindisi, Baden-Baden, Cannes . . .

Cannon Street, to use the words of Sir John Betjeman, is now no more than a contemptible shed. Built in 1865–6 as the terminus of the South-Eastern Railway, the train shed was designed by E. M. Barry and Sir John Hawkshaw. It was demolished in 1958–61, yielding 1,000 tons of scrap metal and leaving the flanking cupola water towers to the iron-arched train shed sticking out incongruously over the Thames. The City Terminus Hotel, also designed by E. M. Barry, survived war damage until the 1960s (it was in a room in the City Terminus, in its later guise as an office block, that Betjeman once discovered a meeting of the mysteriously named Upper Ouse Catchment Board in progress). It has all gone now, replaced by a bland and profitable office tower block. Fenchurch Street is small and hidden away, but is of considerable architectural importance. Designed by the engineer George Berkeley in 1853–4 as terminus for the London and Blackwall Railway, it has one of the earliest iron-arched train sheds in London. The front is a delightful and curvaceous interplay of shapes between the wide segmental arch of the train shed roof, expressed as though it were a wide brick pediment, and the frilly zigzag timber canopy that protects passengers at street level. The effect will hardly be improved by British Rail's intention to replace the train shed (admittedly of little interest) by an office block over the tracks; it is to be hoped that the superb cast iron stairs up to the trains, will survive.

London Bridge, designed by George Smith and extended in 1844 by Henry Roberts, was the station for the first London steam railway, the London and Greenwich, which opened in 1836 and ran to Greenwich on an almost continuously roof-top viaduct of brick arches. Apart from the complex developments of different railway lines that terminated at London Bridge, the buildings themselves have undergone many vicissitudes, including additions in 1850–51 by Samuel Beazley, culminating in the present-barrel-vaulted train shed completed in

1866. A high level station was added in 1864 on the extension to Waterloo and Charing Cross. It is now a profoundly complicated, muddled and architecturally undistinguished assembly of buildings that sits uncomfortably cheek by jowl with Southwark Cathedral. The terminus hotel, built in 1861 and later converted to offices, was demolished following war damage sustained in December 1940, and the station itself has never really recovered from the wartime fire-bomb attacks. The major redevelopment of the station, now in progress, will undoubtedly simplify the planning and

Above *London King's Cross; 1852. The remarkably modern main front built to the design of Lewis Cubitt*
Right *London Cannon Street; 1865–6. Sir John Hawkshaw. The towers incongruously survive following demolition of the train shed in 1958–61*

tidy up the mess, though judgement must be reserved upon its architectural merits.

More than any other London terminus, Marylebone station wears the mantle of times passed by that will never be recaptured. Outside the rush hours it is a nearly deserted red brick hulk that seems to be merely marking time awaiting its fate. To some the hush that pervades the station is one of nostalgia, of ghosts, of intangible but historic atmosphere; to others it is decay, an almost total lack of modernization and the station feels like a stranded dying whale. Marylebone was the vision

of a Manchester cotton magnate, Sir Edward William Watkin, who dreamed of a Great Central Railway linking Manchester, Sheffield and Lincolnshire with London. The station was designed by Sir Douglas and Francis Fox, with architectural advice from H. W. Braddock, and it was opened in March 1899. Never a commercial success, the station was not completed and it was said that the initials MS & L stood not for Manchester, Sheffield and Lincolnshire but for Money Sunk and Lost, and the Great Central initials GC for Gone Completely. The Great Central Hotel, designed by

Colonel Robert Edis for Sir Blundell Maple, is now British Rail office headquarters. The end of steam in 1966 meant the end of through services to Rugby and Nottingham. Suburban diesel trains run now only as far as Aylesbury and Banbury. Three utterly contrasting elements still give Marylebone an air of some distinction: the delicate cast iron canopy across the private forecourt road; the best unaltered station bar in London, serving a multitude of brands of Real Ale; and the survival of the last large steam engine turntable in London in the sidings at the end of the platforms.

The earliest great London terminus still intact is King's Cross, which, apart from the travel centre in the front, remains virtually as it was built. It was the start of the celebrated Great Northern line, founded in 1846, and the station was completed in 1852 to the designs of the architect Lewis Cubitt and the engineers Sir William and Joseph Cubitt, members of a remarkable family famous for civil engineering and speculative building. The front of the station is one of the most simple, direct, functional and surprisingly modern of all major Victorian public buildings: a monumental, plain stock brick screen of two semicircular openings, framed with recessed arches, following the curve of the twin train sheds behind. When it was opened King's Cross was the largest station in England, and the simplicity of the concept of the train sheds is admirable: one for arrivals and the other for departures, separated by a superb arched brick colonnade. In fact the station suffered both operational and structural problems in its early days, necessitating reconstruction of platform layouts, and the replacement of both train shed roofs. These had originally been of laminated wood, a challenging structural experiment on such a scale, inspired by the use of the technique at the Czar's riding school in Moscow. However, before long the horizontal thrust proved excessive, and they were replaced with the present iron-ribbed roofs to the eastern shed in 1869–70, to the western in 1886–7. Nevertheless, the interior of the station carries an atmosphere of mystery and expectancy about it; travelling from King's Cross is still an exciting experience, a quality curiously absent from St Pancras

next door. Similarly, the front of the station, in spite of the recent inadequately designed additions to improve passenger facilities, is a superb architectural statement in its monumental plainness that is all the more effective for being seen in juxtaposition with the High Victorian excesses of St Pancras.

Paddington station followed. Begun in 1850 and completed in 1854, it was built to a design produced by a collaboration between the engineer Isambard Kingdom Brunel and the architect Matthew Digby Wyatt. It was, and is, the terminus of the Great Western Railway, still the British Rail region with by far the most distinctive individual character and feeling of tradition. Brunel was without doubt the greatest of all nineteenth-century engineers, the designer of celebrated bridges like those over the Tamar and the Avon, magnificent stations like Bristol Temple Meads and Bath Spa, major tunnels like Box, and a series of revolutionary steamships. His train shed at Paddington is perhaps the culminating triumph of British engineering and architecture of the nineteenth century.

Brunel's vision was of a vast, glazed, aisled cathedral. Cast iron columns support a gigantic triple roof where every third arched rib rests directly on a slender octagonal pier, the intermediate ones on open cross members; the 'nave' is 102 feet wide and the 'aisles' 70 feet and 68 feet respectively; and there are two pairs of unique 'transepts' along the sides. In 1909–16 a fourth matching shed was added on the north-east side, with a span of 109 feet. Matthew Digby Wyatt, hardly a figure of front-rank importance among Victorian architects, seems to have played a subsidiary role in all this, and his most felicitous contribution is the treatment of the wall flanking platform 1. Paddington station is the only major London terminus without a principal exterior façade; the train sheds are fitted into a cutting, and the adjacent and sadly mutilated Great Western Hotel (designed by P. C. Hardwick) was not part of the original Brunel scheme, although it opened at the same time. Largely thanks to the small proportion of commuter traffic using the station, and the subdued nature of internal modernization schemes, Paddington remains a station in the grand manner where travelling is an occasion.

Although at first glance there is little external evidence of this, Victoria is chronologically the next major London terminus. The original station was the successor to the Pimlico terminus of the West End of London and Crystal Palace Railway, and it developed as two stations: the terminus serving the London, Brighton and South Coast Railway, completed in 1860 to the designs of the engineer Robert Jacomb Hood; and that for the London, Chatham and Dover Railway completed in 1862 and designed by Sir John Fowler. In effect, later alterations now mean that three stations in one

Below *London Paddington; 1850–54. I. K. Brunel and Matthew Digby Wyatt. The splendid roofs of Brunel's train sheds*
Overleaf *London St Pancras; 1865–8. The train shed by W. H. Barlow*

can be appreciated. The oldest is that of the LC & DR, and, in spite of war damage, the original buildings and train shed survive almost intact off Wilton Road where they form the Continental section of Victoria main station. The damaged domestic-scale booking hall block may not amount to much architecturally, but Fowler's airy train sheds with their thin iron ribs are of more than passing historical interest. Next to this is its successor as the terminal building to the South-Eastern and Chatham Continental Line, as it became known, a robust and lively Portland stone Edwardian baroque building with much richly rumbustious detailing, by Sir Arthur Blomfield. Finally, behind the principal forecourt, with its inelegant steel shed of a bus station of 1971, lies the pompous rebuilt headquarters of the SE & CR, begun in 1898, and a monument of overscaled Renaissance detailing in red brick and stone. Beyond this again in Buckingham Palace Road lies the best building at Victoria, the magnificent and now no longer soot-blackened Grosvenor Hotel of 1860–61, designed by J. T. Knowles, a splendid exercise in High Victorian French Renaissance, and in many ways the most architecturally impressive of all London railway hotels. Although this heterogeneous collection of buildings is a fascinating study historically, and few can deny the nostalgia of the traditional way to Paris and the Continent (or the immortality of the discovery of Worthing, in *The Importance of Being Earnest*, in a handbag in the Brighton line cloakroom), Victoria remains an overcrowded and claustrophobic experience at almost any time of the day. It is not helped by the continuing march of modernization in the name of which British Rail have recently mutilated the front with a travel centre wearing its trendy mid-1970s stainless steel sophistication with a certain air of desperation.

The terminus of the South-Eastern Railway, Charing Cross station, dates from 1863–5. The station was designed by engineer Sir John Hawkshaw and the railway hotel by E. M. Barry. The train shed, 98 feet in height, and with a single arched span of 164 feet, was undoubtedly one of the most impressive in London until its sudden collapse in December 1905. The present flat roof is a poor substitute and war damage in 1941 led to the hopelessly misguided reconstruction of the upper parts of the hotel in 1951. Steam finally disappeared from Charing Cross in 1961, and the present reconstruction of buildings flanking the forecourt of the station merely emphasizes the long-tolling death knell of one of London's most historic termini. To the railway enthusiast or historian Charing Cross

London Liverpool Street; 1875. The western train shed, designed by Edward Wilson

station is a sad place, and probably best avoided.

Architecturally the most famous of all London termini is St Pancras, begun in 1865 and completed in 1876, to the design of the engineer William Henry Barlow; the hotel, that most familiar landmark in Euston Road, was the work of Sir George Gilbert Scott. St Pancras was the terminus of the Midland Railway, which until then had had its headquarters in Derby. Barlow was the engineer of the Midland and his train shed is a sensational piece of construction: a single awe-inspiring 240 foot span in cast iron arched braces manufactured by the Butterley Iron Company and tied together by the floor girders of the station floor, which is effectively at first-floor level. For a century this was the largest station roof in the world without internal supports. And yet for all the statistics the train shed at St Pancras does not have the impact of Paddington or the atmosphere of King's Cross. The ribs are in the form of pointed arches, and the whole structure is supported under the platform floor by an amazing grid of iron columns, a space that was dictated when the station was built by the practical need to store barrels of beer from Burton-upon-Trent. The 500-bedroomed Midland Grand Station Hotel was begun in 1868, the year the station was completed, and opened to the public in May 1873, although the curved wing to the west was not finished for another three years. The architect, Sir George Gilbert Scott, was one of the most fashionable of the Victorian era and, appropriately to the prosperity and pretension of the Midland, the hotel was a glorious piece of pompous window-dressing. Externally a preposterous hybrid and profusion of Romanesque and Gothic forms, with its brick and stone spires, gables and turrets, it succeeds by its very scale and its ability still to startle both traveller and passer-by alike. Internally, the vast empty halls, where once magnificent rooms were linked by some of the earliest hydraulic lifts in London, echo emptily to the occasional sounds of a desultory office use. After years of neglect, British Rail has matched government aid and the building is to be cleaned and repaired. An imaginative new use is needed urgently; first-aid repairs are insufficient remedy. St

Pancras is undeniably the most scenically impressive of all London stations; moreover, a century after it was built it still functions admirably whether for commuter or inter-city traveller.

Liverpool Street station, designed by the engineer Edward Wilson for the Great Eastern Railway, was first opened in 1875. Its train sheds survive, forming the western part of the present station, Gothic, ecclesiastical in character and delicately effective, with their rows of paired slender cast iron columns dividing the principal aisles, with lacy fretwork to spandrels and staircase balustrades. They create a marvellously light effect, not of a spectacular iron-arched shed like Paddington or St Pancras but somehow entirely welcoming and human-scaled in spite of the vast size of the spaces enclosed. In 1894 the eastern part, serving the Southend and South Essex suburban lines, was added. This was designed by the engineer John Wilson and the architect W. N. Ashbee, head of the GER Architectural Department. It is a functional and efficient space, little more. The Great Eastern Hotel was built in 1884 by C. E. Barry and much added to in 1901-6 by Colonel Robert Edis in the Anglo-French Renaissance style. The exterior is jolly rather than grand, with a fanciful collection of gables and turrets and a series of fine interiors. The over-all threats of redevelopment to Liverpool Street station, its train sheds and hotel, appear to have at least partially receded. By any standards the western train sheds and the hotel deserve retention in any future plan that caters for the newer post-war image of Liverpool Street as the busiest commuter station serving the City of London.

The predecessor to Waterloo was the terminus of the London and Southampton Railway at Nine Elms, a handsome station designed by Sir William Tite, built in 1838 and only recently demolished, after lengthy disuse, to make way for the new Covent Garden market. Waterloo was reached in 1848 when the first station was designed by Joseph Locke for the same railway, now renamed the London and South-Western Railway. Nothing survives of this, but the station was extended in 1862 to accommodate the Windsor line, and the side wall of this still remains almost unnoticed alongside platform 16. The present platforms 16–21 represent the area of the north station, added in 1885 and retaining its original roof; the south station having been previously added in 1879 on the site of the present platforms 7 to 12. The major part of the existing station was begun in 1900 and opened by Queen Mary in March 1922. The architect was J. R. Scott and the engineers were J. W. Jacomb Hood and A. W. Szlumper. Waterloo is the largest rail terminus in the British Isles. Much of the Edwardian grandeur has now gone, and its rich interiors and bars have been swept away, although the triumphant Victory Arch facing York Road is a magnificent classical entrance in Portland stone and bronze. Sadly, this intended great entrance arch serves only as a way in for a few pedestrians, so convoluted are the access arrangements at Waterloo. The train sheds are not beautiful, or even elegant, and their axis is across the platforms, which seems perverse at first view. Nevertheless the spatial vistas are effective, overriding British Rail's current attempts to minimize their size by the insertion of grossly overscaled electronic indicator boards which are carried, together with advertising mat-

ter, on large continuous overhead gantries. It is particularly regrettable to see the demise of the old hardwood mechanical indicator boards, which were the earliest of their type, of a superbly simple and readable design; and above all they really worked. Nowadays, Waterloo has little atmosphere other than that conveyed by the loudspeakers with their unique repertoire ranging from *The Entry of the Gladiators* to enliven the morning rush hour to the strains of a somnolent Viennese waltz to lull the weary evening traveller. Any attempt to enjoy the vast spaces of Waterloo is

Above *Birmingham Snow Hill; the derelict platform canopies shortly before demolition*
Left *Birmingham Snow Hill; opened 1852. Hotel by W. G. Owen. Station rebuilt 1909–14. Demolished 1976–7*

frustrated by combat with the rush of thronging commuters, and a sense of relief is invariably felt once away from the mêlée.

Outside London it is not merely the great iron-arched train sheds that have suffered: major city stations at Bradford Exchange and Birmingham Snow Hill were demolished in 1973–6 and 1976 respectively. From those that remain three great stations stand out as national monuments to Victorian engineering. They are at least the equal of anything in London: Bristol Temple Meads, York and Newcastle Central.

In some respects Brunel's terminus at Bristol Temple Meads, opened in 1841, was an even greater achievement than Paddington. For a start it is thirteen years earlier, and his train shed is thus without any parallel elsewhere in early railway architecture. Planned ecclesiastically in the form of a nave and aisles, the arches are closely spaced cast iron columns with depressed pointed arches of Tudor character between them. The roof beams are wood and are in the form of mock hammerbeams, a splendidly medieval effect. The block of buildings that originally contained the headquarters and board room of the Great Western Railway is in a stone-faced mock-Tudor style. The train shed has been serving since the early 1960s the rather undignified function of a car park, but it is at least properly maintained. Temple Meads developed over the next century in a most interesting and varied manner. About 1850 the Brunel shed was extended in brick with a much thinner cast iron tie roof; and in 1852 the terminal building of the Bristol and Exeter Railway was added in a mock-Jacobean style by S. C. Fripp. The major alterations and additions came in 1865–78 to the designs of Matthew Digby Wyatt; a gigantic new iron-arched shed not unlike St Pancras, with pointed Gothic trusses but following the relatively sharp curve of the tracks. It is a most exciting space. Large new buildings faced the main forecourt in a castellated Tudor style, and this pattern was amazingly followed as late as 1930–35 when the centrepiece tower of the exterior was completed. Temple Meads remains perhaps the most evocative station experience, both historically and architecturally.

York, for the railway buff, is probably the most thrilling of all. This great station, with its wonderful curving train shed roof, is unforgettable. Its origins are very early in railway history with the creation of the York and North Midland Railway by George Hudson, and his first line from Normanton to York opened in 1840. The original terminus, which was used until the present station was built, was designed by the prolific and talented York architect George Townsend Andrews, and completed in 1841–2. The iron-arched train shed has long gone, but the forebuildings survive, not-

is not spectacular; the interior is breathtaking. Not only are the train sheds another of the great triumphs of Victorian engineering, but they have the rarer quality of a real beauty of line and proportion. Three wide spans curve strongly, it seems almost endlessly, into the distance, a magical effect. The iron columns are solid, of the Corinthian order, and have openwork spandrels; as at Brunel's Paddington every third rib rests on the columns, the intermediate ribs running to the cross girders. None of the great iron-arched sheds has finer spatial qualities, and the gentle cohesion of the curves of

ably the rather later and austere Italianate eastern block of 1853, built as a hotel. The North-Eastern Railway was formed in 1853 by amalgamating three Hudson lines, and a new terminus was built in 1874–7 to replace the old one. The original designs were prepared by Thomas Prosser, architect to the NER from 1854 to 1874 (perhaps using designs by John Dobson), Benjamin Burley and finally William Peachey, to whom the present train sheds should properly be ascribed. Externally the station

Above Bristol Temple Meads; begun in 1865–78 and not completed until 1935, the Tudor Gothic forecourt buildings designed by Matthew Digby Wyatt
Right Bristol Temple Meads; 1840–41. The original train shed by I. K. Brunel. The hammer beam roof is 1.2 metres (4 feet) wider in span than Westminster Hall

the iron roof trusses with the over-all shape of the sheds is railway architecture at its best. It is superbly preserved and maintained by British Rail and nothing could form a better preparation for the glories of the Railway Museum nearby.

Newcastle Central was germinal in the development of railway engineering. There can be no other station anywhere that has such a magnificent approach as that across Stephenson and Dobson's High Level Bridge over the Tyne, an approach that prepares the traveller for spectacular things. The station is no disappointment. John Dobson, the outstanding Newcastle architect, is the man with whom Newcastle Central will always be most closely associated. His grand portico and forebuilding, begun in 1848, were not completed until 1865 by Thomas Prosser, following a somewhat modified design. The train shed roof, as at York, has a pronounced curve, and it is the earliest iron-arched train shed to use the structural concept of curved ribs forming the framework spanning a wide space by themselves, without intermediate supports. The idea finds precedents in Paxton's greenhouse at Chatsworth (1836–40, demolished) and the Palm

Above *Newcastle Central; begun in 1848, completed in 1865, the grand portico by John Dobson to the design of Thomas Prosser*
Right *Edinburgh Waverley; 1874. Looking down on the trainsheds with the North British hotel on the left*

House at Kew of 1844–8 by Decimus Burton and Richard Turner, but this is the first application on such a scale to a railway station. In many ways the shed at Newcastle is the earlier, less refined, model for York, for as well as being curved it also has three wide spans separated by iron arcades with open spandrels and every third rib is resting on the columns and the intermediate ribs on cross girders. How much of the design should be attributed to Dobson alone and how much to the engineer Robert

Stephenson we shall probably never know for certain, but Newcastle is a national, industrial and architectural monument to the whole Victorian age of great building enterprises. The heavy workload of Newcastle suburban train services, plus the main line west to Carlisle, not to mention the many inter-city services to London and Scotland, have exerted pressures on Newcastle that have left it less pristine than York. The platforms and concourses are cluttered, the spatial effects are disturbed by a plethora of hanging signs and advertisements; later alterations and modernization have blurred the

outlines in places and there was a serious fire in the roof in December 1977. With a little love and care in the future, Newcastle could once again take its place as the forerunner of the great city termini.

The other stations that remain to be described are perhaps the division two of the termini league. Several large cities have suffered grievously by loss or mutilation of their major stations, and in Scotland this has happened in both Edinburgh and Glasgow. In Edinburgh the North British Railway terminus at Waverley station, interchange for all London-bound passengers, has been sadly maltreated

in recent years. As the tracks were sited in the deep cutting between the old and new towns the station never had an imposing exterior, and the railway hotel, the North British, was situated on Princes Street. The complex roofs of the station almost escape notice in the view acrosss the valley and are unrewarding internally. However, all the wealth of the company was expended in creating a magnificant booking hall with massive carved hardwood panelling and ticket kiosks and a heraldic design mosaic floor. This has been mercilessly and unnecessarily swept away in the formation of one of British Rail's favourite new playthings, a travel centre. Not far away Haymarket station, terminus and headquarters of the Edinburgh and Glasgow Railway, has been under threat for many years. The beautifully proportioned and simple two-storey stone classical building with Doric portico dates from 1840–42, and is one of the earliest and least altered of main line terminus buildings in Britain. Nevertheless, it seems destined for demolition to make way for an office development over a rebuilt station below. It was only in 1964 that Princes Street station was demolished and its service transferred to Waverley. It was the terminus for the west end of the city and the train shed was a splendid single iron arch in the great tradition of this form; its removal was singularly futile since the site still lies empty and derelict in the heart of the commercial centre of the city. The terminus hotel, the overpowering Caledonian in dour red sandstone, remains to remind us of past glories. To complete a gloomy picture, in the Edinburgh suburbs Leith Central, opened in 1908, was an important terminus, dating from a time when Leith was still a significant port and the station handled many boat trains. Closed in the mid-1960s, it became a diesel depot until 1972 when the development potential of the site was realized by the British Rail Property Board. However, the station still stands empty and neglected, awaiting its fate.

Things are no better in Glasgow. Apart from the loss of St Enoch, Queen Street station is suffering greatly from the construction of a large new development in front of the train shed which will entirely hide it from George Square. The shed itself is a fine wide iron-arched span, straight like St Pancras but nowhere near as impressive. It was designed by James Carswell in 1878–80, but its survival in no way makes up for the loss of the architecturally and spatially much finer St Enoch. Glasgow Central, headquarters of the Caledonian Railway, was designed by Sir Robert Rowand Anderson in the French *château* style. Opened in 1879, it lacks nothing in size or ostentation, but neither terminal buildings nor train sheds are of great architectural merit.

Further north, the Caledonian Railway's showpiece station at Dundee West has been completely demolished, and, north-east, Aberdeen was once a proud city terminus of noble scale. It has been much neglected and part demolished, but the impressive station concourse is being restored (with the addition, of course, of a travel centre). But so much of the train sheds has now gone that it is altogether an unworthy introduction to the new-found oil

Above *Edinburgh Haymarket; 1840–42 by John Miller, a fine and very early station scheduled for redevelopment*
Right *Glasgow Queen Street; 1878–80. Designed by James Carswell, the train shed is now hidden by new development*

prosperity of the capital of eastern Scotland.

Back in England, Darlington Bank Top is another of the great city stations of the North-Eastern Railway. It was designed in 1884 by William Bell, who had become architect to the NER in 1877. But, before this, Darlington occupies an important place in early railway history, for the present North Road station, dating from 1842, is probably the best preserved of all early stations, with a simple stuccoed classical forebuilding and a wide train shed divided into unequal halves by an iron arcade. Bank Top has an impressive forebuilding in the Flemish style, with a bold *porte-cochère*. The train shed is formed of three iron-arched spans, with a strong Gothic influence, and was the last of the great sheds to be built in this form. It is a station of grand scale, but not to be compared with York or Newcastle.

The Liverpool and Manchester Railway was founded in 1829–30, and one of its original termini survives in a much altered form at Liverpool Road, Manchester. Probably designed by John Foster the younger of Liverpool, it is the earliest extant railway station building, although now hardly recognizable as such. Manchester's finest major city station, the Central, has closed. This is distinguished primarily by yet another of the series of magnificent iron-arched train sheds. Manchester Central was the terminus of the Midland Railway, so the great straight single-span shed designed by Sir John

In 1836 the Liverpool terminus of the Liverpool and Manchester Railway at Edge Hill was replaced by the original station at Lime Street, and this was probably the first station to have both cast iron arches and also an over-all roof to platforms and tracks. John Cunningham was the architect and George Stephenson engineer for the train shed. The station did not survive long and was rebuilt on a much larger scale in 1846–51 by Sir William Tite. This has a round-arched iron roof designed by Richard Turner, who had worked with Decimus Burton on the Palm House at Kew. Further major alterations, designed by the engineer William Baker, came in 1867, and at the end of the century the enormous railway hotel was designed by Waterhouse. This has just been restored for future office use. Lime Street is a huge station, but it is muddled in plan and has been so altered and added to over the years that the over-all effect is confusing, although it cannot be denied that the dramatic effect of the twin curving train sheds receding into the distance is almost worthy of York. Liverpool has other notable stations, including the Central, by Sir John Fowler, and more particularly Edge Hill, but they are not in the major station category in size or pretension. The train shed of the Central was demolished in 1976.

Above *Birmingham Curzon Street; 1838–40 by Philip Hardwick. The Ionic Propylaeum was built to match the 1836 Doric Arch (right) at Euston, the work of the same architect*

Fowler in 1876 was a counterpart of the other pointed-arch Midland sheds at St Pancras and St Enoch. However, large terminal buildings were never erected and the shed serves now as a rather dowdy rubbish-strewn car park. Elsewhere in Manchester Piccadilly station is modern, with dull platforms and forebuildings, and Victoria station, with a new front of 1909 by William Dawes, is a mess and hardly important enough to warrant detailed description here.

Birmingham has probably suffered more than any other large city in the decimation of its railway architecture, although only New Street was ever really a great city terminus to compare with the finest elsewhere. New Street has been replaced, Snow Hill has gone, the Great Western Hotel has been demolished, and the optimistically named International station has appeared, a large, brand-new and relatively little-used station serving the exhibition centre. The single monument of importance is Curzon Street, the original opposite terminus to Euston of the London and Birmingham Railway. Designed by Philip Hardwick the elder in 1838–40, the station was superseded in 1854 by New Street, and has been used since then for goods. The train shed was demolished in the early 1960s, but the long-disused forebuilding, an elegant three-storey square stone block with a monumental Ionic portico, survives and awaits a sympathetic user.

Although Brighton is not a city, the great iron train shed of the terminus ranks with the best anywhere. The original station at Brighton was designed by the architect David Mocatta, a pupil of Sir John Soane. However only the forebuilding survives and this has been all but obliterated by the later *porte-cochère* of 1882. The important feature of Brighton is its monumental iron-arched train shed of 1882, a fitting approach to England's most cele-

brated and elegant seaside resort. It is curved, the wide-arched spans are elliptical, and there is much openwork decoration to beams and spandrels, as well as unusually tall and slender iron columns. It is visually entirely satisfying and it is to be hoped that British Rail are not serious in their recurrent threats of demolition.

Within this single chapter all the surviving great iron-arched train sheds have been described, spaces

where the real delights of atmosphere and architectural excitement can be experienced in a manner perhaps unmatched by any other building form. Because of their sheer size, the city stations have survived for the most part with far greater completeness than their more vulnerable and smaller urban and rural counterparts. They stand now as a group of buildings unparalleled in Britain as a tribute to the triumphs of the Industrial Revolution.

Left Manchester Central; *1876. The disused train shed, designed by Sir John Fowler*
Below Brighton; *1882–3. Unusual curving train shed*

LARGE TOWN STATIONS

DAVID LLOYD

THIS CHAPTER deals with the substantial stations of important industrial towns, county towns, ports and resorts – smaller than the great metropolitan termini and junctions, but bigger than country town or village stations.

There is a distinction to be made in every station between the operational parts and the ancillary facilities. The operational parts are the tracks and platforms; the ancillary facilities include booking offices, waiting rooms, refreshment rooms, parcels offices, administrative offices and possibly living accommodation for railway staff. These facilities are often largely or wholly concentrated in 'forebuildings', the parts of stations usually most conspicuous from outside, but may also be dispersed in smaller buildings adjoining the platforms or elsewhere.

Terminal stations usually have forebuildings facing the ends of the tracks and platforms, with a concourse, or circulation space, in between. Through stations necessarily have their forebuildings to one side, unless, as occasionally happens, they are built on bridges which cross the tracks and platforms.

Operational parts and forebuildings provide totally different architectural problems. With operational parts of stations the main problem, once the tracks have been laid out and the platforms constructed, is to roof the platforms. This can be done either by providing over-all roofs covering all the platforms and intermediate tracks, or by roofing the platforms only. Over-all roofs to stations provided Victorian architects and engineers with some of their most exciting challenges, especially when they used curved iron braces to span huge spaces, as in the great and famous roofs at Paddington, Newcastle, St Pancras, York and Liverpool Street. They seldom, however, used this form of construction in the smaller stations covered by this chapter. More often, if they provided over-all roofs at all, these were of simple gable sections with not very wide spans, supported intermediately by rows of columns and horizontal girders, sometimes bracketed to give the appearance of rows of arches. Most through stations, and some of the terminals, had individual platform roofs, often bracketed from buildings facing the platforms and from iron columns on the platforms. The brackets, with their openwork iron construction, provided the Victorian designers with opportunities for decorative schemes to endless varieties of themes, and the columns, too, were usually treated decoratively. Characteristically, platform canopies had vertical wooden perforated edges, the perforations delicately shaped to control the dripping of rainwater.

Forebuildings, and other buildings containing ancillary accommodation, called for more conventional structural treatment. Any of the normal materials used in Victorian commercial or domestic buildings could be used – brick, stone, timber – and

the styles were as varied as with any other type of Victorian building. The classical tradition persisted in railway stations right up to mid-century; two superb examples, Huddersfield and Monkwearmouth, were built just before 1850. Brunel, Thompson, Tite and Andrews – four of the leading early station designers – used simple, basically classical forms for many of their stations but could be more elaborate when occasion demanded;

Monkwearmouth, Tyne and Wear; 1848. Handsome Greek Revival station by Thomas Moore

49

Thompson and Andrews in Italianate, as at Chester and Hull; Brunel and Tite in romantic Tudor as at Bath and Carlisle. The Jacobean manor house style was a particular favourite in the 1840s and early 1850s, as at Stoke-on-Trent and Shrewsbury. Full-blooded Gothic was rarer. Some companies evolved very distinctive house styles, such as the London, Brighton and South Coast after about 1850, and the London and South-Western towards the end of the century.

Naturally railway stations were made as conspicuous as possible to the communities which they sought to serve, so that the forebuildings were often designed with eye-catching façades and striking skylines. Often there were elaborate *portes-cochère*, or carriage porches, inviting the affluent to drive up. However, town stations were not always on particularly conspicuous sites. Usually the railways had to skirt established towns, so that the stations were initially away from their commercial centres, although the towns' central areas often subsequently developed up to the new stations, as at Huddersfield and Hull. At Portsmouth the station provided a new focus for the growing city away from the old centre. Only occasionally did a main railway cut right through the centre of a well established town, as it did at Sunderland and, on a larger scale, at Newcastle.

Southampton is a city which to a very large extent owes its present prosperity to railway enterprises. In the early 1830s it was a decayed ancient port with little to sustain it but cross-Channel traffic and its reputation as a pleasant resort and place for retirement. In that decade a company was formed to promote a railway from London primarily to serve new docks to be built at Southampton. The railway in 1838 reached Woking Heath (then virtually an uninhabited place far from the original village of Woking; the modern town developed round the station late in the century), and Southampton in 1840 – the second trunk line from London to be completed, following that to Birmingham.

The architect for the London and South Western Railway, as it came to be known, was Sir William Tite, a pupil of David Laing, who himself had been taught by Sir John Soane. Tite made himself nationally known – after his first major works for the L & SWR – as the architect of the Royal Exchange in London, finished in 1844. His terminal of 1838–40 at Southampton and its surroundings illustrate the overlap between the world of post-Georgian fashion and that of the early railways. The façade is like that of a simple Italian *palazzo*, stuccoed, three-storeyed, and with a projecting five-arched ground storey, rusticated in imitation of stone jointing. Round the corner is Queen's Terrace, also suave and stuccoed, built in the

Above *Southampton; 1838–40. Italianate terminus by Sir William Tite*
Right *Gosport, Hampshire; 1841–2. A majestic Tuscan colonnade in Portland Stone by Sir William Tite.*

50

early 1830s to enjoy the view over the unsullied Southampton Water. In a very few years the view was transformed by the docks. The railway-age port prospered at first, then its fortunes languished; its present-day major importance dates essentially from the purchase of the docks in 1892 from the independent Dock Company by the ever-enterprising L & SWR, which steadily expanded them. The town's centre of gravity shifted northwards, away from the original station; more and more trains called at the present through station, and the original terminus was closed in the 1960s.

It is still empty, but the forebuilding is intact and the local authorities have expressed their intention to find a new use and conserve it.

Tite designed all the original stations on the Southampton line, but only the village station at Micheldever remains essentially unaltered. The original, straightforward, classically proportioned forebuildings at Eastleigh and Winchester can still be partly seen, much altered amid accretions. Eastleigh was originally a rural junction (the town developed in the later nineteenth and early twentieth centuries when the railway works moved there),

from which branches ran to Gosport (opened 1842) and Salisbury (1847). The Gosport branch was intended to serve Portsmouth, then, with its naval base, a far bigger place than Southampton. Portsmouth is on an island, then defended at its landward approach by the earthen Hilsea Lines, which the War Office did not at first allow the railway to breach; hence the terminal across the harbour at Gosport. Though basically a simple terminus, with an internally plain train shed roofed in timber with iron ties, the station had a splendid flanking forebuilding, with a grand colonnade in Portland stone and a bell in an open turret which tolled the impending departure of trains. Fire destroyed the roof and gutted most of the buildings in the 1960s, and it is now wholly closed, but the ruin, and particularly the colonnade, is impressive. The local authorities are now looking at ways of using the site so as to incorporate the best surviving parts of the building.

Gosport station may at first have been used by Queen Victoria when she reviewed the Fleet at Portsmouth, or embarked for the Isle of Wight. Later a branch line – really an extension – was built into the Royal Clarence Victualling Yard, on the Gosport side of Portsmouth Harbour. This was connected with a special station built within the Yard for the Queen, which she used when embarking for, or arriving from, Osborne on the Isle of Wight. Parts of this building, a fairly simple structure with a gabled iron roof, remain within present-day naval structures.

Tite was typical of the more conservative architects of his age, the earliest Victorian period, in being able to design in romantic Gothic or Tudor as well as classical styles. This was evident in his large neo-Tudor station at Carlisle, opened in 1848, with its collegiate turret and monastic arched porch – still partly surviving though much enlarged and altered. Still more do we see Tite's aptitude for evocative Gothic in his terminal at Windsor (now Riverside), built for the L & SWR in 1850–51. This is on a 'prime site' right underneath the castle cliff, near the river and just over the bridge from Eton College. Furthermore the Queen herself used it (in diplomatic alternation with the GWR terminus up

the hill). The station has been little altered except for the removal of part of the roof over the tracks. The façade of the forebuilding, in rich red brick with stone dressings, has a central gable with a big Tudor mullioned window and a corner porch, with college-like arches between buttresses. The station's special feature was the royal waiting room to one side, with elaborate Gothic entrance windows folded out diagonally, and the initials 'VR' and 'PA' inset in black brick, Tudor fashion, on the adjoining wall.

Windsor was one of the places – Plymouth and Exeter were others – where the GWR and the L & SWR were in deadly rivalry. Nothing however survives of the GWR's original station at

Above *Carlisle, Cumbria; asymmetrical collegiate Gothic*
Right *Windsor Riverside, Berkshire; 1850–51. Fine iron roof carried on columns*

Windsor (its successor is described later in this chapter). It was at the end of a short branch from Brunel's London to Bristol line, opened in 1841.

Brunel's original station at Bath (now called 'Bath Spa', jarringly and unnecessarily) was designed to evoke the age of Bath Abbey rather than the city's then somewhat faded reputation as a watering place. Alas, the original roof across the tracks – a simpler version of the great timber roof at Bristol Temple Meads – was removed long ago, but the two-storeyed forebuilding, with the platform abutting the upper level, is still partly as Brunel designed it. By contrast, some of Brunel's other stations were in austere basic classical style; that at Swindon had hardly any embellishment. Other main town stations which he designed, such as those at Exeter, Taunton and Reading, originally had long platforms with central crossover lines, trains running in different directions using opposite ends. This arrangement was superseded in both Exeter (St David's) and Taunton later in the century, as were the original buildings. Exeter, however, retained until lately a subsidiary station (St Thomas) which remained largely as Brunel designed it, with wooden roof over the tracks and simple flanking forebuilding. Now the roof has gone and little else is left, though the station is still open. At Reading the original arrangement remained till 1899. The oldest part of the present station is the central block with pedimented windows and central cupola, dating (according to H. G. Arnold's *Victorian Architecture in Reading*) from 1865–7; the buff bricks came from Coalbrookdale. Nearby is the original Great Western Hotel of 1844, a fairly simple stuccoed building recently converted into NHS offices and enlarged, but retaining its main façades.

At Cheltenham, appropriately, the earliest station (Lansdown, the only one still open) was in a classical style. Gordon Biddle, in *Victorian Stations*, says it was adapted from a pre-existing villa on the outskirts of the town, but Brian Little, in *Cheltenham in Pictures*, attributes it to S. W. Daukes, a notable Cheltenham architect who designed fine churches there and elsewhere, as well

as Friern Hospital in north London and the now ruined Witley Court in Worcestershire. If the station really is older, then Daukes may have added the very fine Doric portico, running the whole length of the façade, which was wantonly destroyed by British Rail a few years ago.

Two superb classical stations in the north of England have been luckier. That at Huddersfield was opened in 1847 when the through route across the Pennines via the Standedge tunnel was finished. Huddersfield had been quite a small town previously; it had an initial spurt of growth after 1811 when the canal was opened via Standedge, but it was the railway which enabled it to grow big and important – eventually to become the third largest woollen or worsted town in the West Riding. The town centre quickly developed towards and around the station, which dominates a fairly formally planned town square called St George's Square. It has a magnificent façade with a hexastyle Corinthian portico, and for a time contained a hotel. Originally it was a single-platform station, but the tracks and platforms were remodelled in 1886. The service is now much reduced; British Rail wanted to dispose of the forebuilding for redevelopment, but it was bought by the Borough Council, cleaned and restored in celebration of the centenary of their charter in 1968; it is now used for public meetings and exhibitions.

The station at Monkwearmouth, now part of Sunderland, makes an interesting counterpart to Huddersfield. This was a terminal, on the north bank of the River Wear opposite Sunderland proper, opened in 1848 and grandly designed in a classical style by the local architect Thomas Moore, at the behest of George Hudson, the 'Railway King', who controlled the company and wished his recent election as Member of Parliament for Sunderland to be commemorated. (His downfall was soon to come.) Monkwearmouth station was greatly reduced in importance when the line was extended across the Wear into the centre of Sunderland in 1879, and it was closed in the 1960s. Sunderland Borough Council bought it, restored it and converted it excellently into a local museum. With its splendid Ionic portico, its rounded Doric corner

Above *Hull Paragon, Humberside; 1846–8 by G. T. Andrews. Inspired by Italian Renaissance palazzos*
Left *Huddersfield, West Yorkshire; 1847–50 by James Pritchett the elder. As imposing and ambitious as contemporary town halls*

Left *Cambridge; 1847 by Francis Thompson inspired by early Italian Renaissance Loggie*
Below *Chester; 1848 by Francis Thompson, as extensive as a grand hotel*

features and its arched screen wall on either side flanking the railway (which is still very much open) it is, like its counterpart at Huddersfield, the finest secular building in a big industrial town. Both Huddersfield and Sunderland councils behaved in an exemplary way in saving and restoring these outstanding buildings.

The heartland of George Hudson's kingdom was central and eastern Yorkshire. Here he employed the York architect G. T. Andrews, whose practice was already well established (his is the splendid Italian former headquarters of the Yorkshire Insurance Company in St Helen's Square, York), to design a series of stations large and small. The biggest was at Hull, opened in 1848. The operational parts were reconstructed in 1903–5, but Andrews's long-drawn-out original forebuilding, really a whole series of interlocked structures, survives on the southern, flanking, side. Two- and three-storey ranges, in strongly detailed Italianate style, alternate with single-storey ranges, all built of golden-brown magnesian limestone – a very fine composition. In 1851 Andrews designed a hotel at the end of the station which, recently altered and extended, now provides the main elevation of the station complex towards the main streets of the city.

Andrews and Tite both designed many buildings besides railway stations; Brunel was a great engineer; Francis Thompson, by contrast, is known today only as a railway architect. He was for long an enigma; it is now generally thought that he was a tailor in the West End of London who somehow came to design railway buildings, but there is no indication of how he obtained his architectural expertise. He designed stations on three lines: Derby to Leeds for the North Midland; London to Cambridge for the Eastern Counties; and Chester to Holyhead; on the first and last he worked in association with Robert Stephenson. His stations, large and small, are or were outstandingly good of their kind. His Derby Trijunct (of which nothing significant now survives; the present Derby station occupies the same site) was a landmark in architectural history. Of it Gordon Biddle wrote in *Victorian Stations*: 'Francis Thompson,

probably in collaboration with Robert Stephenson, showed how light iron roofs could be used to cover large areas in several spans, at the same time creating an atmosphere of airy elegance. The Derby Trijunct station roof of 1840 covered 140 feet in three spans on two lines of fluted columns and decorated cross girders substantial enough not to require brackets.' Thompson's station at Cambridge (*not* by Sancton Wood, as Pevsner says even in his 1970 edition of *Buildings of England: Cambridgeshire*) has a splendid loggia of fifteen arches, well treated recently by British Rail; the station, uniquely, retains the arrangement of one long platform with central crossover. Thompson's surviving *tour-de-force* is the station at Chester, externally intact. It is a junction of several lines, well outside the walled city (one corner of which is penetrated by Stephenson's Holyhead Railway, to more dramatic effect than has been achieved by the nearby relief road). It shows how masterful Thompson – like Andrews at Hull – was at designing an immensely long façade, giving it architectural interest through bold articulation (projection and recession of stretches of façade in alternation). The style is restrained Italianate in dark red brick with stone dressings; the main part is two-storeyed, with boldly treated, slightly projecting blocks at either end, each arched on the ground storey and crowned with a pair of round-arched turrets. The façade continues on a lower key in either direction, ending in two-storeyed pavilion blocks projecting well forward. There is little of interest inside, except for a long round-arched arcade which divided the two halves of the station, then each operated by a different company. This monumental station has more in common with Chester's outstanding neoclassical architecture of the late Georgian period, such as the castle and courts, than with its romantic half-timbered buildings.

The Jacobean manor house style was a favourite for several early station architects. Probably the most notable in this style is Stoke-on-Trent, originally the hub of the small but enterprising North Staffordshire Railway. This station was designed by H. A. Hunt and opened in 1850. The façade is a superb three-gabled composition in dark brick with stone dressings, with Flemish curves and finials; the central gabled bay is larger and contains a huge oriel window which lit the company's board room. The ground-floor façade has a loggia-like arcade. The station behind was reconstructed in 1893. Even more than Huddersfield, Stoke station is the centrepiece of an impressive townscape. Opposite, across a square (Winton Square) and symmetrical to the station is the North Stafford Hotel, just like a Jacobean mansion outside, while the sides of the square are defined by two-storeyed railwaymen's houses. This is a unique example of a whole urban composition focused on a railway station and designed as a whole, but it is effectively self-contained and unlike the square at Huddersfield does not form an integral part of any town centre. (The city of Stoke-on-Trent is an amalgamation of six towns; the small-scale centre of Stoke proper is nearby, but Winton Square is cut off from it by the railway itself.)

Few of J. W. Livock's stations on the London and North-Western system survive, unfortunately; those that do are small. His Northampton (Bridge Street) and Peterborough (East) were elaborate

Far left *Stoke-on-Trent, Staffordshire; 1850 by H. A. Hunt, inspired by Jacobean country houses*
Left *Bury St Edmunds, Suffolk; 1847 by Sancton Wood. Jacobean side by side with Baroque*
Below *Shrewsbury, Salop; original 1848 by T. K. Penson, substantially rebuilt in part-facsimile, 1903*

Jacobean compositions with tall chimneys; Northampton had twirly Flemish gables and Peterborough straighter ones. Peterborough East – now abolished altogether – contrasted with the main line Peterborough North (1850), with its rather pinched classical forebuilding typical of early Great Northern stations.

Further into East Anglia, Bury St Edmunds has a splendid and unusual station by Frederick Barnes, the Ipswich architect who also designed the smaller country town stations at Stowmarket and Needham Market. Bury, built in 1847, has a pair of baroque turrets, one on each side of the tracks, entrances through three splendid recessed arches in brick, and a neo-Jacobean stationmaster's house looking for all the world as if it were a Cambridge college master's lodging.

At Shrewsbury the station was designed by the Oswestry architect T. K. Penson, who also did smaller stations on the Chester line (Gobowen, for example), and buildings in Chester itself. Its scholastic Jacobean style, with mullioned windows and central thinly pinnacled tower, must have been suggested by the nearby old building of Shrewsbury School (now the public library). It stands on an awkward site, on the hump of land linking with the river-girt peninsula on which the historic town stands and overshadowed by the Georgianized castle. In 1903–4 it was treated in a curious way; the ground was lowered in front of it and the original two-storeyed forebuilding underpinned on a new lowest storey, in the same style. At the same time the operational parts, at the convergence of several lines, were reconstructed. It is worth going, by a devious route down a steep lane or steps, to the river towpath to see the main platforms spanning the Severn in a dramatic manner.

Buxton formerly had a remarkable pair of stations, both opened in 1863 as terminals of separate lines operated by the London and North-Western Railway and the Midland Railway. Each had the same general outline though differing in details – an iron-framed shed with stone flanking buildings and an end elevation, towards the town, with a striking semicircular window subdivided fanwise. Sir Joseph Paxton, who began his career at Chats-

worth and was financially involved with the Midland line through the Peak District, is thought, without certainty, to have been involved in this pair of stations, where company rivalry was subordinated to a desire for external symmetry in a fashionable town. Alas, the Midland station (at the end of a branch from Miller's Dale) was demolished some years ago and the L & NWR station, still used by trains from Stockport, is in a sadly reduced state.

The Midland was particularly notable for its platform ironwork; the best surviving displays are to be found on the platforms at Bedford and Kettering (both 1857); the former is due for rebuilding, but it is hoped that the latter will survive.

Scotland has relatively few large town stations of special architectural interest. Perth, a complicated junction, has a central building of 1848 by Sir William Tite, somewhat inappropriately in an English Tudor style, rather like his work at Carlisle; as at Carlisle the original part now stands amid later accretions, mainly of 1884 and 1893. Recent alterations and curtailment have not improved the station's appearance. Stirling, rebuilt in 1913–15 by the Glasgow architect James Miller, has a fairly modest neo-Jacobean façade and a semicircular

Above Birkenhead Woodside, Merseyside; 1878 by R. E. Johnston. Like the great hall of a medieval house with polychrome stonework and massive roof trusses. Demolished Left Buxton, Derbyshire; c. 1862. Joseph Paxton is said to have advised, hence perhaps the ironwork window

concourse behind, recalling Miller's more fantastic concourse of the same shape at Wemyss Bay, described in the next chapter.

In the later part of the nineteenth century railway companies tended to employ their own architects and so developed distinctive 'house styles'; fewer architects with outside interests and practices were employed. The London, Brighton and South Coast Railway's architecture became particularly ebullient. A typical example of their style is Portsmouth and Southsea, used jointly with the London and South-Western Railway but rebuilt by the LB & SCR in 1866. The first station had been opened in 1847, after the military authorities had at last allowed the railway to breach the Hilsea Lines on the north coast of the island on which the city stands – the railway passes through the now overgrown earthwork by a pair of brick arches. The present station has a façade of the rich red Fareham brick, recently cleaned to reveal its brilliance, with a restless pattern of larger and smaller rounded windows on the first floor of the main central block, a French *château* roof rising behind a balustrade, and a big eaved but frilly-topped *porte-cochère*. It is right in the centre of the city, since Portsmouth developed during the nineteenth century away from the original medieval and Georgian streets alongside the harbour mouth towards the centre of the island, with the surroundings of the station becoming the focal area. The station was built as a terminus, but in the 1870s the ancient earthworks and moats which had surrounded the older town were removed, and over part of their site a railway extension was built to a new station beside the harbour mouth, connecting directly with the departing ships for the Isle of Wight. This meant that through lines had to be provided alongside the original terminal station at a higher level, since they had to cross the main street, Commercial Road, immediately to the west. The present twisty high level platforms between the two through lines, with their ironwork canopy, date from then.

Now most trains use these two platforms to go to or from Portsmouth Harbour. Portsmouth Harbour station itself, remarkable in being built on piles, over tidal water, was rebuilt between the wars.

Eastbourne is a particularly exuberant LB & SCR terminal station, relatively little altered. The town was a late starter as a major seaside resort; until well into the nineteenth century it was an inland village with loose seaside appendages. From about 1850 the Duke of Devonshire, the principal landowner, began to develop it as a superior resort, and in 1861

what was originally a branch line was opened, ending at a discreet distance from the sea-front, though in a good position at a bend in the main shopping street. Nikolaus Pevsner and Ian Nairn (probably the latter) wrote of the station in *Buildings of England: Sussex*: 'Yellow brick, low and with an inexorable multitude of funny motifs, basically medievalizing but not shunning a French pavilion roof either.' It has indeed a multitude of motifs, including a corner clock of the miniature Big Ben type, a series of greenhouse roofs over the external canopy (this could be later) and a tall upper roof tier, pagoda-like, rising over a clerestory on top of the booking hall. The yellow brick is variegated with red and black. The station has an affinity with that at nearby Lewes.

In the far north-east, Tynemouth station served a resort which was fashionable in mid-Victorian times, particularly, so it was said, for Scotsmen coming south. An enormous station was built by the North-Eastern Railway in 1882. As with other NER stations, particularly York, the forebuilding is not very imposing, but the interior is a huge labyrinthine space subdivided by numerous columns and openwork girders, with a repeated 'greenhouse' type roof. All it serves now is a frequent suburban service (soon to be taken over by the Tyneside Metro), and the wide side platforms for holiday excursion trains are empty. Tynemouth, despite its unspoiled beach, was in the end considered to be too near industrial Tyneside for discriminating holidaymakers, and by the end of the century Whitley Bay, just to the north, had become the main Northumbrian seaside resort. Both Whitley Bay and its appendage Monkseaton have pleasing Edwardian stations in brick with elaborate stone dressings.

The NER paid considerable attention to roofs all through its existence. Newcastle, York and Darlington are, of course, major examples. At Stockton, William Bell, then the NER's architect, designed a latter-day round-arched roof of wide span in 1893 (as he had earlier done in the bigger station at Stockton's inseparable brother Darlington). At Hull, Bell reconstructed Andrews's station behind the latter's forebuildings in 1903–5;

Above *Eastbourne, Sussex; 1884. Boldly asymmetrical classic design with central clock tower. Note the top-lit booking hall on the right*
Left *Tynemouth, Tyne and Wear; fine filigree ironwork*

it is roofed by a busy series of narrow round-arched spans supported by columns and lattice steel girders. Nothing is now left of Bell's round-arched roof at Sunderland, rising from about ground level over a station set in a cutting in the heart of the town, to which the railway originally terminating at Monkwearmouth across the Wear had been extended in 1879. Sunderland station was bomb-damaged, like its even more remarkable iron-roofed counterpart at Middlesbrough; what survived at Sunderland, including a rather wild Gothic forebuilding, was swept away for rebuilding a few years ago.

Perhaps the Queen of railway stations, certainly one of the best in the provinces for restrained elegance in the mid-Victorian period, was Green Park (originally Queen Square) in Bath. This was a terminal for two lines approaching from different directions, the Midland from Mangotsfield, connecting there from Gloucester and the Midlands, and the long-lamented Somerset and Dorset, which climbed so majestically, through sinuous valleys, to the Mendip summit and then descended to the misty Vale of Avalon (at least Glastonbury Tor always appeared rising amid mist whenever I took that journey), and over the Shepton viaduct to the remote rural junction of Evercreech. Through trains, most notably the Pines Express, actually went into Bath Green Park and out on their way from Manchester or Sheffield or Brad-

ford to Bournemouth. Now the station is derelict, awaiting the decision of a prevaricating planning authority as to whether it should be converted into a hypermarket. The forebuilding is impeccably Bath Georgian long out of its time; through it one enters a train shed which, though designed apparently without embellishment, is one of the most effective of its kind, with its simple segmental

Above *Middlesbrough, Cleveland; 1873–7 by William Peachey. Railway Gothic at its most original*
Left *Carlisle, Cumbria; 1848 by Sir William Tite. Graceful structural ironwork, shorn of ornamental detail*
Far left *Tynemouth, Tyne and Wear; 1882. Fine ornamental ironwork*

ribs rising from plain octagonal columns, the roof structure itself resting, tent-like, tangentially to the ribs.

Iron-arched roofs gradually went out of favour in the latter years of the nineteenth century with a preference for more complex systems of over-all roofing, as at Tynemouth. At Stoke-on-Trent and Carlisle the new over-all roofs erected behind Hunt's and Tite's forebuildings respectively in 1893 and 1873–6 were of the ridge-and-furrow or 'repeated greenhouse' style, supported on close-spaced steel girders (the same system as was adopted at Waterloo and Glasgow Central during the present century). Much more usual were individual platform canopies, with their often profusely decorated ironwork. The Great Eastern favoured for their platform canopies a series of narrow-spanned 'greenhouse' roofs at right angles to the spans, with repeated gable-shaped perforated bargeboards facing the line. A good intact example is on the central platform at Ipswich.

The latter-day stations of the Great Western are not, on the whole, particularly interesting architec-turally. Slough is a special case. This was always an important junction (for Windsor) even before Slough became big as a town. It was rebuilt in 1879 as if it were a small, but elaborate, French *château* and retains its splendid skyline intact, with bulbous roofs and profuse ironwork. Long may it remain undiminished. The GWR's terminal in the heart of Windsor was belatedly rebuilt in 1897 as if to outdo the rival terminus of the L & SWR. Its chief features are the round-arched shed (surely one of the very last of its kind to be built), constructed over a curving viaduct, and, peculiarly, an adjacent round-arched *porte-cochère* entered end-on from the street. One comes out of this arched space straight into the heart of the town, right opposite the castle walls in all their Victorian glory (this part of the curtain wall and the Curfew Tower were refaced by the Victorian architects Edward Blore and Anthony Salvin).

Both the Midland and, to a lesser extent, the London and South-Western developed exuberant styles of station architecture towards the end of the century, generally of rich red brick with profuse

Left Slough, Berkshire; 1879 in French *pavillon* style with *oeil de boeufs* and fishscale roofs
Right Nottingham Midland; 1904 by A. E. Lambert. *Edwardian baroque with the full swagger of Empire*

dressings of stone or sometimes terracotta, the more florid examples of Flemish and French Renaissance styles often providing the precedents. Leicester (London Road) is perhaps the Midland's latter-day *tour-de-force*, with its tremendous façade of one tall storey in red brick and terracotta with round-arched openings, balustrade and bulbous turret. A series of large arches leads from the street into what amounts to an inset *porte-cochère*. The façade is fortunately to be retained when the rest of the station is redeveloped behind. Nottingham is a later (1904) and even more ebullient Midland station, faced in dark red terracotta.

The L & SWR's later Flemish and French styles are found particularly at smaller stations. Bournemouth (originally Bournemouth Central, opened in 1885) is rather special. It is essentially a huge train shed over four tracks and two side platforms, with tall side walls, and ancillary facilities set into, or abutting on to, the main structure on either side. The roof was extraordinary, resting on a series of wide open lattice girders partly supported on brackets fixed to the side walls but otherwise with-

out intermediate support. The central part of the roof itself has been removed, but the girders remain. The upper part of the south façade is in effect a clerestory, with triple groups of thin segment-headed windows between buttresses which take the thrust of the girders. The walls and buttresses are of a harsh local red-brown brick.

At Salisbury an interesting comparison can be made of three different styles. The main part is a 1900 L & SWR rebuilding in dark red brick set off by thin stone dressings, with a series of big round-arched windows. Adjoining is the façade of the more modest earlier forebuilding (1859), stuccoed, in a simple classical style following the Tite tradition. Round the corner and under the bridge can be seen the former goods shed of the original GWR terminal (of a line from Westbury opened in 1856) which adjoined the through L & SWR station; with its thin stone pilasters and door and window surrounds standing out against the red brick walling it is in unmistakable Brunel style – an example of a quite modest building with basic elements achieving real distinction.

SMALL TOWN STATIONS
PETER BURMAN

ETWEEN THE GREAT TERMINI and the large town stations on the one hand and on the other the tiny stations and halts which once served so many hamlets or groups of houses all over Britain, there lies the extensive group of medium-sized stations serving the market or smaller industrial towns. In this chapter an attempt will be made to show something of the variety of style and character of these stations; something of the work of the principal architects in the field of railway design; and of the relationship of the stations to other types of buildings, especially those which were evolving *pari passu* in the nineteenth century. Something will be said also of the stations in this category which are currently, for one reason or another, at risk in the sense of being possible candidates for demolition (not a few, as will later become apparent, are already closed and either in use for temporary purposes such as storage or gently mouldering away).

The relationship of stations to their communities is a point which is immediately striking. Many stations appear to be in the middle of nowhere, but in fact serve sizable towns as well as catchment areas of a predominantly rural kind. One example of this is Audley End which, although in its unexpected grandeur it obviously reflects the proximity of Audley End House and the convenience of Lord Braybrooke and his guests up until the 1930s, also serves the township of Saffron Walden. Another example of this is the station of Kemble, serving Cirencester and Tetbury.

'The coming of the railway to Cambridge would be highly displeasing both to God and myself,' a nineteenth-century Master of Magdalene is said to have remarked, and his confidence in the value of his insight into the workings of Providence is merely on a par with the self-confidence of those directors of railway companies whose determination increased the extent of the railway system by leaps and bounds in the 1840s and 1850s. The result of opposition from the University however is that the station in Cambridge is at a considerable remove from the colleges and commercial centre of the city. In Oxford the station is likewise at a dignified distance from the High Street and the

Greenwich, London; 1840 by G. Smith, re-erected 1878. Restrained Italianate, complete with a piano nobile to impress

majority of the colleges. Similar opposition to the physical location of stations was exerted elsewhere by privileged bodies or individuals: at Stamford, for example, by the all-powerful Marquess of Exeter – so that the railway went instead through Peterborough, then a smaller place.

It must be admitted that, in cases such as these, the railway companies seem to have been prepared to make extra efforts to secure the erection of buildings of some architectural dignity, which would enhance rather than mar the architectural environment of which they formed a novel part. Hence, perhaps, the choice of Gothic – though admittedly

late Tudor Gothic – for Durham City station, which has a crenellated portico on five mildly Perpendicular arches. In this case the Dean and Chapter seem to have played a significant delaying role, by asking exorbitant prices for the land through which the projected railway ran. The station at Cambridge was in its original form one of the finest works attributed to Francis Thompson: the frontage to the street presented a continuous arcaded ground storey which happily still survives; while the original station at Newmarket, where fashionable society came for the racing, was one of the most impressive of all stations in this category for its architectural grandeur. What still precariously survives is the seven-bay single-storey building which has been aptly likened to a baroque orangery – an immensely powerful composition with coupled Ionic columns bearing a boldly projecting entablature, and above it eight chunks (especially in their eroded state) of attic storey. The dismal red brick station at Oxford cannot be said to have lived up to this standard, though it was certainly a good

deal better than the exceptionally meagre replacement which British Rail have recently provided.

In many towns the erection of a station has gradually altered the planning balance of the town, so that from beginning as a building perhaps virtually in the fields (as at Tonbridge, for example) the station has become a fulcrum of commercial and other related activities which naturally found it beneficial to be close to the railway.

It is worth bearing in mind, in the context of location, the point made by David Lloyd in his essay on 'Railway Architecture: small stations' in

Steam Horse: Iron Road that 'until the invention of the motor car, electric tram and motor-bus, railway stations had to be reached by horse-drawn transport, or else on foot. So they were usually built at relatively short intervals – every two or three miles, or less where the population was relatively dense.'

Turning to the designers of the railway stations, it is immediately apparent that the challenge of evolving a new form of building type lay less within the sphere of a conventional architect (who, in the 1840s and 1850s, would probably have been producing schools, vicarages and churches) and more within the sphere of the man who was something between an architect and an engineer. In the High Victorian period *The Builder* from time to time inveighed against the railway companies for having stations designed by men who were not architects, and it is true that the use of styles (Jacobean, Tudor, East Anglian Flemish, various forms of classical and Italianate, and occasionally Gothic) was often ill digested and sometimes illiterate.

It is difficult to think of architects distinguished for their work in other categories of architectural

Above *Great Malvern, Worcestershire; 1863 by E. W. Elmslie. Enchantingly decorative spa station*
Left *Windermere, Cumbria; minimal Gothic executed in two colours of brick*

design who contributed significantly to the architectural history of the small town railway station, and this seems a pity: greater cross-fertilization between the designing of, say, churches and railway stations would surely have produced some exciting spatial experiences and a more confident handling of the range of styles – a station concourse vaulted by J. L. Pearson, the designer of St Augustine's, Kilburn, and Truro Cathedral, for example; or a stationmaster's house designed by William Butterfield or William Burges in their best 'vicarage' manner.

One architect who did cross the boundary between church work and the railways is E. W. Elmslie, designer of the sumptuous early Gothic revival church of St Thomas, New Southgate Street, in Winchester (1845–6, the steeple over the crossing completed in 1857). At that date the leaders of the Gothic revival in its early period – A. W. N. Pugin, George Gilbert Scott and Benjamin Ferrey – were introducing tracery of the Early Pointed period and Elmslie's handling of the vocabulary is no less convincing than theirs. Moreover, the siting of the church and the ambitious scale of the tower and spire make it one of the key visual elements in the townscape of Winchester no less now that it is the County Records Office for Hampshire than when it was still a parish church.

This same architect was responsible for the station of Great Malvern (1863) on the Worcester and Hereford line, which later became part of the Great Western. He may also have designed Malvern Link, described by Gordon Biddle as being 'in quiet Tudor with matching buildings and ridge-and-furrow awnings on both platforms', but Malvern Link has now largely disappeared and it is Great Malvern which is unquestionably the more memorable; and, like St Thomas's church in Winchester, it is a carefully considered part of its setting, since it embraces also a landscaped approach road and gardens, a bridge over the railway, and the Imperial Hotel.

As one might expect, the station reveals a knowledge of Gothic – handled in a manner which recalls the schools and vicarages designed by George Gilbert Scott, William Butterfield and George Edmund Street. The entrance façade comprises a long rambling range, with subsidiary ranges at either end set at right angles to it. Like many contemporary schools it is built of random stone with freestone detailing, single-storey and with steep roof pitches covered by slates. Prominent features of the skyline are the profusion of strongly moulded chimneys and a cresting along the roof ridges of a pierced quatrefoil pattern. The door and window openings are asymmetrically disposed along the façade, and include both flat and triangular-headed openings – the latter having a circlet punched in the head, recalling the plate tracery used by some architects in the 1850s and 1860s. One of the subsidiary doorways has a round-headed arch, evoking the twelfth century, with a single order of attached colonettes. There are two small angular gables in the long main façade, set close together at one end; and these play point counter-point to the larger gables of the ranges at either end. Most striking of all, but now alas removed, was the dominating feature of a clock turret set diagonally on the roof ridge over the main entrance. Above the clock turret was a deep pierced frieze, topped by a steeply pitched miniature roof; and the whole was capped by a flying spirelet springing from the four corners of the frieze and ornamented with crocketed pinnacles – a delightful piece of fantasy, and one which was entirely successful in forming a visual climax to the composition. Once inside the station the visitor still encounters the other most memorable and visually fantastic feature in the shape of the marvellous capitals supporting the awning. The capitals are of wrought iron, richly inventive in their design, and have been painted up in yellow, blue and red so as to maximize their effect.

Another memorable station in the Gothic style is that at Battle, in Sussex, designed by William Tress in 1852. Tress was a pupil of the distinguished classicist, Sir William Tite, but the proximity of Battle Abbey (part of whose ruins were turned into a Gothic mansion by Henry Clutton in 1857) no doubt encouraged Tress to turn to Gothic here. The main façade of dark stone trimmed with lighter stone gives the impression of a vicarage (the station-

SMALL TOWN STATIONS

Left *Battle, Sussex; hooded fireplace*
Below *Battle, Sussex; 1852 by William Tress*

master's house) combined with a church hall, the booking office having a gabled front elevation with two tall windows, of two tall trefoiled lights each with a circlet in the head. The original beautiful slate roof coverings survive, with intriguing patterns in different-toned slates.

G. T. Andrews's Richmond station, in Yorkshire, was a most inspired essay in the Gothic vein: the *porte-cochère* has almost become a cloister, with five bays punctuated by convincing buttresses.

Other Gothic stations which deserve at least a passing mention are Stamford Town, where the bell turret evokes an echo of the Abbot's Kitchen at Glastonbury and elements of eighteenth-century Hawksmoor's Gothic can be discerned; and the tiny former station at Nailsworth, Gloucestershire,

built of yellow stone ashlar, which has a Gothic porch and foliated caps to the columns.

The best known of the architect-engineers is of course Isambard Kingdom Brunel. Brunel's work is closely identified with the expansion of the Great Western Railway, but he designed also for the smaller companies in association with the GWR, so that his stations are encountered over a wide area which includes not only the West Country but the west Midlands and South Wales. Beginning in the late 1830s, Brunel's designs were numerous but followed well-defined patterns and continued to be built even after his death in 1859.

The earliest examples of decorated valancing in railway stations are attributed to Brunel. Valanced awnings over the platforms, now all too frequently

Left *Stamford East, Lincolnshire; 1856 by William Hurst. Attention to detail worthy of the great Elizabethan house at Burghley on the edge of the town*
Right *Nailsworth, Gloucestershire; abandoned station with* Gothic *porte-cochère*

swept away in the interests of economical maintenance, served both to give delight to the eye and to fulfil the severely practical functions of deflecting driving rain or snow from the platform and of piercing the clouds of smoke and steam which an effort of the imagination is now required to conjure up.

Ealing, and then Maidenhead, were most likely the earliest manifestations of decorative valancing, though sadly in neither case does anything of Brunel's work now survive. The all-round awning appears with dog-tooth valancing – virtually a signature of Brunel's designs at this time – in his early stations; and the supports of the awning in the form of ironwork spandrels, mass-produced by Macfarlane's of Glasgow, are an important feature of the design. The use of decorative ironwork, mass-produced, in railway station architecture spread all over the British Empire: examples are legion in South Africa, New Zealand, Australia and India, and in those countries the same patterns were also used in domestic architecture to create the single-storey or two-storey stoeps or verandahs which so well suited their benign climates and were, in effect, the direct domestic descendants of Brunel's awnings.

A somewhat later station, Bradford-on-Avon in Wiltshire, which was opened in 1858, may be taken as a good example of a surviving town station by Brunel. This is a pleasant Tudor-style gabled building with mullioned windows, echoing the traditional weavers' cottages in the town, in the local

Above *March, Cambridgeshire; a dramatic perspective of matching canopies*
Right *Kettering, Northamptonshire; 1857 by C. H. Driver. Ironwork growing organically from the columns*

Bath stone, partly enveloped by Brunel's original canopy.

An important link between this station and its contemporaries and the world of domestic house-building is the use of the Tudor style. It is inconceivable that Brunel was unaware of the writings of the theorists of the picturesque landscape, and of the work of its practitioners; and if it may be too fanciful to discern a link between the Tudor window of Culham station and the Hermit's Cottage at Stourhead, it is not difficult to see a link between it and the work of John Adey Repton and John Nash. Now that our urban landscapes have changed so radically since the 1840s it is difficult to recapture a sense of the picturesque vision, but there seems no doubt that in his choice of Tudor (essentially an 'English' style) or, mostly later, greatly simplified Italianate, and still more in his choice of natural materials reflecting the indigenous use of local stone, wood or brick, Brunel was consciously intending his stations as designed elements in a landscape, not simply as isolated intrusions. It was not until the 1860s and onwards, after Brunel's death, that the indiscriminate use of mass-produced brick far from its place of origin became prevalent, owing to the ease with which it could by then be transported around the United Kingdom by rail, and also to the facility with which the increasingly standardized designs could be executed with a minimum of craftsmanship and skill. Hence, in Brunel's sphere of influence, the brick and flint of Oxfordshire and Berkshire stations was replaced further westwards by the appropriate Cotswold or Mendip stone, as at Wootton Bassett (1841, no longer surviving), Brinscombe (1845, closed) and Melksham (1848, closed).

For his second phase, Chepstow, perhaps the most engaging of the surviving Brunel stations, may be taken as an example. In this second phase the flat awnings were replaced by the device of a broad-hipped roof extending outwards on all sides to become, in effect, awnings. This device was generally combined with the use of a simplified Italianate style characterized by round-headed windows and doors, the surfaces of the walls being

Top *Bradford-on-Avon, Wiltshire; railway furniture emblazoned with the insignia of 'God's Wonderful Railway'*
Above *Tweedmouth, Northumberland; gabled Jacobean pavilion*
Right *Stone, Staffordshire; 1848 by H. A. Hunt, a handsome example of gabled Jacobean*

articulated by flat pilasters and the brickwork often being enriched with bands of darker brick.

An intriguing aspect of Brunel's technology is his use of timber for the structural elements of stations. He handled timber with such confidence, and such mastery, that many of his buildings in this uncertain medium have survived remarkably well. As an example, we can cite the station and its ancillary buildings at Frome in Somerset. Here the use of timber was occasioned by financial stringency, the Wiltshire, Somerset and Weymouth Railway being then on a shoestring budget. For greater strength the wall of the train shed is divided horizontally into an upper and a lower stage, and the square panels thereby produced are strengthened both by vertical struts and by diagonals. The pleas-

ing but straightforward carpentry of the roof is given a modest visual interest – in a place where the public eye was unlikely to penetrate – by the curved brackets which link the main tie-beams and the wall-plates. The main part of the station consists of a range of buildings on the entrance side and a smaller range on the opposite platform linked by an over-all roof to form the train shed. Beyond the main structure is a free-standing awning on columns, edged with valancing. Valancing also appears, restrainedly, in the openings of the gable at either end of the main structure, the roof of which is raised up, and glazed, in the centre to form a kind of continuous lantern or clerestory. Another example of Brunel's use of wood is the unspoilt station of Lostwithiel in Cornwall, still painted

brown and cream, where the Cornish palm trees on the platforms add a touch of the exotic. At Dorchester West, also by Brunel, the main structure in timber survives, but not the canopies.

The multiplicity of rooms provided for a relatively small station serving a small market town is analogous to the strict separation of function in a Victorian country house – game larder, butler's pantry, housekeeper's room, and so forth – in that waiting and refreshment rooms were provided (often on every platform) for first- and third-class passengers (second-class passengers were expected to pay first-class prices), and sometimes also with a differentiation between the sexes. No wonder they proved difficult to run in the straitened circumstances of the post-war period. But, while there are understandable difficulties in adapting a system designed and given architectural expression in social circumstances quite different from those of the present day, it is surely the case that far greater effort and ingenuity could have been exercised in finding new uses for the superfluous spaces?

An extensive essay could be written on the use of the Jacobean style in railway station architecture, more especially as it produced some of the most attractive buildings in the genre. Louth, for example, in Lincolnshire, is one of the handsomest stations built by the Great Northern Railway: in red brick, with sharply curved gables and paired chimneys, it consists of a long single-storey main building with a two-storey block at either end. It was provided with a stone porch in the form of a shallow three-bay *porte-cochère*; the porch has Renaissance detailing taken up by the corner pilasters of the main building and is now in very poor shape. Surely it would make a splendid house? Sadly, the station was closed in 1970.

Maldon East, in Essex, is one of the most exciting of the Jacobean stations. Biddle tells of the bid for political influence which may account for the astonishing amount of money clearly lavished on what has every appearance of being a substantial country house – it is built of brick with stone dressings, and its façade has a frontispiece in the form

Far left *Market Weighton, Humberside; an elegant classical pavilion*
Left *Burntisland, Fife; c. 1842, the terminus of the North British Railway made redundant by the building of the Forth Railway Bridge*
Below *Gobowen, Salop; 1846 by T. K. Penson. Italianate*

of a nine-bay arcade, breaking forward at the sides so that there is a rhythm 3:3:3 and capped by a continuous balustrade. The side bays have shaped East Anglian-Flemish gables (formerly flanked by stubby stone finials, which have now mostly disappeared) and tall polygonal chimneys. The line from Witham to Maldon East was closed to passengers in 1964 and to freight in 1966. After some years of lying unused the station was adapted as a restaurant, the Great Eastern, but this has now been closed. This swashbuckling minor masterpiece well deserves careful restoration for some other suitable alternative use.

A stone-built example of the Tudor merging into Jacobean style is Stamford East, terminus of the Stamford and Essendine Railway, built by William Hurst in 1856. Again there are three elements in the design of the façade, with gables (ornamented by big stone urns) for the side bays, mullioned and transomed windows, and a centrepiece with a strapwork balustrade in the middle of which is a coat of arms. Stamford East has long been closed, and is now used for storage purposes.

The Jacobean style was sometimes mixed with earlier, Tudor, motifs as in the remarkable series of stations designed by Frederick Barnes of Ipswich for the Ipswich and Bury Railway of 1846. Needham Market, reopened in December 1971, is one of these, and resembles nothing so much as a Tudor mansion in miniature. It is built of red brick with quoins of white Suffolk brick and there are three gables on the approach front, with towers flanking the outer gables. Stowmarket, also by Frederick Barnes, is more Jacobean in feeling, with shaped gables echoing the sixteenth- and seventeenth-century Dutch-Flemish influence in East Anglia. Other outstanding Tudor–Jacobean stations include Wateringbury and Aylesford, the former in red brick and the latter in flint.

Francis Thompson was a designer who worked in classical Italianate and Tudor veins, straying occasionally into Jacobean. After working for the North Midland he was later taken on by the Chester and Holyhead Railway, opened in 1846–50, where the stations he designed were classical in style, the larger ones consisting of a central block with flat verandah roofs at front and rear between the flanking pavilions. Holywell Junction, closed since 1966, is one of the most pleasing of these. Another example, with the same motif of projecting pavilions at either end of the two-storey main block, is at Mostyn.

Thompson also worked for the Eastern Counties Railway. *The Builder* attributes Audley End, Great Chesterford and Cambridge to him; and others which seem likely on stylistic grounds to be by him include Bishop's Stortford (which has been extensively altered), Lakenheath, Waterbeach, Ely and Whittlesea, all dating from 1842–7. Ely is classical, in the Chester and Holyhead manner, but of white brick and plainer than Holywell or Mostyn.

Another architect associated with the development of a particular line was G. T. Andrews, who flourished under the patronage of George Hudson. Andrews had been Sheriff of York at the time of the election in 1847, when he exercised his political influence in favour of Hudson's nominees, and from this unpromising relationship a good deal of

Above *Whitley Bay, Tyne and Wear; 1910 seaside Jacobean*
Right, above *Rye, Sussex; miniature Italianate villa with loggia inset*
Right, below *Clacton, Essex; between the wars Georgian*

fine railway architecture developed. Apart from designing the major stations at York and Hull, he evolved for the country towns of the East and and North Ridings of Yorkshire a standard design of train shed, exemplified at Scarborough (1845). This shed has a handsome stone exterior and a complicated internal roof structure, of thin iron ties supported on a central iron arcade. The Scarborough arcade seems to be the earliest surviving example in a railway station of a range of iron piers and horizontal girders, bracketed to appear like arches, although several earlier examples, dating back to the 1830s, once existed. Bridlington, Filey (both 1846) and Pocklington (1847) have similar train sheds. Malton (1845) is a very handsome plain classical stone building; it had a large one-road (that is two-way traffic, one line) train shed, a type which also occurred elsewhere in the North-Eastern Railway system. (Redcar was another example.) Pocklington, now a sports centre, was a fairly typical NER station. Large in scale, for a town with at most approximately 3,000 people, it has a handsome Renaissance-style entrance with five arches.

Another example of Andrews's work, with the five-arched motif appearing in the *porte-cochère*, is the station at Whitby Town (1847). This is surely an evocation of the Renaissance, with a nod in the direction of the Loggia dei Lanzi in Florence? Combined with this Renaissance exoticism is a moulded cornice and the comfortable homeliness

Left *Market Harborough, Leicestershire; 1885 'Wrenais-
sance'*
Right *Alnmouth, Northumberland; iron brackets with quatre-
foils*
Below *Oban, Argyllshire; more North American than
Scottish*
Overleaf *Crystal Palace, London; 1854. The booking hall*

of Georgian-style sash windows. Andrews's Gothic Richmond station has already been mentioned. But his work is so extensive and so consistently high in quality that it is almost invidious to single out particular examples for attention in such a brief survey.

Examples have been mentioned of the use of Gothic styles, various aspects of classical or Italianate, and the more specifically native styles of Tudor or Jacobean. Exceptional, but worth noticing, are the occasional instances where a French flavour is discernible – as at Crystal Palace (Low Level, 1854) which was in the French *château* style, with Renaissance details; Welshpool (1860) in equally determined French Renaissance style; and Shanklin, Isle of Wight, with its very splendid cast iron brackets. The London, Brighton and South Coast Railway was seemingly fond of the 'French style', with examples at Eastbourne, Lewes, and Denmark Hill as well as at Crystal Palace.

Occasionally a still more exotic note is struck, associated in very many cases with the seaside or other holiday places – where, no doubt, the restraints of the everyday world could safely be set aside in railway architecture as in other matters. A famous example of this is the station at Matlock Bath in Derbyshire (1880s), which is Swiss in style, reflecting the almost Alpine character of the scenery: this is a delicious fantasy, and consisted originally of as many as five Swiss chalets, deploying timber-framing with brick nogging in herringbone pattern and big overhanging eaves to deflect the snow. A remarkable seaside trio is to be found at Saltburn-by-the-Sea (*c.* 1860–61), in Yorkshire; Wemyss Bay (1865), a popular resort from Glasgow; and Whitley Bay (1910), the 'Southend on Sea of Newcastle'. Saltburn might be described as 'Lombardic classical', and has a big three-arched *porte-cochère* evolving (like G. T. Andrews's Whitby) from the Loggia dei Lanzi in Florence. The booking hall has determinedly bold Lombardic tracery, and there is structural polychromy in the window heads of the side walls. A pleasant feature is the relationship of the station front with the spire of the church behind. Wemyss Bay has red-tiled roof coverings, homely gables and timber-framing, unexpectedly combined with an asymmetrically placed and uncompromisingly tall clock tower. At Whitley Bay the clock tower forms the focus of the composition, with splendid baroque stone swags round the clock and an ogee cap on top. These three deserve to be better known.

Not so wilful, but uncommon in their styles or treatment, are Hertford East (1888) and Market Harborough (1885). Hertford East has elegantly shaped Flemish-inspired gables which look back to our East Anglian group. But the feeling is quite different, more cosmopolitan and sophisticated, with superb detailing in red brick and white stone. The *porte-cochère* is on a grand scale, with two arches, one semicircular and the other segmental. There is strapwork over the windows (perhaps an allusion to Hatfield House?), and over the main part of the station building is a lantern or bell-cote which makes it look like the hall of an Oxford or Cambridge college. Market Harborough, at a junction of the London and North-Western and the Midland Railways, is notable for being a rare and particularly successful example of the Queen Anne style: of red brick, with white pilasters and window surrounds, and a tiny out-of-scale dormer in the centre of the sweeping roof. This is one of the most endearing of the small town stations.

Finally (and once more illustrating the distinctive part played by the patronage of the smaller companies) two Welsh examples, also returning us to seaside exotica, at Barmouth and at Tenby. In both cases the support for the awnings is shown, the cut-out style being typical of the Cambrian Railways. At Barmouth the bracket (which is found also at Aberdovey) almost defies description: perhaps the cut-outs depict, or suggest, a bird in flight, a fish and a tadpole? All evoke redolently the Victorian seaside holiday. And at Tenby the large trefoil shapes are outlined by tiny punched circles.

It would be possible to continue almost indefinitely the catalogue of quirks and oddities, and the delights and charms, of the town railway station. Enough has been discussed, and illustrated, to show just how varied and impressive a group of buildings it is – one to be jealously guarded, and kept in good repair, and needing (in all too many cases) the sympathetic restoration of all-important detail.

COUNTRY AND SUBURBAN STATIONS
ALAN YOUNG

DESPITE THE STEADY STREAM of station closures over the years and the recent trend to replace old station buildings with smaller and simpler ones, Britain retains a fascinating collection of small stations. The vast majority were constructed during the nineteenth century, and they were the product of numerous independent companies, each of whom provided a brand of station reflecting its financial state, its pretensions and the taste of the architects it employed. Since the station building era has stretched over a 150-year period which has seen both the introduction of new building materials and remarkable changes in architectural fashions, it is not surprising that station architecture has reflected these developments.

The first country stations were experimental and simple, their buildings being small and functional. It soon became apparent to the companies that resident station staff should be in attendance, so the station house became a common feature, early examples being at Wylam and Riding Mill on the Newcastle and Carlisle Railway (1835). At Mitcham, Surrey (now Greater London), an existing house was adopted for the station. For the issuing of tickets and the handling of parcels, offices were built either within the structure of the station house or as an appendage. Passenger shelters were provided either as buildings in their own right or within the station house structure. Many station buildings had a recessed area on the track side, covered to shelter passengers, or an awning extending beyond the building towards the track. Platforms were not always provided at the earliest stations, but were added later, as at Wylam and Riding Mill. Platform construction, or the raising of original low platforms, could create a comic effect of dwarfed buildings with ground-floor windows almost level with passengers' feet on the platform, as at Cleland, Lanarkshire (now Strathclyde). Numerous stations have the house standing at some distance from the platform and other buildings; this may be seen at some Midland Railway stations including Irchester, Northamptonshire (closed), where access to the station was from a road-over-rail bridge. The plain brick station house was built

at road level, high above the platforms, which had their own buildings.

In contrast to the major city stations, whose size and, in some cases, magnificence can overawe the passenger, in country and suburban stations the structures approach a more human scale. The station house is normally the largest part, so the platform furniture and fittings, which on a larger station are easily overlooked, achieve greater prominence. A footbridge, for instance, can dominate a small station, whereas in a larger station it nestles discreetly beneath the train shed. Similarly

Left *Mitcham, Surrey ; house c. 1800 converted into station c. 1855*
Below *Etchingham, Sussex ; unusually deep canopy valences*
Overleaf *Pen-y-Groes, Gwynedd*

a station garden, of which there are few today, could make a small station special. Indeed it was by the standard of the garden, rather than the architecture, that the public judged a station's appeal.

The buildings at a suburban station would be only offices, workshops, lavatories, waiting rooms and shelters, possibly with awnings, yet the overall bulk of the structures could be considerable. This is the case at some London stations, for example Eltham Park. Certain rural stations have been engulfed by suburban growth yet have kept their original character; Benton, Northumberland (now Tyne and Wear; temporarily closed), which still has its station house, is a good example.

Early this century 'halts' were first built. These were usually tiny, unstaffed stations, in town or country, with simple buildings. The Great Western Railway favoured corrugated iron 'pagoda' huts whose roofs curved concave-upwards to a ridge, as at Goonbell, Cornwall (closed) and Radipole, Dorset, halts, but they were more ambitious at Wood End in Warwickshire (strictly a 'platform',

Left *Fenny Stratford, Buckinghamshire; herringbone half-timbered and ornamental bargeboards*
Above *Charlbury, Oxfordshire; overhanging roof canopy*

not a 'halt'), where they erected a grotesque assemblage of shacks. The Great Eastern Railway reused old railway coaches as shelters, for example at Brundall Gardens, Norfolk. A few halts are more substantial. Emerson Park in Essex (now Greater London), on the London, Tilbury and Southend Railway, has a booking office and large awning.

As well as contrasting in building styles and facilities offered, stations also differ in layout. The number of tracks through the station normally dictates the number of platform faces which will be required. Single-track railways, except at passing places, have single platform stations. Double-track railways usually have two flanking platforms, but can have one island platform between the tracks. The Great Central Railway's London Extension has numerous island platform stations such as Rothley in Leicestershire (preserved by the Main Line Steam Trust), which has simple buildings and a short awning. The North British line to Fort William is another case, with delightful single-storey platform buildings notable for their gambrel roofs and glazed end screens, as at Rannoch, Perthshire (now Tayside). In a very few cases double-track railways

have platforms on one line only, as at Seghill, Northumberland (closed). West Auckland, County Durham, now regrettably demolished, had two platforms for a double track, both facing in the same direction, one sandwiched between the tracks and backed by a fence. Some companies favoured the staggering of platforms, often with one each side of a level crossing, as at Spooner Row, Norfolk. An extreme case is Dilton Marsh, Wiltshire, where diminutive platforms with simple shelters stand many yards apart, either side of a bridge. Junction stations have been built with a

Left and above Chathill, Northumberland; *gables, bay windows, chimneys and finials make this small station an eventful design where wooden columns support the canopies*

variety of layouts depending upon whether they are situated before or beyond the parting of the lines, and whether platforms are provided for terminating trains. In London Tooting (formerly a junction) has flanking platforms on a double track. Helsby, Cheshire, is beyond its junction.

Much of the most flamboyant architecture was reserved for major town stations, where rival companies were anxious to outclass each others' buildings and the admiration of architectural masterpieces was assured by virtue of the sheer numbers of passengers who would use the stations. There are, however, numerous minor stations of architectural merit.

Possibly our most strikingly designed small stations are of the *cottage orné* style. The railway passenger between Bedford and Bletchley is treated to a succession of charming buildings at Millbrook, Ridgmont, Woburn Sands and Fenny Stratford. Each is an extravagant composition of half-timbering and fancy bargeboards, and, of the four, Fenny Stratford is the best. Its half-timbering is in a mixture of herringbone, lattice and other geometrical patterns, and the platform elevation has a bay window at ground-floor level, a tiny dormer with fancy bargeboards, and there are lean-to porches flanking the building, providing shelter for waiting passengers. The *cottage orné* style is found too in the upland settings of Central Wales and the Yorkshire Dales. The Cambrian Railways stations at Cemmes Road and Pontdolgoch in Montgomeryshire (now Powys; both closed) have large, dignified villas in dark stone, but their sombreness is relieved by their delicate bargeboards. On the Midland Railway, near Skipton, Yorkshire, Clapham and Giggleswick stations have small, charming *cottages ornés*, incorporating recessed waiting shelters. Whether these two stations are really at home in an area noted for its austere and functional architecture is questionable.

Many railway companies erected fine Tudor buildings at their stations, and a lot of these have survived beyond closure owing to their aesthetic qualities, sound structure and usefulness as houses. The Newcastle and Berwick Railway built a splendid collection of Tudor stations, including Chathill and Acklington, which were designed by the northern architect Benjamin Green. The stations have a strong family resemblance, all stone-built with tall chimneys and ball finials on their gables, but they differ in detail. Acklington's building appears, at first glance, symmetrical, with a pair of two-storey pavilions projecting on to the platform and a covered waiting area (or 'integral awning') recessed into the building between them. However, to add interest, the ground floor of one of the pavilions has a bay window, and, further destroying symmetry, another integral awning is added to one end of the building. Chathill's composition shows no attempt at symmetry. It has only one two-storey pavilion on the platform elevation, each storey having a bay window; a dormer with a ball finial breaks the eaves, and there is only one integral awning. To add to its charm, Chathill is one of the very few British stations to retain antique oil casement lamps on its platforms.

The North Staffordshire Railway's Churnet Valley line possessed good Tudor stations, but some, such as Oakamoor, have been demolished. Fortunately, although they have closed, Cheddleton and Rushton remain, both stone-built and elegant. Cheddleton's building has an interesting towering quality produced by a tall dormer and immense chimneys, while Rushton, also notable for its chimneys, has a more substantial appearance, more like Green's Newcastle and Berwick stations. On the Birkenhead Joint Railway in Cheshire, Little Sutton and Ince and Elton stations have stone Tudor villas on their north platforms, sturdily constructed with finialled gables and tall chimneys, looking very much like the Newcastle and Berwick stations, if slightly less ornate. The small waiting shelters on the south platforms are intact, complementing the main buildings.

Making an interesting contrast with the majority of Tudor railway stations, which possess an austere grandeur, are Thurgarton and Lowdham, both in Nottinghamshire. These stations were built by the Midland Railway, whose standard of architecture was generally good, and they have a pleasingly delicate appearance thanks to the combination of steeply sloping chalet-style roofs and charming elaborate bargeboards.

The Jacobean style, with curving gable ends as a dominant feature, is found at a few small stations, and Sandon, Staffordshire (closed), Brocklesby, Lincolnshire (now Humberside), and Thurston, Suffolk, are among the best examples. At Thurston there is a fascinating Tudor–Jacobean building; from the elevated platforms it appears unremarkable, but it possesses a splendid exterior with a three-arched porch, a pair of three-storey gables, and a central portion with a weathervane.

In southern and eastern England in particular, elegant Italianate buildings, characterized by their solid symmetrical appearance and round-headed openings, stand at various stations. Sir William Tite provided the original design of large, hipped-roofed structures which are found on the former London and South Western Railway, for instance

Above *Thurgarton, Nottinghamshire; a picturesque station with steep roofs, bargeboards and hexagonal glazing*
Right *Thurston, Suffolk; an unexpected essay in Mannerism with a tall upper storey over a mezzanine*

at St Denys, Southampton, and Chertsey, Surrey. Although, like the Tudor stations of the Newcastle and Berwick Railway, these Italianate buildings are superficially alike, some are symmetrical while others are not entirely so, and the quoins and eaves brackets differ in detail from station to station. Francis Thompson is believed to be the designer of a number of Italianate railway stations scattered around England, and a few in North Wales. Perhaps they are not as elegant as those based upon Tite's designs, but many of them are quite dignified. Great Chesterford, Cambridgeshire, has a large, imposing, two-storey building, almost box-like, with a near-flat roof; the austerity of its appearance is reduced by the flat awning stretching the whole length of the building's platform elevation, supported by end screens and straight brackets. A different Thompson style can be found at Bodorgan on Anglesey. The flat roof and awning of Great Chesterford are replaced at Bodorgan by a pitched roof and a sloping integral awning. The design is a very well balanced one, having a two-storey house flanked by single-storey wings, between which the roof continues to form the awn-

ing. An interesting feature that Bodorgan shares with some other Thompson stations in North Wales is a stone tablet with the station's name engraved on it, set into the back wall of the platform. One further station by Francis Thompson deserves mention. Wingfield, on the former North Midland Railway in Derbyshire, is a particularly satisfying design which Biddle in *Victorian Stations* uses to show Thompson's concern in providing symmetrical buildings with an attractive platform elevation. The building is fairly plain, 'relying for effect on the exact proportions and restrained styling of the central pavilion and lower flanking wings'. The central pavilion formerly carried the station's name in gilded letters, but these have regrettably been removed.

Although they were formerly elegant, the Italianate buildings at North Woolwich and Collingham have been spoilt in recent years. North Woolwich is the terminus of a run-down branch through London's dockland, where only the booking office has been in regular use. At Collingham, in Nottingham, an ugly platform shelter now stands in front of the fine main building.

Towards the close of the nineteenth century some railway companies, under the influence of the Arts and Crafts movement, erected imaginative buildings which cannot easily be related to any particular historic style. Such a station is Privett in Hampshire, possessing a large, elegant building with a fine frontage. Two carefully shaped gables stand forward from a hipped roof which is also interrupted by two dormers, while a tiled entrance porch adds interest to the lower half of the building. 'Stockbroker' Tudor appears in various stations, ranging from a modest half-timbered gable at West Jesmond, Northumberland (now Tyne and Wear; temporarily closed) through the single-storey building with timber-framed brickwork, gambrel roof and half-timbered gable which formerly stood at Sandling, Kent, to the exotic rambling two-storey structure at Saughall, Flintshire, now Clwyd (closed).

Here timber-framing is widely used, the roof has a lantern, and there is an integral awning, making one of the most remarkable buildings at any small station. In Sussex, Cocking and Lavant (both closed) have massive station buildings notable for their half-timbering and pargeting in a pot-plant design, which show the Arts and Crafts influence.

During the twentieth century railway buildings have continued to reflect contemporary architectural ideas. The inter-war period was one of interesting developments, notably the replacing of straight lines and right angles with curves, and this produced some striking designs in new London Transport stations such as Arnos Grove. The main line station at Hoylake, Cheshire (now Merseyside)

Above *Menai Bridge, Gwynedd; a profusion of chimney stacks provide the architectural accents, far more than were actually required*
Right *Matlock Bath, Derbyshire; timber framing, zigzag brickwork and low-pitched overhanging roofs*

is in the same idiom, the booking hall rising one storey above the rest of the building as a squat circular tower. Bishopstone, Sussex, is similar, though the tower is octagonal. In London the main line Highgate station was rebuilt in the 1930s with austere box-like structures of brick and a flat concrete awning. It closed to passengers in 1954, and vegetation is now overwhelming it. At its Chessington branch stations in Surrey (now Greater London), built on the eve of the Second World War, the Southern Railway erected amazing futuristic curved concrete awnings, springing forward from restrained platform buildings. Malden Manor station, one of the intermediates on the branch, has retained its 1930s character particularly well. It still has its original concrete lamp standards.

In addition to those station buildings which have some clearly defined architectural style there are numerous others which lack such pretensions but are nevertheless attractive. Large straightforward two-storey stone houses are found at many Scottish stations, for example at Georgemas Junction, Caithness (now Highland). Greater distinction was given to others by gables on the front elevation, as at Garve, Ross and Cromarty (now Highland) and three dormers, as at Lairg, Sutherland (now Highland), two at first-storey level and a further one slightly above ground-floor level. At many of the minor stations in Britain's wilder and more remote areas, particularly simple, but entirely appropriate, buildings were erected, which could easily pass for roadside cottages. Deadwater (closed), standing in the bleak landscape of the England–Scotland border, is such a station. Its single-storey stone building with a shallow pitching roof (formerly housing the office and waiting room) and small stone sheds at either end is entirely without decoration.

It was partly owing to the coming of the railways that bricks became widely available. Nevertheless railway companies often preferred to use stone, for aesthetic reasons, or because the stations were built before the tracks were laid over which bricks could be imported. As new building materials have become available so they have been adopted in the construction of stations, and progressively glass,

concrete and plastic have been added to the traditional materials.

The use of local stone allows the station to blend with existing local buildings. This is well illustrated at Bow and North Tawton stations (both closed) at the foot of Dartmoor. Although their Italianate buildings with round-headed windows are reminiscent of some stations in the south-western suburbs of London (such as Strawberry Hill) the choice of granite in their construction allows them to fit comfortably into the Devonshire landscape. The attractive rambling building at the Dorset

station of Corfe Castle (closed) is constructed of rock-faced Purbeck limestone, as is practically every other structure in the village. The two-storey station house is at one end of the building, then follow offices whose roofs drop in height from that of the house in two stages; the higher of these two roofs is broken by a dormer, and the lower one is enlivened by a small wood and tile lantern. The platform elevation is partly obscured by a simple ridge awning. Random, rather than layered, stone construction has produced attractive buildings at Aylesford, Kent, and also at Brentor, Devon

(closed). In or near chalklands flint facing adds character to station buildings; this treatment has been given to the charming Italianate station building at Micheldever, Hampshire, where, apart from the quoins, the entire frontage is flint-faced. County School (closed) in Norfolk has a hexagonal flint-faced tower springing from one side of the station house, whose upper storey is tile-hung – a feature one associates particularly strongly with architecture south of the Thames. In Sussex tile-hanging can be found on a number of stations. The closed and derelict Barcombe station is a good

Alton, Staffordshire; rugged Italianate, the former station master's house has a three-storey tower

example, with tiles hung on the upper storey of the two-storey station house. A large wooden entrance porch which projects from the single-storey office wing adds elegance to this station. At Wanborough station, Surrey, tiles clothe the frontage from ground to eaves level which, although interesting, is possibly excessive. Slate-hanging produces an austere effect at some London and South Western stations such as Tisbury, Wiltshire, where the walls of the entire platform elevation are a sombre grey; eaves corbelling and a curved awning make the composition more attractive.

Red brick was chosen for many stations, including Shenton, Leicestershire, which has a delightful platform building with a bracketed hipped roof and a tall chimney. Yellow or buff brick is preferred in some areas, although it is usually combined with red for decoration. The large villa at East Barkwith, Lincolnshire (closed), for instance, is of yellow brick with red brick bands, and the single-storey ridge-roofed structure at Cross Inn, Glamorgan (closed), is made attractive by red brick quoins and two red bands on the chimney stacks. The goods shed at Cross Inn has the colour scheme reversed,

Above *Petworth, Sussex; timber-clad with a zigzag frieze and dado – evocative of a Russian dacha*
Left *Bucknell, Salop; triple projecting gables provide shelter; the roof has bands of fish-scale tiles*

the greater part of the building being of red brick, with yellow reserved for detailing.

Railway companies wishing to economize on construction costs could choose wood rather than brick or stone. The South Eastern and Chatham Railway erected many 'Kentish clapboard' stations with simple single-storey hipped-roofed buildings, such as can be found at Headcorn, or at East Farleigh where there is an added awning. On the London and North Western Railway small wooden

buildings were erected on the platforms of some of the stations on the Lichfield City branch, for instance at Wylde Green, where the shallow-hipped roof of the single-storey building projects outwards slightly as an awning. Some wooden stations are built in the style of sports pavilions; there are good examples in Scotland. Carrbridge, Inverness (now Highland), has twin pavilions with bay windows and a long integral awning, while Plockton, Ross and Cromarty (now Highland), has a single pavilion, integral awning, decorated bargeboards and finials – a delicate-looking building in a bleak and rugged landscape. Petworth station in Sussex, built by the London, Brighton and South Coast Rail-

way, has an especially fine wooden building, which is unfortunately now derelict, and its platform elevation is obscured by vegetation. It is a long single-storeyed structure with a low-hipped roof. The corbelling under the eaves, the narrow panels of a herringbone pattern in the woodwork and a small lantern at one end of the building make it distinctive. Clearly it was essential to provide brick or stone chimneys in an otherwise wooden building, and at Petworth, as elsewhere, the brick chimneys contrasting with the woodwork and projecting high above the roof add considerable charm to the composition.

Corrugated iron is not usually chosen as an

attractive or durable building material, but a simple iron building survives in the Welsh upland setting of the closed station of Derry Ormond in Cardiganshire (now Dyfed). Concrete as a building material is best illustrated on the Chessington branch, whose stations have already been described here.

It is remarkable how an awning can lend dignity to the most simple station building; without its awning the building at Cressing, Essex, would be a plain brick box. Awnings differ greatly from station to station, although railway companies had their own preferred styles. The Midland favoured ridge-and-furrow awnings, as at Elstree, Hertfordshire; so did the Great Eastern in its London suburban area, for instance at Bruce Grove and Lower Edmonton, where awnings give distinction to otherwise unremarkable buildings. Elsewhere, as at Dersingham, Norfolk (closed), the GER erected flat awnings with serrated valancing. Brackets decorated with geometric designs or the Company's initials supported the awnings. In southern England curved awnings (as at Tisbury) and ridge awnings with straight gables (as at Corfe Castle) are common. Hipped awnings still survive at the closed Scottish stations of Dyce, Aberdeenshire (now Grampian), and Drybridge, Ayrshire (now Strathclyde). Awnings can rise or fall away from the building and, surprisingly, these two styles can be found at the adjacent closed stations of Radstock North (rising) and Wellow (falling), in Somerset (now Avon). At Hellifield, Yorkshire, there are possibly the finest examples of awnings which 'fall away' from the building, supported by large, elaborate brackets; it is a matter for regret that these awnings may soon be removed. The device of integrating the awning into the structure of the station building has been mentioned above with reference to Francis Thompson's stations. For some of his stations the great railway engineer Brunel used the device of a hipped roof which was too large for its building and extended forward as an awning; Mortimer, Hampshire, is an excellent example. Possibly the most interesting building to have an integral awning is the Furness Railway's station at Askam, Lancashire (now Cumbria),

where the roof descends from above second-storey level to form the awning, supported by wooden brackets. Flanking the awning are a gable facing the platform at one end of the building and a two-tier wood and tile lantern at the other end.

Minor architectural features add interest at numerous stations. Entrance shelters can range in size from the fully fledged awning at Severn Beach, Gloucestershire (now Avon), and the *porte-cochère* at Sandon, Staffordshire (closed), down to the wooden porch at Barcombe, Sussex (closed). Roy-

Above *Cressing, Essex; canopies and ironwork give character to even a simple station*
Left *Maxwell Park, Glasgow; low-pitched cantilevered roofs*

don, Essex, has a curious, possibly unique, curved wooden verandah with attractive valancing and columns. At some stations the windows are decorated, those at Glendon and Rushton, Northamptonshire (closed) having delightful lattice patterns. At the stations at Insch, Aberdeenshire (now Grampian), and Flixton, Lancashire (now Greater Manchester), there are rare surviving examples of drinking fountains; the Flixton fountain has been tastefully painted and could be mistaken for a small shrine!

So far the impression might have been given that there is a random geographical scattering of railway architectural styles. This is not entirely true, for definite styles were favoured by each company and generally there is some similarity between the stations on a line. In the early days, when numerous small companies built short local lines, the result was a great variety of buildings in a region, but larger companies eventually absorbed most of the smaller companies, so later buildings will often show uniformity over greater areas of the country. A few company styles will be described to illustrate these points.

In East Anglia the Great Eastern Railway was the dominant company, created by an amalgamation of various companies in 1862. One of the minor companies involved was the Waveney Valley Railway, whose first section (between Tivetshall and Harleston) opened in 1855. This railway produced a distinctive design of minor station building, which is interesting not only for its appearance but also for the fact that it is also to be found on the Colchester to Walton-on-Naze line, which opened a decade later, in GER days. This design is basically a red brick villa with a pitched roof. The upper storey on the front and platform elevations has one centrally placed round-headed window to which prominence is given by an ample, bracket-supported gable. At ground-floor level the front elevation has a large, centrally placed arched entrance flanked by paired round-headed windows, while on the platform elevation a shelter with a gently sloping lean-to roof is provided. This style of building can be seen, for example, at Weeley and Wivenhoe stations on the Colchester to Walton line, and on the closed Waveney Valley line there are well preserved specimens at Ditchingham, Geldeston (where all the walls, apart from the platform shelter, are rendered), and at the derelict Starston, closed as long ago as 1866, where buff brick quoins add elegance to the composition. The round-headed windows and tiled integral awnings of these station buildings are reminiscent of Francis Thompson's designs, and elsewhere on the lines which combined to form the GER there are stations which bear a faint family resemblance to those just discussed. The apron style of integral awning can still be seen at Oulton Broad South and Darsham stations on the East Suffolk line, and at the closed, derelict Belton and Burgh station in Suffolk, while plain two-storey buildings with integral awnings supported by end-blocks are still to be found at Marlesford and Melton stations in Suffolk (both

closed). Great Chesterford, perhaps the finest Francis Thompson style East Anglian station, has already been described, but Harleston (one of the more important stations on the closed Waveney Valley line) must also be mentioned as an extremely attractive Italianate building. Here, to use Biddle's words 'clever use was made of curving balustraded steps to an entrance midway between ground and first-floor platform level, creating an "area", flanked by gabled end-sections, to give the impression of a recess in a flat wall'.

While it adopted more than one existing design

Above *Glendon and Rushton, Northamptonshire; Norman window with diamond and hexagon glazing*
Left *Hellifield, North Yorkshire; 1880. Note the asymmetry of the brackets*

of building for new stations, the GER was not slow to develop what could be called its standard country station design, and many examples of the style can be seen on the disused system of lines linking Cambridge, Long Melford, Sudbury and Bury St Edmunds, on the former Bishop's Stortford to Braintree line, and also on the Ongar branch which is now on London Transport's Central Line. For the stationmaster a two-storey hipped-roofed house with rectangular openings was provided, and the station offices and public rooms were accommodated in a single-storey block recessed from the station house at the front and platform elevations. The single-storey roof was carried forward slightly as a platform awning. Buff bricks were used at the now disused stations of Pampisford, Cambridgeshire, and Takeley, Essex, while at Felsted (also closed) and Blake Hall, both in Essex, a more satisfying effect was obtained by using warm red brick with buff brick reserved for quoins. At the closed stations of Stoke, Suffolk, and Sturmer, Essex, as a variant on this design, typical GER awnings, supported by iron columns and wall brackets and surrounded by decorated valancing, formerly

stood over the platforms. To indicate their greater importance, certain stations had their small platform awning enclosed by a screen, and a single-storey hipped-roofed end-block was appended. These stations also benefited from the use of the two colours of brick, and closed but well preserved examples survive at Lavenham, Clare and Long Melford in Suffolk.

An interesting later addition to the GER stock of stations came from 1879 to 1882 when the East Norfolk Railway built its Wroxham to County School line. Although this company was nominally

Left *Glendon and Rushton, Northamptonshire; an unusual station on a T-plan*
Below *Eridge, Sussex; ironwork supporting the canopies*

independent the line was operated, and eventually absorbed, by the GER. Its station buildings (all of which are still standing twenty-five years after the closure of the line to passengers) are ample and handsome 'suburban' villas built of buff brick, with red window heads and string courses and simply decorated bargeboards. Buxton Lamas is a good surviving example. As befitted its greater importance, the station building at Aylsham South was an enlarged version of the villas at the other stations on the line.

The Midland Railway enjoys a good reputation for its architecture. Perhaps its best known country station style is the single-storey twin-pavilion platform building with a tall pitching roof and elaborate bargeboards, such as are found between Settle and Carlisle and at a variety of other locations throughout the Midland's former territory. These buildings usually face smaller structures without pavilions on the other platform, and the stationmaster's house stands away from the platforms. Main and subsidiary buildings are constructed of whatever material was thought most suitable to the locality. Cumwhinton (closed) is a good example of such a station, built of local Cumbrian red sandstone. On its Leicester to Hitchin line (now closed between Bedford and Hitchin) the Midland combined a two-storey house and single-storey offices at its stations; once again, care was taken to blend the stations in with existing local architecture, and at Glendon and Rushton this meant that local limestone was used. This station building has a pitched roof and the delicately detailed bargeboards found on so many Midland stations, as well as a variety of other attractive details including the lattice windows already mentioned. Entry to the platform from the building was gained through a curious low four-gabled structure occupying the corner between the house and the offices. Although less elaborate than the Leicester to Hitchin line stations, and built of brick, some of those on the Bedford to St Pancras line are broadly similar in combining station house and offices in one building: Flitwick, Bedfordshire, is such a station. Some stations

Appleby, Cumbria; old photograph of a cottage-like station

110

between Bedford and St Pancras, such as Radlett, Hertfordshire, have only the offices and waiting rooms on the platform, with awnings appended to the building or free-standing.

In contrast to the GER and the Midland, the Great Northern Railway has rather a poor reputation for the architectural standard of the stations it erected. It owned a number of large, plain, two-storey station buildings built of brick, the large villas with offices at Hertingfordbury, Hertfordshire (closed) and Swineshead, Lincolnshire, being good examples. On the GNR – GER joint line some of the stations were slightly more interesting, and Postland, Lincolnshire (closed), is one of these.

Above *Wooler, Northumberland; rugged stonework set off by delightful finials*
Right *Sandon, Staffordshire; curvilinear gable and diaper brickwork inspired by East Anglian vernacular*

It is the basic GNR villa, but a small integral awning is provided between a projecting section of the station house and a single-storey wing, and the over-all appearance of the brickwork is enlivened by light-coloured string courses. In Lincolnshire a few of the more important small stations were given the distinction of a three-storey hipped-roofed tower, in which the stationmaster lived, and this style of building can be seen at the closed Woodhall Junction. Although the GNR is not celebrated for unnecessary adornment of its station buildings, the large brick villas at Morton Road and Rippingdale, in Lincolnshire (both closed), were given dormers and fancy bargeboards; a little frivolous decoration of this kind would have been a welcome addition to the other GNR villas. One charming GNR station building which was given such frivolous decoration is Ashwell and Morden, Cambridgeshire, where no fewer than four gables at various levels face the platform and one of them is extended well beyond the building, supported by enormous brackets, giving shelter to passengers on the flight of steps which leads down to the platform. The building is of buff brick, with one gable rendered.

The Great Central Railway owned many twin-pavilion stations inherited from the Manchester, Sheffield and Lincolnshire Railway, some single-storey, as, for example, Habrough, in Lincolnshire (now Humberside), and some with one single- and one two-storey pavilion. Woodhouse, Yorkshire, is an example of this latter type, with fine barge-boards. The Manchester, Sheffield and Lincolnshire Railway had an interest in the Liverpool–War-rington–Manchester line, and here the Woodhouse-type building reappears at several stations. The finest example is at Flixton, where the bargeboards are exquisite.

The North-Eastern Railway's territory contains stations ranging from the mean to the magnificent. At one end of the scale tedious wooden single-storey buildings with glass screens were erected, as at Gilberdyke, Yorkshire (now Humberside), where small gables provided a little interest. As a contrast, the NER inherited some excellent Tudor station buildings (such as Chathill) from the New-

castle and Berwick Railway, and a collection of well conceived stations in Yorkshire designed by G. T. Andrews. This architect was responsible for some good small town stations in the north-east and his rural stations were of a pleasing design, consisting of a simple house set at right angles to the railway with a bay window facing the platform and an adjacent small porch over the platform side of the offices. Holme Moor station in Yorkshire (now Humberside; closed) was of this type. To indicate the greater importance of some of his stations, Andrews gave them a small stone portico, and one of these survives at Stamford Bridge, Yorkshire (now Humberside; closed). If a 'standard' NER building style can be identified, it is probably the two-storey structure combining the stationmaster's house and offices. Lealholm station, Yorkshire, illustrates one version of the standard style, consisting of a large villa with a pitched roof and a ground-floor bay window facing the platform, and single-storey extensions at either end. The entire building and the platform back walls are of stone, and a particularly delightful feature is the 'crow-stepping' of all gables, which is an architectural tradition associated with Scotland rather than England. The other version of the standard can be seen at Ebberston, Yorkshire (closed). Again this is basically a villa, but there the similarity ends. At both ends of the main building single-storey pavilions project on to the platform, ending with a bay window and a finialled gable, and a sloping integral awning stretches between them. Brick, rather than stone, is used at this station.

The Great Western Railway has undoubtedly been the object of more enthusiastic study than any other British railway. As far as the architecture of its small stations is concerned it has possibly been overrated. Buildings are usually rather small, and houses are not a prominent feature on the platforms within its territory. However, the closed Burghclere and Litchfield stations, Hampshire, both have houses which are notable for their dormers, and delightful *cottages ornés* stand at Lodge Hill and Draycott in Somerset (both closed). Brunel designed some early GWR stations: Mortimer has already been mentioned, with its hipped roofs forming in-

tegral awnings. Small, functional, but elegant stone buildings, again by Brunel, can be seen at Culham and Heyford stations in Oxfordshire. Gara Bridge, Devon (closed) and Fawley, Herefordshire (now Hereford and Worcester; closed), typify the minor GWR stations, their awnings adding distinction to rather ordinary buildings. The disused Wellington–Market Drayton line in Shropshire has fine classical single-storey buildings at Hodnet and Crudgington, where pediments crown each end of the structure on both the frontage and the platform elevation, and the window openings are paired and round-headed.

Mention must be made of some of the styles used by minor railways. The Midland and Great Northern Joint Railway, virtually all of which is closed, had twin-pavilion single-storey buildings, not dissimilar to those of the Midland, for instance at Hindolveston, Norfolk, large plain villas (as at Clenchwarton, Norfolk), Francis Thompson style houses with integral awnings (as at Fleet, Lincolnshire), and some villas with gables facing the platform (as at Moulton, Lincolnshire). The Furness Railway produced nice subsidiary buildings with half-timbering above local stone, for example at Silverdale, Lancashire. The Highland Railway owned some attractive standardized stations between Inverness and Wick, of which Ardgay, Ross and Cromarty (now Highland), is a surviving example. The two-storey stone building presents a gable end to the platform, with two ground-floor bay windows sheltered by a simple front-supported awning. At each end there is a single-storey wing with a ridge roof at right angles to the line of the main building. One of the smaller companies, the Hull and Barnsley, erected unnecessarily large, but dignified, villas, which may still be seen at the disused stations of Little Weighton and South Cave in Yorkshire (now Humberside).

Many small stations are interesting; some are exceptionally good. The following are, in the writer's opinion, among the best minor stations. Askam and Saughall, both of which have already been mentioned, must be included. Sandon station, although closed, retains a noble building in the Jacobean style with an integral *porte-cochère*: as with some other fine minor stations, this one was designed to please a local magnate who had interests in the North Staffordshire Railway which built the station. Similar circumstances surrounded the building of the fine Jacobean station at Brocklesby, Lincolnshire (now Humberside). Somerleyton station in Norfolk was built in the grand manner, with a tower and decorated windows, to please Sir Morton Peto, a leading railway contractor and local resident. Castle Howard station, Yorkshire (closed), had a villa with a balcony overlooking the railway and a *porte-cochère* in the facade, serving the

Box Hill, Surrey; 1877 by C. H. Driver. Steep roofs with alternate bands of tiles

residence of the same name, and considered suitable for the patronage of royalty. It was specifically for the benefit of the royal family that Wolferton, for Sandringham, Norfolk (closed), received special treatment, with unrestrained half-timbering and a clock on the roof of the 'public' section, and careful stone and brick construction of the royal building. The regal associations of Hampton Court meant that its station, now a suburban terminus of Greater London, had to be distinguished. The station building is of brick in Jacobean style. The Dukes of Sutherland had a private halt named after their seat of Dunrobin Castle, in Sutherland (now Highland). Until its closure in 1965 the public were allowed to use this charming little half-timbered station. Alton Towers, the Staffordshire stately home, was provided with a smart Italianate station of rock-faced stone, whose highlight is a three-storey tower to house the stationmaster. This station is now closed. The private estates of Cressington and Grassendale in Lancashire (now Merseyside) were thought worthy of a rather special station, and what they received was an ample villa with fascinating roof lines, half-hipped gables, decorated bargeboards and tall chimneys. The station closed in 1972, but was reopened in 1978 with its buildings tastefully restored. A delightful survival in Cheshire is the closed station at Waverton, which was built to blend in with the local buildings of the Duke of Westminster's estate at Eaton Hall. The single-storey station building is of sandstone, and it possesses a steeply pitching roof whose central portion is elevated and carried forward over the entrance to form a porch supported on four brackets. The roof line is further enlivened by four spiked finials and tall barley sugar twist chimneys. As a final example of the delightful stations which could result from the presence of important local residents, Box Hill and Westhumble station in Surrey is worth mentioning. To placate the owner of the Mickleham Valley the London, Brighton and South Coast Railway built him an ornate French-style station, with a booking hall of barn-like proportions entered by a large porch; the steep roof of the building rises up to a turret with delicate iron cresting.

115

Some other stations are remarkable for their turrets. Aboyne, Aberdeenshire (now Grampian; closed), has a pair of large Franco-Scottish turrets, an adornment appropriate to a station on the line to Ballater (for Balmoral). The stone station building with turrets at Carcroft and Adwick-le-Street (closed) and South Elmsall are particularly interesting in the light of the fact that they serve Yorkshire coal-mining villages. Cromford, serving an early industrial village in Derbyshire, has an unremarkable building with an awning on one platform, but on the other is an amazing stone building with a

steeply sloping hipped roof, a pointed turret, dormers and lattice windows; at a higher level is the station house, in similar style. In London at Hatch End a dignified building in red brick with white stone quoins, built in 1911, is topped with a small clock turret. The façade is very well proportioned, the door and windows being enclosed within arches, and a moulded railway company crest (L.N.W.R.) is central to the composition of the station.

Again in London, Battersea Park station is unusual for its palatial booking hall, with narrow paired columns supporting elegant arches. Attractive, but totally different, is Port Sunlight station, serving the Lever Brothers estate in Cheshire (now Merseyside). The weatherboarded building has complex roof lines, including dormers, and the roof drops steeply to form an awning of the Askam type over the entrance. At Golspie, Sutherland (now Highland) the station building, though of stone, resembles that of Port Sunlight in its delightfully complex roof lines. The sheer height of the building at Hunts Cross, Cheshire (now Merseyside), merits its inclusion in a list of the finest small stations; it rises four storeys from the platform, with a second-storey road entrance. The third-storey windows are dormers, and the bargeboards are decorated.

Although it is by no means beautiful, New Holland's strange station at the end of a wooden pier, jutting out into the Humber, deserves mention. Access is by rail, footpath, or road from New Holland Town station via the pier, or by steamer from

Top *Hatch End, Greater London; 1912. Suburban station by Gerald Horsley in best 'Wrenaissance'*
Above *Battersea Park, London; the top-lit booking hall with blind windows and an arched screen supported on columns*
Right *Battersea Park; deep window recesses create a sense of mass*

Hull. Its buildings are wooden, with ridge awnings. In the Derbyshire Peak District, Darley Dale (closed) warrants mention as a delightful ecclesiastical Gothic station built of stone. There are buildings of similar style on each platform, the main building having a steeply pitching roof and lancet windows.

To conclude the list, three Scottish stations deserve attention. Taynuilt and Connel Ferry stations in Argyllshire (now Strathclyde) have enormous wooden shed-like buildings, painted, in the case of Taynuilt, to give a half-timbered effect, and both have large tiled awnings continuing the slope of the roof, with end screens. Dunkeld in Perthshire (now Tayside) has a splendid collection of features. Its large stone building ends with decorated bargeboards, and its massive lean-to awning contains some of the very few surviving pendant gas casement lamps at a British station.

Of the many thousands of small stations which exist or have existed it has been possible to mention only a small proportion by name. These few should, however, serve as a guide both to some of the standard features and to some of the delightful eccentricities of British country and suburban stations.

RAILWAY HOTELS
CHRISTOPHER MONKHOUSE

THE BRIDGE House Hotel's proximity to London's first permanent railway terminus at London Bridge was not overlooked by the London and Greenwich Railway Company. After they formally opened their terminus on 14 December 1836, the chairman of the Company and 'about three hundred ladies and gentlemen sat down to a splendid *déjeuner*, prepared in the great room of the Bridge-house Tavern, Southwark'.

It is not coincidental that the Bridge House Hotel and the London Bridge terminus were first projected in 1832: both obviously wanted to take advantage of the splendid new entrance to the City afforded by the opening in 1831 of Sir John Rennie's London Bridge. However, the hotel and terminus were quite separate developments, and this would generally be the case for the rest of the 1830s: it was quite enough for a railway company to find the requisite funds for building termini and the tracks, bridges and intermediate stations to link them.

In the case of the Bridge House Hotel the independent developer was John Humphrey, who in the course of building the hotel became an alderman, sheriff and Member of Parliament, and hence a politically powerful personality. This meant that Humphrey was able to take a rather cavalier attitude towards the development of the hotel and buildings adjacent to it in Wellington Street at the south-west corner of London Bridge. Although his lease from the London Bridge Committee was quite specific that his buildings should conform to a uniform plan for the approaches devised by Sir Robert Smirke, Humphrey and his own architect, George Allen, did pretty much as they pleased.

When the hotel opened in 1835 Allen's architectural elevation of it was exhibited that summer at the Royal Academy; this showed the ground floor treated as a rusticated base for giant pilasters and engaged Ionic columns which linked the next two floors, and sitting atop the entablature was an attic storey of five round-arched windows flanked by half-storeys. A tavern was housed in the basement storey below the bridge and facing the Thames, and this was punctuated internally by a series of free-standing Ionic columns. The main entrance on

Wellington Street gave access to a coffee room and smaller function rooms, while the side entrance facing the Thames, and directly above the tavern entrance, gave access to a stone staircase which threaded its way through a series of paired Ionic columns to the top floor which housed the 'great room'. The two floors in between were given over to a series of bedrooms and sitting rooms, some arranged *en suite*, and it is said that the hotel was able to make up a total of seventy beds. Despite changes in taste, and the Second World War, the interiors were remarkably well preserved until 1971 when they were systematically destroyed by the owners. For this we owe thanks, I am afraid, to the inefficiency of the present system for listing buildings. In the process some of the most exuberant plasterwork to be created in nineteenth-century London was lost for ever, and in turn one of the first hotels built specifically with an eye to catering for the railway age was reduced to a shell of its former self.

The first railway company to provide its own

Bridge House Hotel, London Bridge; 1835 by George Allen

hotel accommodation was the London and Birmingham at Euston Terminus, in 1838–9. Before this decision was made, however, Philip Hardwick's Doric arch had already been erected as a monumental frontispiece for the Euston terminus. Therefore, it became necessary to divide the hotel accommodation between two separate buildings which would flank the arch, and create a sort of cour d'honneur. Again, the architect was Hardwick.

The building to the west of the arch was called the Victoria Hotel, and that to the east the Euston Hotel, and in appearance they were nothing more than Regency terrace houses of the plainest sort, relieved only by a cast iron balcony on the first storey. In a book which deserves to be far better known in the literature of English railways, titled simply About Railways (London, 1865) the author, William Chambers, observed that the hotels were 'simple erections as regards architecture, being nothing more than white painted walls, pierced with numerous windows, of which there are no less than 350 on the several frontages'. As their total number of windows was impressive to contemporary observers, so, too, was their over-all size in comparison with earlier hotel architecture. To quote Mr Jorrock: 'But look first at the dimensions of the Euston – why it's a town in itself! Take its opposite neighbour and twin brother, the Victoria, with it, and they are a city of themselves; in olden times they would have returned a Member of Parliament between them.'

Although the hotels and arch together formed an impressive composition, the division of the hotel accommodation into two separate units was a disaster from a functional point of view, as is borne out by the need early on to link them by an underground tunnel. In 1880 they were linked above ground by a six-storey addition which effectively destroyed the view of the arch. Furthermore, the London and Birmingham Company tried to run the Victoria themselves as a 'dormitory', and hired the steward of the Athenaeum Club, Mr Bacon, to manage it for them. The Euston, however, was intended from the start to be leased as a first-class hotel, and not only was its overnight accommodation more elaborate than that across the way at the

Victoria, but its coffee room was licensed to sell wine and spirits, while the Victoria's was not. Despite these differences, the threat of competition was such that the Railway Company found it extremely difficult to find suitable tenants for the Euston Hotel: finally Messrs J. Dethier and Zenon Vantini became the proprietors, and in 1843 Vantini became sole proprietor of both hotels. The fact that Vantini was a Corsican and had served as a courier for Napoleon may well account for his success in conquering the catering industry connected with railways: apart from the Euston and Victoria hotels, he established the first railway refreshment room at Wolverton, and became proprietor in 1841 of the North Euston Hotel at Fleetwood, Lancashire, and, in 1844, of the South-Eastern Railway's Pavilion Hotel at Folkestone, Kent.

As had been the case with the Euston terminus, the London and Birmingham Company came to appreciate somewhat after the fact the need for a hotel at their other terminus at Curzon Street, Birmingham. In March of 1839 the board of directors asked Philip Hardwick to consider the problem and shortly thereafter he demonstrated that for about £1,000 he could convert the board room in the main terminus building for hotel use. The conversion was complete by the end of December, and, apparently, the demand was so great that a wing was added in 1840–41 from the designs of Robert B. Dockray, the Company's engineer. The terminus hotel was called the Queen's, and the erection of the Dockray wing was less than flatteringly recorded by A. W. N. Pugin in his Apology for the Revival of Christian Architecture in England (London, 1843). Thanks entirely to the fact that this terminus was eclipsed in 1854 by the Central station, which, as its names implies, was built in the heart of Birmingham by the London and North-Western Railway Company, successor to the London and Birmingham, the hotel buildings designed by Hardwick and Dockray are still intact at Curzon Street, although they are badly in need of imaginative reuse. On the other hand, over the last fifteen years Birmingham Central (which had a hotel, also called the Queen's, designed by J. W. Livock, incorporated into its main façade) and London's

Euston have both disappeared without a trace in the wake of redevelopment.

Although Euston and Curzon Street were the exceptions in the 1830s, in the 1840s hotel accommodation became an essential part of the plan of new railway stations. Among the first was the Midland Hotel at the Derby Trijunct station. Begun in 1840 by the North Midland Railway Company, the hotel was designed by Francis Thompson, who had designed the station. He tried to overcome the disadvantage of the station's location on the edge of Derby by making the hotel appear as much as possible like a country house sitting in its own grounds.

In order to achieve this result, he not only resorted to what would have then been a liberal use of architectural detail for a hotel, but also adopted a typical country house 'H' plan. Furthermore, the main entrance was oriented away from the station and instead looked on to its own forecourt, replete with an ornamental fountain. It was hoped that in this way the Midland Hotel would serve as much as a resort as a station hotel, and here at least this was apparently a successful formula because it has the distinction of being the oldest purpose-built railway hotel in the British Isles with a record of continuous operation in its original building.

The necessity of building railway stations on the outskirts of towns caused other railway companies to adopt the country house as a model for their hotels. One of the most impressive was the Victoria Station Hotel, erected in 1843 for the Eastern Railway Company at their Colchester station, from the designs of Lewis Cubitt. Doubtless using Charles Parker's *Villa Rustica* (1832–41) as a pattern book, he devised an Italian villa, complete with tower, not unlike Osborne House which two years later his brother, Thomas, created, with the assistance of Prince Albert, on the Isle of Wight. *The Builder* was impressed enough by the hotel to publish an illustration of it in its issue for 26 August 1843, and the accompanying text noted, among other things, that 'The novelty of a tower to an hotel must be considered worthy of notice, and as such forms a very beautiful feature in the building. Those resorting to the hotel may be enabled to have a fine view of the surrounding country from its great height, which approaches one hundred feet.'

But the novelty of a tower was apparently not enough to make the hotel a financial success. By 1850 it had been transformed into a hospital for the mentally retarded, and has continued to be used as such to the present.

Equally impressive architecturally, and equally unsuccessful financially, was the Royal Hotel, built in 1843 at Slough station, which also doubled as the station for Windsor and Eton for the Great Western Railway. The architect for the hotel was the GWR's renowned engineer Isambard Kingdom Brunel, and, like Lewis Cubitt, he might well have consulted Parker's *Villa Rustica* in arriving at his version of an Italian villa, with not one but two towers nestled into its hipped roof. Despite, or perhaps because of, the fact that no expense was spared in fitting up this hotel, it did not prove profitable, and it became a school before being demolished.

As early as the 1840s railway companies came to appreciate the need to develop resort hotels for themselves. Resort hotels were another way to increase passenger traffic along a line, especially in an area where the passenger and goods traffic might be limited, or even non-existent. The new port and resort town of Fleetwood, Lancashire, is one case.

Begun in the late 1830s as an estate improvement by Peter Hesketh-Fleetwood in conjunction with the Preston and Wyre Railway Company, Fleetwood was intended to be a port which would link the north of Ireland, the Isle of Man and the west coast of Scotland with Euston terminus in London. To make this point more explicit, the Preston and Wyre Company called their principal hotel the North Euston. This was erected with an eye to capturing the resort market for Fleetwood. It was designed by the fashionable young neoclassical architect Decimus Burton, who took the crescents of eighteenth-century Bath as his model, and then turned them inside out so that the convex façade would follow the shoreline, giving all the windows along the front an uninterrupted view of the sea. As already mentioned, Zenon Vantini, the proprietor of the Euston Hotel, London, was entreated to be proprietor here as well. For reasons that are

Above *The North Euston Hotel, Fleetwood, Lancashire;*
1841 by Decimus Burton
Right *Duke of Cornwall Hotel, Plymouth, Devon; 1863 by*
Charles F. Hayward

too complex to go into here, Fleetwood failed
totally as a resort and did scarcely much better as a
port. Vantini discontinued his proprietorship of the
hotel as early as 1844, and the doors were closed
completely in 1859. It reopened in 1861 as a
government school of musketry. In the 1890s the
North Euston once again became a hotel, catering
to the overflow of visitors from nearby Blackpool;
it has remained one since.

The Welsh Coast Railway was also keen to build
a string of resort hotels at scenic points along the
coast of North Wales, in order to augment its
passenger traffic. Thomas Savin was largely responsible for this programme of hotel building, and in
1864 he consulted with the architect John Pollard
Seddon about the completion of an unfinished
hotel at Borth. While he was engaged on this project Savin asked him to transform Castle House,
Aberystwyth, into a truly palatial hotel to serve as
the flagship of his hotel fleet. Although this transformation took place at Aberystwyth it resulted
not in a hotel but in a university, as Savin
apparently had more ambition than ability to see
his hotel project through to completion. Even so,
as a major 'might have been', it was a striking
endorsement of the Gothic style for hotel architecture, and along with C. W. Hornes's now
demolished Ilfracombe Hotel, Ilfracombe, Devon,
of 1863, and Charles F. Hayward's Duke of Cornwall Hotel, adjacent to the railway station at Plymouth, also of 1863, it can be said to have helped
pave the way for George Gilbert Scott's winning
design of 1865 for the Midland Grand Hotel at St
Pancras, London. Scott, of course, would have us
believe that the Midland Grand was entirely the
product of his unsuccessful design for the Foreign
Office.

Thanks to the passage of the Limited Liability
Act in 1862 the early 1860s were generally a boom
period for the development of hotels throughout
the British Isles, both in town and country, and so
it is not surprising to find other railway companies
indulging in resort hotel developments during this
decade. In the north of England the Stockton and
Darlington Railway sought to exploit Saltburn-
by-the-Sea in the North Riding of Yorkshire as a

fashionable watering place, and as its centrepiece built the Zetland Hotel in 1861–2 from the designs of their architect, William Peachey of Darlington. The result was a somewhat conservative Italianate pile of yellow brick relieved by a cast iron balcony running round the second storey and a semicircular projection in the centre of the front façade which formed a tower for housing a 'telescope room' for viewing the North Sea and 'the terribly-beetling brow' of Huntcliffe Nab. The line and platform of Saltburn station were extended to within a few feet of the back entrance of the hotel, to enable guests to alight or depart at its very doors, 'thus avoiding any trouble or inconvenience in cab or bus transit, and the removal of luggage', as an 1869 guidebook noted. The other noteworthy feature of the Zetland's arrangement was that it was designed not just for the moneyed minority but rather 'as a home for all classes, and the tariff is so adjusted that the humble tradesman may be accommodated as comfortable and as economically as at an ordinary inn'. Ever since Euston the high charges at railway hotels had been a constant complaint, and so this was a particularly welcome attempt at reform, and one

all too infrequently put into practice by other hotels since then.

The 1880s was another boom period in the hotel industry, and this may well have encouraged the London and North-Western Railway, in conjunction with the Lancashire and Yorkshire Railway, to build the Preston Park Hotel in 1882. Designed by Arnold Mitchell, the hotel was situated in extensive pleasure grounds overlooking the valley of the Ribble. Many of its architectural features had more than a hint of Richard Norman Shaw about them, along with certain Scottish

Above *Gleneagles Hotel, Auchterarder, Perthshire; 1926*
Left *Preston Park, Lancashire; 1882 by Arnold Mitchell*

baronial touches which were not at all inappropriate for an hotel intended to serve as a half-way resort for those wishing to break the long train journey between London and Scotland. However, the running of fast through trains soon obviated this need and as early as 1904 the hotel was seen as something of a white elephant: it was eventually adapted for County Offices.

One of the last and without a doubt the most palatial of all railway resort hotels was Gleneagles. Although it did not open its doors until 1926 it was begun before the First World War, and this may explain why its scale and architectural detail have more in common with the Edwardian era. Gleneagles' superb situation near Crieff, reinforced by 'the last word in modern golf course construction', has made it popular with visitors from the south and overseas ever since.

The last railway resort hotel to be built before the Second World War was Oliver Hill's Midland Hotel for the London, Midland and Scottish Railway at Morecambe, a popular seaside resort on the Lancashire coast. The Midland was designed in the International style and was thus, when it opened its doors in 1933, in the avant-garde of English architecture. However, in a characteristically ambivalent English way, it also looked backward to the inverted crescent shape of Decimus Burton's North Euston Hotel at nearby Fleetwood.

The railway resort hotel, as we have seen, developed out of the need to overcome the disadvantages of railway stations far removed from the city centre. Beginning in the 1850s, however, a combination of political pressure and the ability to assemble the necessary inner city sites made it possible in some instances, such as Birmingham, to abandon remote locations. On the other hand, in the instances when the railway station had no choice but to remain on the outskirts, the amount of activity it was able to generate often encouraged the city to grow around it. Thus it became a formidable rival to such traditional centres of attention as the city hall and the market place.

With the railway station and its attendant hotel playing an increasingly important role in the city plan, it became necessary to give them a suitably dignified architectural appearance. A closely related building type, the club house, beginning with Charles Barry's Travellers' Club in 1829, had successfully adopted the Italian Renaissance palace as its model. The city terminus hotel was quick to follow this example: one of the first and most elaborate hotels to emerge as a Renaissance palace was the Paragon Station Hotel at Hull.

The Paragon Station Hotel was built between 1847 and 1850 by the North-Eastern Railway, to the designs of G. T. Andrews. The hotel's design not only included the customary quoins, string courses, heavy console-bracketed cornice and low-hipped roof, but the central parts of the two principal façades were recessed in order to incorporate Doric and Ionic arcades in front of the ground and first storeys, and everything was executed in stone. The interior courtyard, sixty feet square, formed a central hall which was roofed over with a skylight between the ground and first storeys, and all public rooms opened directly off it. The architectural display of the Paragon Station Hotel did not go unnoticed. Queen Victoria expressed a desire to stay there during her official visit to Hull in October of

1854, and thereafter it has been known as the Royal Station Hotel.

Another station hotel which used the Renaissance palace as a model was the George Hotel, Huddersfield, built between 1849 and 1850 by the local landowning family of Ramsden to the designs of their estate architect, William Wallen. The hotel fronted the newly laid out St George's Square, which had been especially created to accommodate J. P. Pritchett's Palladian revival railway station, built in 1847–50 by the Huddersfield Railway Company, which shortly after amalgamated with the London and North-Western.

Other station hotels in the Renaissance palace mode which should be mentioned, however briefly, are Samuel Beazley's 1850–53 Lord Warden Hotel at the Dover terminus of the London and South-Eastern Railway and Lewis Cubitt's crescent-shaped Great Northern Hotel, opened in 1854 just to the side of the London terminus of the Great Northern Railway at King's Cross.

The North Staffordshire Railway Company seems to have made a point of defying the dominance of Renaissance Italy. They came to build their stations almost uniformly in the Jacobean style and for their headquarters at Stoke-on-Trent their architect, H. A. Hunt, laid out a square entirely surrounded by Jacobean buildings, including the splendid North Stafford Hotel.

When the Great Western Railway finally decided, in the wake of the 1851 Crystal Palace Exhibition, that a hotel was needed at their London terminus at Paddington, their architect, P. C. Hardwick, united Italian Renaissance detail with a pair of Jacobean towers inspired by those at Westwood and Crewe, and for good measure capped the building with a massive mansard roof from the reign of Louis XIV. With this building the era of eclecticism may be said to have arrived in London.

Several reasons can be found to account for why the GWR's terminus hotel, or, as it came to be called, the Great Western Royal Hotel was such a radical departure from what had gone before. First, the nature of the GWR's patronage must be considered; this is nowhere else better analysed than

Above *Great Western Hotel, Paddington, London; 1852–4 by P. C. Hardwick*
Left *Great Northern Hotel, King's Cross London; 1854 by Lewis Cubitt*

127

Great Western Hotel Paddington; the coffee room

in J. C. Bourne's *History and Description of the Great Western Railway* (London, 1846):

> The case of the Great Western is in some respects peculiar, it differs from the London and Birmingham, in the possession of a large intermediate traffic, and it differs from the Grand Junction and most of the railways traversing manufacturing districts, in the fact that much of that traffic is of the description called 'first class'. Upon the Great Western Line, Windsor, Reading, Oxford, and the Cheltenham and Gloucester Junction, and Bath, are all places of great magnitude, and many of them of sufficient importance to claim a railway on their own account. They are also the centres of districts abounding in landed gentry, and Bath and Cheltenham are supported by persons living on their own resources. A traffic of this kind requires arrangements of a totally different description from those upon any other line.

The reference to Windsor implied that the GWR had Queen Victoria as its foremost patron.

Although the Great Western Royal Hotel was the first hotel whose construction was actually paid for by the GWR, the directors of the company, and especially their engineer, Brunel, had considerable experience of hotel construction. Brunel worked closely with Hardwick in designing the Great Western Royal Hotel at Paddington, and when nobody could be found to lease it from the GWR after it was finished, he and a few other shareholders 'being unwilling that the hotel should remain empty and be a loss to the proprietors, formed themselves into a company to lease and work the hotel'. Brunel was made a director and, shortly after, chairman of this company; and in the hotel's first half year, it paid at a rate of 10 per cent, with an additional bonus to the proprietors.

As well as superior patrons and enlightened company directors, the Great Western Royal Hotel had the benefit of the young, talented and extremely well informed architect P. C. Hardwick. Not only was he the son of Philip Hardwick, who had designed the only other railway hotel in London

at Euston, but in the 1840s, as part of his architectural education, he had travelled extensively on the Continent, filling up numerous sketchbooks with his impressions; these were to form a rich quarry of ideas which he would draw upon for the rest of his life. Indeed, the eclecticism of his design for the hotel might well be explained as a young man's trying to show off how much he had learned about architecture while studying and travelling at home and abroad.

The interior of the Great Western Royal Hotel, was as innovative as the exterior. With regard to technology, in which Brunel doubtless had a hand, the staircases and passages were made fireproof, an elaborate bell system was installed throughout the hotel, electric clocks were to be found everywhere and hot water pipes were run through the linen closets on each floor; all of which prompted the *Civil Engineer and Architect's Journal* to observe prophetically: 'The construction of such establishments has led to many ingenious

Above The Grosvenor Hotel, Victoria Station, London, before cleaning in 1978; 1861 by J. T. Knowles
Below Charing Cross Hotel, London; 1863–5 by E. M. Barry. The roof was rebuilt following war damage

appliances which will have their future place in domestic architecture. . . .'

As for interior decoration, it is hard to appreciate just how advanced it was on the basis of P. C. Hardwick's one surviving view of the coffee room, which he exhibited at the Royal Academy in 1852. As can be seen, Hardwick originally designed it in a rather stodgy late neoclassical fashion, reminiscent of the club house coffee rooms by Charles Barry and others from the 1830s. But trips made by Hardwick to Paris in the early 1850s while the hotel was still waiting to find a tenant, revealed to him that stylistic changes were taking place there under the influence in part of Eugénie, who had come to identify with Marie Antoinette. She had had the interiors of St Cloud redesigned in the style of Louis XVI, and the heavy detail of the late neoclassical style left over from the Empire period suddenly seemed very old fashioned. On Hardwick's return from Paris he enlisted at the eleventh hour the help of Holland and Company, one of the foremost cabinet-making firms in mid-nineteenth-century London, and also of Henri Alphonse Remon, a Parisian decorative painter who conveniently happened to be living in London at the time. It was their task to transform the hotel's coffee room, along with the Queen's private waiting room, in order that they would conform with the current rage in Paris for the revived decoration of Louis XVI. P. C. Hardwick and Isambard Kingdom Brunel had left no stone unturned in their efforts to make sure that their hotel was a leader, rather than a follower, of fashion.

The Great Western Royal Hotel happily survives, although two twentieth-century renovations have completely obliterated the Louis XVI coffee room at Paddington, and presently, by way of a thin veneer of Viking décor, it masquerades as Oscar's Coffee House.

London's next major railway hotel, the Grosvenor, next to Victoria station, was built from the designs of James T. Knowles between 1860 and 1861. Its dominant architectural feature was once again the mansard roof. Its richly sculptured façade, marvellously revealed since cleaning in 1978, incorporates portraits of Victoria, Albert, and Baron

*Lime Street Chambers, Liverpool; 1867. Designed by
Alfred Waterhouse as a hotel*

von Humboldt, testifying to that mid-Victorian
phobia of surfaces devoid of ornament.

The South-Eastern Railway's two London termini hotels at Charing Cross (1863–4), and Cannon
Street (1864–6) were both designed by E. M. Barry,
eldest son of the architect of the Houses of Parliament. Both sported mansard roofs and architectural detail which 'may be called, broadly, Italian'.
In each case the hotel also served on the ground-
floor level as entrance gate and booking hall. To
be sure, it is preferable to avoid integrating the
station and hotel in this way, but the nature of the
sites made this impossible, and similar sites produced similar solutions at Lime Street station,
Liverpool, and St Pancras station, London.

Despite the similarities in site plans and elevations, the City Terminus Hotel at Cannon Street differed from Charing Cross in that the former had only 84 bedrooms, while the latter had 250. The remaining space in the City Terminus Hotel was devoted to banqueting rooms. The other striking difference was Charing Cross's forecourt: it was dominated by a highly picturesque Gothic revival monument designed at considerable expense for the SER by E. M. Barry, with the assistance of Arthur Ashpitel. This was a bit of historical fabrication on the part of the railway, which hoped that it would lend greater interest to their station and that it would serve to offset the criticism they had received for destroying a large number of buildings, including some of historical interest, in order to build their two London termini on the north side of the Thames. The original of this monument had been erected in a slightly different location by Edward the Confessor as a memorial to his wife, Eleanor of Castile: needless to say, this original had long since disappeared. Although the City Terminus Hotel was demolished in the 1960s after suffering bomb damage during the Second World War, Charing Cross Hotel still flourishes as a British Transport hotel, and its remarkably well preserved coffee room has happily come into its own again as a smart French restaurant.

The hotel boom taking place in London in the 1860s had its reverberations in the provinces as well. 1862 saw exhibited at the Royal Academy Thomas Allom's elevation for the Great Eastern Railway's terminus hotel at Harwich, in Essex; its sculptural pediment and mansard roof obviously owed a debt to the Great Western Royal Hotel at Paddington, as did the 1869 design by John Norton for the London and South-Western Hotel at Southampton. One feature more or less unique to the latter hotel was a highly mechanized laundry for the benefit of transatlantic travellers.

Liverpool, as Southampton's rival port of entry for American visitors, had a hotel with 400 bedrooms projected in 1861 by W. and A. Moseley, but in the end it was not built. Its loss was largely compensated for by the London and North-Western's competition for a hotel to front their Lime Street terminus in 1867, and the laurel this time went to Alfred Waterhouse, a local architect with a growing national reputation ever since he designed and built the Assize Courts at Manchester.

All the above provincial hotels could be described as partaking of the Italian Renaissance in varying degrees, and uniformly they adopted mansard roofs. Charles F. Hayward's Duke of Cornwall Hotel, adjoining the Plymouth terminus in the Millbay Road, was exceptional in going the Gothic route in 1863. Gothic must have recommended itself over Italian Renaissance for the Duke of Cornwall not only because it was a national style but also because on the local scene the only other important hotel was the Royal, a neoclassical pile of 1812, with lumbering Ionic porticoes casting many of the rooms into perpetual shadow. While the Royal met the fate of most other buildings in Plymouth during the Second World War, the Duke of Cornwall miraculously survived the holocaust and so many of its singular features, such as the spiral staircase, can still be studied; they make us realize that Charles F. Hayward was a far more original practitioner of reform Gothic principles than he has generally been given credit for.

While the Duke of Cornwall Hotel was designed as a free-standing building directly across the street from the terminus, its London equivalent in the Gothic style, the Midland Grand Hotel at St Pancras, was totally integrated with the life of the station. Its screen-like façade was punctuated by entrances and exits for the station shed behind, and a large portion of its ground floor was given over to railway refreshment rooms. The saga of the Midland Railway's limited competition in 1865–6 for the design of the hotel has been told many times, beginning with George Gilbert Scott's autobiography (London, 1879), and most recently by Jack Simmons in his admirable monograph entitled *St Pancras Station* (London, 1968). In short, Scott claimed that his winning design was merely a rolling-out and dusting-off of his rejected Gothic scheme for the Foreign Offices competition in the 1850s, not to mention the fact that he ignored the guide-lines for the competition, both in terms of size and cost. Even though, or perhaps because, his design included two extra storeys, and cost £50,000 more than the next most expensive design, the Midland Railway selected him as architect, so intent were they in making a splash as part of their grand entrance into London. Furthermore, the hotel was intended not merely to provide overnight accommodation, but also to serve as an advertisement for Midland products, such as brick, slate, and iron. John O'Connor's well-known painting of 1884 showing St Pancras station and hotel rising above the houses and shops along the Pentonville Road gives an excellent idea of how successful George Scott was at promoting the Midland Railway and the products of that region.

Because the Midland Grand Hotel has not been used as a hotel since 1935 (some of it has been used as office space by British Rail, the rest left empty),

its interior decoration is not nearly as well known as it should be, with the possible exception of the fantastic cast iron staircase, which zigzags its way through the stairwell as if it were inspired by engravings from Piranesi's *Carceri* series. Except for the rood screen, which formerly set off the reception desk, cashier's desk, and manager's office in the hotel entrance lobby, the interiors depend far less upon ecclesiastical Gothic decoration than one might expect from a work by George Gilbert Scott. Instead they emerge as an extremely early application of Queen Anne revival decoration. Perhaps Scott's son, George Gilbert Scott Junior, who was known as 'a master and leader in the "Queen Anne" revival', was partly responsible for placing the Midland Grand Hotel's interiors securely in the Queen Anne camp, thus sunflowers and peacocks

Left Midland Grand Hotel, St Pancras Station, London; 1863–73 by George Gilbert Scott. The ladies' room
Right Midland Hotel, St Pancras; the coffee room

disport themselves amongst the cusped Gothic tracery in a highly 'aesthetic' way. The importance of these interiors was recognized at the time, with several details appearing in the French periodical *Matériaux et Documents d'Architecture*, edited and published by A. Raguenet and H. Cagnon in Paris in the 1870s. The American Moncure D. Conway has left a detailed impression in his *Travels In South Kensington* (New York, 1882):

> The front part of the building is a hotel. It has been decorated by Robert Sang, and furnished by Gillow, in the most expensive style, and certainly presents some rich interiors. The reading-room has green cloth-paper, and a ceiling gay with huge leaf frescoes; it is divided by a double arch with gilded architraves. The mantel-pieces are of dark marble, with two small pillars of yellow marble set on either side. The coffee-room has a general tone of drab, with touches of gold in the paper, and a sort of sarcophagus chimney-piece, surmounted by an antique mirror of bevelled glass. The sitting-room has red floral paper, and an imitation mosaic ceiling. One of the bedrooms which I visited had deep-green paper, with gold lines and spots, and bed-curtains somewhat similar. The furniture was of heavy oak, tastefully carved. The halls and corridors have a dado of fine dark-brown tiles, and bright fleur-de-lis paper above. All of which was rich, costly, and, with slight exceptions, by no means gaudy. Yet I could not altogether like it, or think the decorations entirely appropriate for a hotel. It looked as if there had been more exercise of ingenuity to find things costly than to find things beautiful. The *salon*, the reading-room, may naturally be made gorgeous, but the bedroom ought to be more quiet. One does not desire to sleep amid purple and gold. The traveller who needs rest may well spare these things – which, however, he knows will not spare him; for if there is gold paper on the wall, there will be gold paper in the bill.

Midland Hotel, Manchester; 1898 by Charles Trubshaw

All of this is to say that the Midland Grand Hotel was to the Queen Anne revival what the Great Western Royal Hotel was to the Louis XVI revival. The railway hotel emerges once again as a leader of fashion.

When it came time to open the Midland Grand in 1873, the Midland Railway Company had to look as far afield as Venice to find a suitable manager in Mr R. Etzensberger; by 1884, however, they were able to find his replacement, William Towle, within their own ranks. Under Towle, and his two sons, Frank and Arthur, who were to join him in managing not only the Midland Grand, but all the Midland Railway hotels, an era of improvement and expansion was entered upon. An early sign of William Towle's desire for improvement occurred shortly after his arrival at St Pancras. In order to eliminate the strong air currents endemic to tall buildings Towle was quick to perceive the advantages of the newly invented revolving door, with the result that one of the first to be introduced into a London building was at the front entrance of the Midland Grand.

George Gilbert Scott's ineffectual screen for absorbing smoke and noise from the adjacent railway shed was one aspect of the Midland Grand's design Towle was not able to improve upon until he was given the opportunity to build two Midland hotels from the ground up: at Manchester, to the designs of Charles Trubshaw, between 1897 and 1903, and at Liverpool, to the designs of Frank Atkinson, between 1911 and 1914. In both instances Towle made sure the sites selected for the hotels allowed for free-standing structures well removed from the railway sheds.

Inside the Midland Hotel, Manchester, and the Midland Adelphi Hotel, Liverpool, the influence of César Ritz could be clearly seen in the emphasis on eighteenth-century French and English decoration. With the help of the architectural firm of Mewès and Davis, he had brought about a revolution in the furnishing and decoration of hotels when he opened the Ritz in Paris in 1898 and the Carlton in London in 1899. For the first time the simplicity and refinement of Robert Adam and Louis Seize had been given full reign, and no hotel to open in the wake of either the Ritz or the Carlton could deviate from this stylistic norm if it hoped to be in the forefront of Edwardian fashion. Furthermore, Ritz determined that of all the public rooms decked out in dix-huitieme decoration the palm court or winter garden should form the centre stage for the enactment of Edwardian hotel life. That this was the case at the Midland hotels is borne out by the fact that the palm court of the Midland Hotel, Manchester, served as the setting for the first meeting of Charles Rolls and Henry Royce in 1904.

In terms of building technology, William Towle and his sons were equally determined that Midland hotels should be as much in the forefront of that field as they were in the revival of eighteenth-century interior decoration. Again, César Ritz paved the way with the help of Mewès and Davis by erecting the first steel-framed structure in London, if not the British Isles, the Ritz Hotel of 1904–6. Then came Selfridges Department Store of 1908, with Frank Atkinson assisting Daniel Burnham of Chicago, and this first-hand knowledge of steel construction doubtless recommended him to the Towles for the Adelphi.

After the First World War the Towle family on behalf of the newly organized London, Midland, and Scottish Railway showed their steadfast commitment to architectural excellence by employing Sir Edwin Lutyens to design an annex for the Midland Hotel, Manchester, in 1930. Although it was not actually built owing to the economic depression, the rebuilding of their Queen's Hotel in Leeds did go forward in 1937 with the assistance of another distinguished architect, Curtis Green. But no hotel better expressed the desire of the railway to remain in the forefront of fashion and architectural design than the already mentioned Midland Hotel at Morecambe of 1933. With Oliver Hill as

architect, and the involvement of such renowned designers as Eric Gill and Marion Dorn, Lord Clonmore was able to observe in an article in the *Architectural Review* for September 1933 that the Midland Hotel 'is something quite new as far as this country is concerned, with that extreme simplicity of design which has done so much to beautify modern Germany and Austria, but which is so criminally lacking in most of our modern buildings'.

Above *Adelphi Hotel, Liverpool; 1912 by Frank Atkinson*
Right *Adelphi Hotel, Liverpool; the entrance hall*

BRIDGES AND VIADUCTS
RICHARD HUGHES

IN NINETEENTH-CENTURY BRITAIN the railways gave rise to a new architecture, based on engineering. British railway works led the world in size, materials, engineering design and complexity of construction. Perhaps even more important was the part they played in a revolution of attitudes. The men of genius, like Brunel, Stephenson and Locke, were continually pushing forward the frontiers of engineering practice and Britain truly became the workshop and the envy of the world. The new age started with the construction of canals and received a further boost with the formation of the Institution of Civil Engineers in 1818. With the rapid expansion of the railway industry there was created a demand for engineering skills and with it came the need for a quality of work based on science rather than empirical knowledge.

By far the most spectacular of all railway engineering works were the viaducts and large bridges. In size, materials and position they made an unparalleled impact on the landscape. Some of the viaducts may remind us of such earlier works as the Roman aqueducts, but on the whole they represent a new architectural form, one not using the architect, unconnected with local traditions.

Viaducts are extensions of embankments, a means of traversing the ground using minimum land surface. They were of course expensive to construct, but in the natural landscape they provided the only answer and in the urban environment the price of land made them relatively cheaper.

The town viaduct enabled stations to be placed centrally. The width of the land taken was only a little more than that needed for the tracks. The height of the structures varied considerably. For example the viaduct built in 1836 between Bermondsey and Deptford was a mere 40 feet high and consisted of 878 stock brick arches on very short piers. At the other end of the scale the Stockport Viaduct strides out above slate roofs and cobbled streets below. It consists of 22 arches, 110 feet high, covering a length of 1,800 feet. It was built in 1841.

Monsal Dale Viaduct; 1860. It completed a difficult route between Ambergate and Manchester originally engineered by George Stephenson

At the time, and perhaps even today, the town viaduct was considered to lower the tone of the neighbourhood. Parliament preferred them, because they avoided wholesale street closures and level crossings. However, they crossed the existing street patterns at odd angles, leaving a minimum of headroom. In areas where the communications were still poor or incompletely formed, they curtailed the possibilities for future road-widening.

The most striking of the town viaducts was Manchester South Junction, 'a species of bridge' to provide cross-town communication. By the 1860s it was so crowded with traffic that an hour's wait on its arches was not unusual. The condition of the arches was notoriously bad. When the Union Railway put forward a proposal for a viaduct in Glasgow in the 1860s the fear of depreciating property values in Glasgow led to extensive inquiries and the Railway lost. The termini were placed on the city's outskirts.

Another type of viaduct was that constructed to cross deep inland valleys. The occurrence of one of these deep valleys between long lengths of plateau lands made it necessary either to have a series of cuttings and falling gradients, so as to get down to a low level, or to erect a high level work to maintain the height of the rail already attained. A very good example of this type of viaduct is at Leamside, County Durham. It crosses the Wear with nine brick arches. Viaducts were also used where a gradual descent was required in an area of rapid change in relief, for example at Welwyn Garden City (100 feet high, 4,560 feet long and 40 brick arches). It was normal in this case to extend an embankment from each side of a valley to the point where the embankment's cost or consumption of land made it preferable to substitute a viaduct. To retain the embankment soil at the point where it joined the viaduct abutments were constructed and these were of various forms: a simple front wall with curved wing walls, or with wing walls taken back into the tipped material.

Balcombe Viaduct; 1839 by Rastrick and Mocatta. Perhaps the most elegant viaduct ever built, with fine Italianate pavilions at both ends

143

The type of viaduct depended on the raw materials available. Local stone was the most suitable and where this was not available brick was the best substitute. These two materials formed the most substantial and hence permanent works and if properly used the viaducts have normally required minimal expenditure on maintenance and repair.

Perhaps for the railway era it was Stephenson's Earlestown (opened in 1830) that was the archetypal form: it consisted of red-brick stone-faced 70 feet high piers at 40 foot centres with pier bases 20

Above *London Road Viaduct, Brighton; 1841 by Rastrick and Mocatta. It consists of 37 arches, built on a curve*
Top *Hanwell Viaduct across the river Brent; 1838 by I. K. Brunel, dedicated to Lord Wharncliffe. His coat of arms can be seen on the south side of the viaduct*
Right *Viaduct on the Highland Railway between Perth and Inverness 1898*

feet square. Over the next seventy years only the sizes varied. For example, it was normal that with increase of height the span would also increase. In one case 30 foot spans were suitable, whereas in another it was more economical to introduce spans of 66 feet or more so as to reduce the number of lofty piers. There was however a distance beyond which it was not economical to span with classical arches; the cost increased rapidly beyond 66–70 feet and at this point girders became cheaper. Nevertheless some of these works reached a vast size. For example, the viaduct at Ballochmyle, Ayrshire, built by John Miller in 1848 in local sandstone, had a semicircular central span 181 feet wide and 163 feet high. This was for some time the largest viaduct in Europe. And certainly the most spectacular piece of railway engineering in Britain is the Settle to Carlisle railway line, known locally as the Long Drag. The seventy-two mile route is the highest main line in Britain and twenty viaducts were constructed along its length, the most famous being the Ribblehead, over 1,200 feet long, over 156 feet high and having twenty-four arches. It was constructed in local stone, and some of its blocks weighed more than eight tons each.

The classic form developed by Stephenson continued to be used into the twentieth century, the brick and stone being replaced by concrete. The first concrete viaduct was the Glenfinnan Viaduct on the Fort William to Mallaig extension of the West Highland Railway. It was constructed 1897–1901 as an early McAlpines' contract – twenty-one arches 90 feet high and with spans of 50 feet. Another famous Scottish concrete viaduct is at Lockearnhead. Crouch and Hogg were the consultant engineers and the viaduct was built of mass concrete but finished to imitate stonework. The first English concrete viaduct was at Carrington, near Lyme Regis, built in 1900–1903.

The other form that developed for viaducts was that where the arches were replaced by girder work. In some cases the roadway was carried on the bottom of the girder (through girder), as with William Baker's 305 foot lattice girder spans at Runcorn-Widnes, and some on the top (slung girder), as for example in the Horseshoe Curve Viaduct on the West Highland Railway, Llanbradach Viaduct on the Barry Railway and Taffs Well Viaduct north of Cardiff. Having the roadway in the bottom of the girder meant greater security for the engine, while the roadway on the top of the girder made it easier to brace the girder elements securely together. One particularly important type, with strut members pinned rather than riveted, was developed by R. H. Bow and used for example on Glen Belah and Deepdale viaducts (Barnard Castle to Tebay line). The Charing Cross Railway Bridge also makes use of this construction

Overleaf Crumlin Viaduct across Ebbw Vale; by Thomas Kennard. It was part of the Newport, Abergavenny and Hereford Railway serving the South Wales coalfield. Dismantled in the 1960s

148

method. In some later examples the masonry piers were superseded by metal trestles; for example the Ebbw Vale–Crumlin Viaduct constructed in the 1850s by Thomas Kennard had such piers. Glen Belah and Deepdale were the last great works in the age of cast and wrought iron. As with most others, for example at Crumlin and Taffs Well, corrosion and abandonment have forced their demolition.

In the early days of railways many viaducts and large bridges made use of timber and up to the 1830s and 1840s the size of individual pieces of wood governed the general dimensions of the structure. It was to overcome this limitation that the timber truss and the laminated arch were developed.

The timber trusses were used to form a framework in which the individual pieces of timber were arranged in a geometric pattern. This style was extensively used by Brunel between 1845 and 1860 as a means of cutting down the initial capital outlay. About thirty such structures were built, mostly in Devon and Cornwall but also a few in South Wales. Some of the timber trusses were carried on stone piers, as for example at Treviddo, Cornwall, others were carried on timber piers, as at St Germains, Cornwall. The viaduct at Dove in Glamorgan was somewhere in between, with short stone pillars raised to the road level by timber piers. Ivybridge Viaduct, 1,200 feet long and 150 feet high, was perhaps the last example of this type. This kind of structure was very susceptible to both fire and decay. The decay of one member in the truss effectively makes the whole structure dangerous. Surprisingly, the last example went out of use as late as 1934. Dove Viaduct was noted as still being in existence in 1940.

The lamination method consisted of gluing and stapling together individual pieces of timber to make a component which was not limited by the size of the individual pieces. An additional advantage was that using this method it was possible to produce curved members. The pieces were glued in their curved position and the shear stresses between the laminations were resisted by the glue. About thirty-four laminated bridges were built by a number of different engineers for some twenty

railway companies during the period 1835–50. None have survived.

It was Benjamin Green who first thought of the idea of laminated arches, as a means of decreasing the number of spans needed over fast-flowing rivers. After experiments in the late 1820s his designs were accepted for the Ouseburn and Willington viaducts on the Newcastle and North Shields Railway. Ouseburn had three arches of 116 foot span and two of 114 foot, each arch having three laminated timber ribs. The laminations were formed from best quality Dantzic deals 11 in. × 3 in. and 20–46 feet long. The timber was coated to prevent decay. The fourteen laminations of each rib were nailed at 4 in. centres and also glued together with a layer of strong brown paper dipped in boiling tar.

Another exponent of laminated arches,

Above *Chirk; an example of the lamination method – it lasted only ten years*
Left *Treviddo Viaduct; Brunel's use of timber trusses for the Cornwall Railway Company was intended as a cheap temporary solution while the line's viability was in doubt*

149

Charles Vignoles, was responsible for the design of two viaducts using them, Etherow and Dinting Vale (Sheffield), Ashton-under-Lyne and Manchester Railway). Perhaps the most famous of Vignoles's laminated works was the viaduct crossing the Lune river on the North-Western Railway. He used laminated bows to carry 12 in. rails from which the platform of the bridge is suspended by means of $1\frac{5}{8}$ in. wrought iron rods at 3 ft 6 in. intervals. It was built on a skew of 500 foot radius resulting in 10–60 foot spans. Locke, in conjunction with Errington, was also responsible for a viaduct across the Lune (on the Lancashire–Carlisle line). At either end of the viaduct were multiple brick arches with the central portion being three laminated timber arches of 130 foot span.

All the laminated viaducts and the smaller bridges have been replaced. The average life was about twenty-four years, ranging from ten years at Chirk to thirty-nine years over the River Wissey. However, it is still possible to get an impression of the timber work for the replacements were often copies of the original. Ouesburn Viaduct still exists as perhaps the best example.

'The size of bridge is too commonly the popular standard by which the eminence of its engineer is measured.' This quotation from the 1870s refers to those large spectacular bridges built to carry the track across water, an obstacle that could not be passed by a level road, embankment or the more standard viaduct. Because of clearance restrictions stipulated by the Admiralty, the bridges normally had to cross the water at high level. And the aim was to cross with as few piers as possible, firstly because they caused obstructions and secondly because they presented great difficulty in foundation construction.

The engineer turned to cast iron, wrought iron and later mild steel for the large bridges because these were the only materials capable of producing the required long spans. Reducing the number of piers to a minimum concentrated the dead loads (weight of the bridge) and the live loads (weight of the train, wind, etc.), and part of the engineer's art was to direct and distribute the applied loads through the structure to the piers without overstressing the metal. However, for each type of bridge there was a maximum span length determined by the ratio of the weight of the material to the strength of the material. In the early railway era the design of these long span bridges was based on trial and error accompanied by the frequent building of scale models. The engineer maximized the bridge length by the obvious solution of cutting down the dead loads; the live loads were normally insignificant. In the short span bridge, about which a little will be said later on, the variability of live loads was often the most important factor.

Above *Britannia Tubular Bridge; 1849 by Stephenson and Fairbairn. The development of the box girder system advanced engineering methods. Restored after a fire, 1970*
Right *Royal Border Bridge, Berwick on Tweed; 1849 by Stephenson. It has 28 arches in traditional style*

An analysis in the 1870s showed that over the previous decades when they were conceived and first used the various types of girder, cantilever and suspension bridges usually had too much metal (over-designed – fortunately for us because they are capable of surviving the modern higher loads) or too little metal and failed. For both long and short span bridges the determining factor in keeping the weight to a minimum and strength to a maximum is the strength of the metal related to the depth and thickness of the girder. For example the box girder on the Britannia Bridge is very un-economic because of the amount of metal used to get the necessary girder depth. With the lattice girder it is possible to obtain a much greater depth for the same amount of metal and therefore build a longer span. This aspect was not fully appreciated and all around the country can be seen massively structured lattice girders of shallow depth. They should be compared with the spider-like trussing of American lattice girder bridges.

No matter how much theoretical work went on into the depth of girder, as well as experiments with models (between 1845 and 1868 at least nine struc-

tural model tests were carried out), the only true test of strength was to put the bridge in use. A typical test for a completed structure was set up for the Crumlin Viaduct on 7 May 1857. As one can imagine from the photographs there was much discussion regarding its stability. 'First one engine was run on, then a second, then a third and so on until six engines and a waggon weighing in the whole 380 tons were placed upon one span of 150 feet in length. The worst deflection observable was from one inch to an inch and a quarter.' The same method was used in 1962 for the testing of the new Chepstow bridge.

The famous Britannia Bridge built by Stephenson was opened in 1849. Its originality becomes apparent when it is compared with two other more conventional Stephenson bridges opened in the same year, Royal Border Bridge (Berwick-upon-Tweed) and High Level Bridge (Newcastle-upon-Tyne). It was the two main spans of 460 feet constructed in box girder technique that made the bridge unique. The boxes consisted of rolled plates and angles hand-riveted together with over two million rivets. The top and bottom had a cellular structure for added strength. Doubt in the bridge's performance was sufficient to suggest that suspension cables might need to be used and Egyptian-styled pavilions were constructed on top of the towers to take the cables if it proved necessary. In 1970 the bridge was burnt and the repair work by British Rail changed its appearance beyond all recognition.

The fact that the Britannia box girders could be constructed away from the bridge site and then hoisted into position appealed to Brunel, who faced similar problems at two places a few years later. At Chepstow Brunel used a novel wrought iron girder form much like the straight link Bollman truss extensively used in the United States. The 300 foot span crossed the Wye in an unusual position, a cliff on one side and a plain on the other. On the plain side the pier foundation was constructed using the technique developed by Brunel's father for the Thames Tunnel. A circular caisson with cutting shoe was lowered into the soft river silts and the material inside was excavated to allow its gradual

settlement. This bridge was partly replaced in 1962 when a new bolted and welded steel truss was lifted up under the old deck and attached to the original cast iron columns.

The Chepstow bridge was a prototype for Brunel's last great work, the Royal Albert Bridge across the River Tamar. The two nearly horizontal beams at Chepstow were modified into highly convexed tubes each 465 feet long and weighing 1,500 tons. These, like the Britannia box girders, were hoisted into position by hydraulic jacks. A suspension system, making use of the salvaged chains from

Forth Railway Bridge; 1890 by Fowler and Baker. The first bridge to use mild steel – an engineering triumph

the Clifton Road Bridge, was hung below these.

The 'Beautiful Railway Bridge of the Silver Tay', designed by Thomas Bouch, was opened in 1878 and only one year later it collapsed in a storm, taking with it a 110 ton train and carriages. An enquiry concluded that its failure was caused by faults in the design, construction and maintenance, and not, as had been suspected, by foundation movements. The recommendations that there should be comprehensive site investigations prior to construction, loading tests during construction and research into the influence of wind loading were important for future bridges. The present bridge (designed by W. H. Barlow) was opened in 1888 and was constructed using many of the earlier techniques and even some of the original materials. Just over two miles long, it rests on eighty-six piers, oriented to take account of a complex scour pattern and thick deposits of soft material. The deep foundations required the Brunel technique of sinking iron cylinders lined with bricks. The inside of each was pumped dry and the soft bottom materials excavated away to allow the cylinder to sink to firm bedding material.

Left *Royal Albert Bridge across the Tamar at Saltash,*
Cornwall; 1859. Brunel's last great work
Below *Royal Albert Bridge under construction*

The Forth Railway Bridge was opened in 1890 and at the time was regarded as one of the engineering wonders of the world. Work had started on a suspension bridge, but when the Tay Bridge collapsed work stopped and it was totally redesigned, by the engineers Baker and Fowler. The resultant bridge based on the cantilever principle was the first British bridge to use mild steel. Each of the main spans was over 1,700 feet long and over 150 feet above water level. The structure is so large and complex that painting maintenance is a never-ending job.

Perhaps the best known example of a multiple bow string bridge was that crossing the River Severn at Sharpness. The three-quarters of a mile long bridge was built in 1879 and only went out of operation in 1960 when it was hit by a large oil tanker.

Before the drastic rail closures of the 1960s British Rail had over 60,000 bridges of all shapes

Below *Kew Bridge, London; designed by W. R. Galbraith and built by Brassey and Ogilvy for the South Western Railway Company*
Right *Newport Transporter Bridge; suspended platform across the River Usk*

and sizes. The short span bridges which made up the majority were normally unspectacular in style and position. They presented no problems in construction. The main design criterion was the necessity to ensure that they would stand the active loads imposed by the train on 'over-bridges' or other forms of transport on 'under-bridges'. The spanning systems that were used were the same as those used on the long span bridges. Many of the old masonry and brick arched bridges are as good as when constructed; others have developed a variety of defects and have been replaced. The more usual faults, such as bulging spandrels, cracked arches, perished brickwork, decomposed mortar, foundation settlement and distorted arches, can all now be repaired. However, up to recent years it was cheaper to replace than to carry out sophisticated remedial work. One of the finest brick arched bridges to survive is that across the Thames at Maidenhead. The bridge is formed of two very flat elliptical arches each with a 128 foot span and a rise of 24 feet with four semicircular arches of about 28 foot span at each end. Work started in 1837 and had just been completed when the centring was blown down during a storm in late 1839. In 1890 it became necessary to quadruple the line, the widening being carried out to the same design by addition on each side. The three units were then tied together with metal rods. Since then it has required only superficial maintenance. Another interesting surviving bridge is near Cullompton on the Bristol–Exeter line. It is an over-line bridge built on the skew in 1843, the work controlled by I. K. Brunel, with mechanically correct spiral tapering courses.

A few of the earliest bridges were in cast iron. Surviving bridges, less than two dozen, show they ranged in form from the girder bridge of the Cromford and High Peak Railway in Derbyshire to the arch and spandrel under-bridge across the Grand Junction Canal. George Stephenson experimented with cast iron girders which were truss-braced with wrought iron rods. However the Dee Bridge collapse of 1847 virtually put an end to this idea. Drawings of examples on the London–Birmingham line have fortunately survived to show us the elegance that was achieved in cast iron.

Most of the oldest metal bridges are of wrought iron and are now over a hundred years old. These have some of the characteristics of the old soldier, but they do ultimately expire, as do the less aged steel structures. As a result mainly of corrosion the smaller metal bridges are constantly being replaced. Perhaps it is time that more examples of these less well known bridges were conceded to be worthy of preservation.

Failure of a bridge or viaduct can cause a major disaster and they must, therefore, be maintained at

Right Leeds; small railway bridge over the canal just outside the Central Station

a high level of safety. Of the 178 civil engineering works listed by the Department of the Environment, 141 are still in use. This is fortunate, since use is normally the best form of preservation. Unfortunately, however, this implies that there are only a few abandoned examples recognized as being of historic importance; it is these abandoned relics which are now rapidly decaying. At present British Rail maintains responsibility for the upkeep of the abandoned works. But as British Rail says, it is not in business to preserve the past; its attitude, therefore, has been to demolish or to close access to the public and await the process of demolition through decay.

In the future, I suspect the survival of these engineering works will depend on the recognition of their historic importance. Finding alternative uses for these structures is not easy. A few bridges and viaducts have survived because of their reuse as footpaths in national nature reserves. The drooping arches of the London–Greenwich viaduct now create the atmosphere of the London Horror Museum. These examples, if ingenious, are isolated. But surely the problem cannot be intractable.

ENGINE SHEDS
CHRIS HAWKINS AND GEORGE REEVE

ENGINE SHEDS were a unique, and to many people uniquely interesting, form of industrial building. They housed the much-loved steam locomotives that powered virtually every train on the railways of Great Britain for some 150 years. They had their own distinctive servicing and maintenance equipment and their own special atmosphere – and unmistakable combination of odour, noise, light and smoke. An extraordinarily large number of these fascinating buildings must have been built at one time or another; if those in private industrial and coal-mining sites are included the total is probably in excess of 4,000.

Many of the earliest bore a typically Victorian ornate and built-to-last aspect, and indeed many of these substantial structures survived till the 1960s in rather better condition than their cheaply built descendants of the 1930s. Though constructed purely for the servicing and maintenance of an undeniably dirty, oily and smoky form of motive power, many were surprisingly elegant in appearance. A well-known example is the roundhouse at Inverness, with its arched, separate entrance looking like a cross between a medieval city gate and some mill-owner's folly. The London, Brighton and South Coast Railway shed at Brighton possessed a number of graceful arched entrances, as did the much smaller London, Chatham and Dover establishment at Gillingham. A garden with a fountain was placed alongside the Midland Railway sheds at Leicester, and a similar formal garden adorned the shed of the same company at Manningham, Bradford. Simple designs, once despised as the ugliest expression of a generally lowly regarded period of architecture, have come to be much admired – the aptly named Roundhouse theatre in Camden, London, being perhaps the best known example.

Engine sheds were built from the very earliest days of the railway, buildings where locomotives could be serviced and repaired during working trips being essential for the efficient running of a railway system. The engines also had to be coaled, turned and watered, of course, and various types of layout quickly developed, few of which were particularly logical or efficient. One of the first shed types adopted was the roundhouse, where a turntable was placed centrally in a (round or square) building with an exit/entrance line and a number of stub tracks, termed stalls, radiating off like the spokes of a wheel. Here the locomotives were stabled and repaired, while a coaling platform and water crane were provided outside. Increase in size and numbers of locomotives quickly made these redundant and the Camden Roundhouse (1846) is one of very few surviving examples from the early days, due to its conversion to a goods depot well before 1900.

'Straight' sheds came to be the most common type employed, being literally straight, rectangular buildings, with one or more roads parallel to the longest side. The tracks could terminate at one end or run right through the building.

Few of the first sheds survived very long, as the rapid increase in traffic and thus locomotives in the nineteenth century made larger and more efficient sheds essential, but many of the best known latter-

Marylebone Station, London; late nineteenth century turntable, the last in the London area

day establishments occupied original sites. Nine Elms and Stewarts Lane in south London, for example, while not the original buildings, both stood on sites used since the arrival of the main lines in the capital.

However, nearby building development, itself stimulated by the arrival of the railway, often boxed in and restricted the sheds, and it was frequently found that by the time a shed needed enlargement or the provision of a more efficient layout land was just not available. New depots could only be built much further out, but this would place them too far from the termini and goods depots their locomotives were supposed to serve. The companies had to make do and a pattern developed whereby the first sheds, built near the termini, were backed up by secondary depots further down the line, associated with new freight yards built on the then outer, less built-up areas of the city. This had the advantages of both relieving congestion at the inner depot, which could concentrate on passenger work, and allowing new, better designed layouts for marshalling work and the necessary freight engines.

Understandably, this is best seen in London, where many of the main line companies found it necessary to take this course. Hornsey, by the Ferme Park goods yards, complemented King's Cross on the Great Northern Railway, while Willesden performed a similar role with regard to Camden on the London and North-Western Railway. On the Midland, roundhouses were built adjacent to the new yards at Cricklewood, while passenger engines tended to operate from much nearer St Pancras, at Kentish Town. A similar pattern existed on the Great Western Railway, Southall having mainly goods types with Westbourne Park (replaced in 1906 by one of the country's biggest sheds, Old Oak Common) taking care of passenger locomotives at the Paddington end of the line.

Thus a circle of marshalling yards and engine sheds delineates a former developed limit of the capital in the same way as the better known 'ring of North London termini' marks the Euston Road as a one-time northern margin of the built-up area.

Sheds appeared at all sorts of locations for various reasons. They were naturally placed at junctions for interchange traffic, as at Rugby, Crew, York, Carlisle, and so on, where each individual company built its own depots – at Carlisle there were at one time seven sheds, owned by six separate companies! Sheds were also to be found at country junctions, from tiny Kingham in Oxfordshire to the fairly substantial establishment at Redhill, the only point on the major cross-country link between Reading and the Kent coast where engines had to be turned.

Sheds were also provided for purely operational reasons, as at Salisbury on the London and South-Western Railway, where a large shed was provided for servicing and repairing the engines of the West of England main line trains, which for historical reasons always changed engines at Salisbury.

Local sources of lucrative freight also spurred the railways to provide sheds at otherwise obscure locations, servicing facilities being required for the engines tapping the coal or whatever local mineral was being extracted. Several examples of this could be found in the South Wales valleys, at Westhouses and Kirkby-in-Ashfield in the Midlands, in the Fife coalfields and many other coal and mineral areas of the country.

The tiny single-road engine shed at the end of a country branch, often flimsily built in wood or corrugated iron, was a familiar sight. It housed the single tank locomotive between trips or overnight and was to be found in most abundance and at its most picturesque in the West Country, where virtually every winding branch was provided with its engine shed at the terminus.

By 1900 the general design and size of sheds had become largely set, with each company developing in the next few decades a standard 'unitized' design which they believed best suited their needs. Basically the choice lay between roundhouses and straight sheds for the more important depots while a variety of two or three road buildings in stone, wood and corrugated iron sufficed for the less important places. The design of sheds was often the

Stoke-on-Trent, Staffordshire; former engine roundhouse

responsibility of the chief mechanical engineer, like Hughes on the Lancashire and Yorkshire Railway, and Dean (later Churchward) on the Great Western Railway. Hughes designed a number of brick-built straight sheds, standardized down to turntables, water columns and tank, coal stage and office windows, and Churchward evolved a similar scheme from the designs of his predecessor, Dean. The GWR was one of the comparatively few (but very large and economically important) companies to employ roundhouses on any kind of scale. The typical depot consisted of a square brick building with a tall pitched roof, which contained a turntable, and an adjacent repair shop with lifting hoist, machinery, and so on. The repair shop was a more or less standard unit erected alongside any type of depot (in fact the few survivals are all associated with straight sheds). Coal waggons were propelled up a lengthy ramp provided in the yard. Inside the shelter at the top the coal would be transferred to tubs and emptied into the tenders of the engines parked alongside, a time-consuming process but viable in times of unlimited labour.

The London and North-Western Railway de-

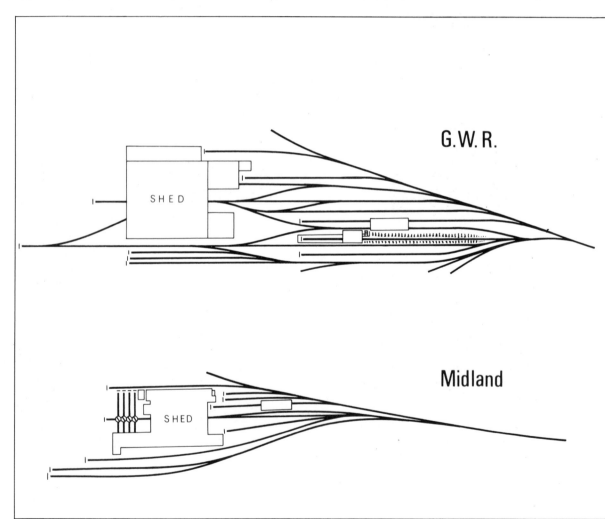

G.W.R.

SHED

Midland

SHED

veloped some of the largest straight sheds seen, with multi-road buildings like the twenty-five track example at Rugby. This shed covered a large area but since the elimination of steam has disappeared completely. The sheds at Crewe North covered a huge expanse of land in the town centre, and were demolished and cleared in the mid-1960s, to remain an empty waste of bulldozed rubble.

Two other railway giants, the North-Eastern and the Midland, concentrated on roundhouses for the stabling of their locomotives. Some of these were particularly attractive, employing a maze of

wrought iron columns to support the cavernous roofs. Possibly the largest British shed ever, at Hull Dairycoates, included six roundhouses arranged in line and each accessible to the other. Perhaps the most famous of these roundhouses is the pair at York, converted as the perfect setting for the new National Railway Museum and proving very popular with the public. Most, however, have disappeared and though presumably they are eminently suitable for conversion to industrial use, being adjacent to the railway (though not so often to roads, it must be said) and capable of holding

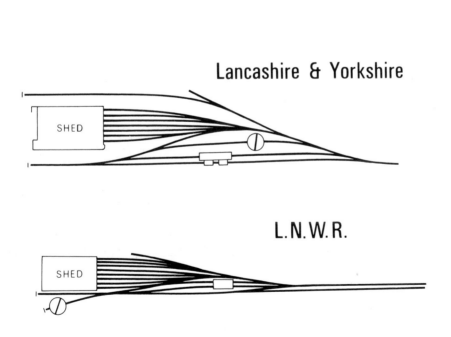

Four different engine shed designs used by major railway companies

two or three floors, relatively few of the hundreds built now serve any useful purpose. Many are now just cleared sites, like Hasland near Chesterfield (partly a rubbish dump) and Newport Ebbw Junction. Some, though, have been put to profitable use, like the giant complex of three roundhouses at Kentish Town, north London, taken over by a building firm after closure and used ever since. Their shape seems to make them eminently suitable for lorries – the old roundhouses at Battersea Park were converted for this use in 1934 and today the vehicles are still parked grouped around the central turntable area, in the same fashion as the original steam locomotives. The original inspection pits under the stalls provide ready-made access to the undersides of the vehicles.

The sheds were an integral and vital, if little known, part of railway operations. The concentrations of locomotives were often a source of local pollution and annoyance, but they provided much work, though admittedly of a hard and dirty nature. Labour, however, was always plentiful in difficult times and there was no problem in obtaining staff until after the Second World War. Sheds

Above *Stratford-on-Avon; the former Great Western Railway shed*
Left *Leeds Central, Yorkshire; former waggon-drop buildings for lowering trucks of up to 20 tons on to the line below*

had been largely starved of investment until then (apart from a noble effort at mechanization by the London, Midland and Scottish Railway in the 1930s) and, amazingly, probably something like over half of the larger depots in Britain employed some degree of hand-sorting of coal, even in the 1950s. This, in one of the most vital industries (then!) of an advanced industrial state.

Alongside the engine sheds the companies also developed their own rolling stock construction factories, always known simply as 'works'. Except in the very early days each private company built its own rails and sleepers and maintained its own civil engineering structures, bridges, tunnels, and the rest. New buildings like sheds were one of the few large capital items to go regularly to outside tender. The private locomotive builders of Glasgow, Leeds, Manchester and other industrial towns depended on overseas markets, and generally were used by British railways only for urgent orders.

The works of the larger railway companies covered huge areas and manufactured everything the railway needed, from locomotives to cap badges, from steel rails to cutlery. Some included their own steel foundries, rolling mills and gas works, and in total they represented a significant segment of British heavy industry and an enormous reservoir of skill and invention, often initiating engineering techniques that came to be adopted elsewhere in the country.

The grouping of the railways into the four main companies in 1923 rendered many of the small works redundant, especially during the enforced economic recession of the 1930s. Several were closed and many more found much of their work

taken away, with remaining facilities concentrated on repairs to engines employed locally, rather than entirely new construction. An early casualty was the Somerset and Dorset Railway's works at Highbridge in Somerset, a catastrophic blow to the small community.

Although railways remained busy enough for many of the large locomotive factories to remain operational under British Rail into the 1950s and 1960s, decreasing traffic and new forms of traction meant cut-backs were inevitable here too, and many of the greatest engineering establishments of

Top *Overseal*; *London and North Western Railway straight shed*
Above *Hasland, near Chesterfield, Midland Railway*
Left *Wellington; the austere former GWR shed*

the nineteenth and twentieth centuries were wound down. This decline paralleled that of the private locomotive builders, famous firms like North British and Beyer Garrett also becoming casualties. The London, Brighton and South Coast Railway factories at Brighton are now a rubble-strewn wasteland high above the town centre, the Great Central plant at Gorton has disappeared under a council housing scheme and the famous North-Eastern works at Darlington also closed its doors in the 1960s. Barry, Caerphilly, Wolverhampton,

Oswestry, Worcester and Newton Abbot closed in the Western Region alone, leaving only a much reduced level of work at Swindon. Cowlairs, Bow, Ashford, Horwich and Inverurie are only some of the other railway factories either closed and demolished or surviving from year to year on much reduced work and staff levels. Virtually all British Rail's locomotive needs are now met from the plants at Derby, Crewe and Doncaster, reorganized under the separate British Rail Engineering Limited. Since 1976 Britain has been importing locomotives from Eastern Europe, the first foreign locomotives to be imported in any numbers for decades.

In the transformation of British railways following the announcement of the Modernization Plan in 1955, there was even less place for the steam shed than for the old works. Coaling, watering and turning facilities were obviously redundant (the shorter turn round period required by diesel locomotives was one of the major factors in their superiority over steam traction), while some of the

Left and below *Glasgow; railway workshops*

buildings themselves were the wrong size, in the wrong place for changing traffic patterns, or just decrepit. Agecroft in Manchester, for instance, had to be closed prematurely because of the dangerous state of the roof, and it was not the only shed to all but fall down before closure.

Thus for many sheds closure was a merciful end after decades of neglect, bomb damage and the corrosive effect of generations of steam engines. Nevertheless large numbers of substantial buildings remained, when their last locomotives were scrapped or transferred away, with varying periods

of useful life left to them, and a portion of these found further use under British Rail or private owners. A few, like Hither Green in south London, were converted to house the new forms of traction which had ousted the old occupants, but most found use only as somewhat ignominious stores for various items of heavy equipment. Hornsey stood empty for years and has only just recently been tidied up to house electrification equipment, and a similar use was found for the shed at Springs Branch, near Wigan.

The majority, however, were simply bulldozed

flat, at enormous cost, after standing empty and derelict for various periods. The huge buildings at Patricroft, Heaton Mersey and Edgeley, near Manchester; Bank Hall, Edge Hill and Speke Junction in Liverpool; Nottingham, Colwick, Bolton and dozens of others are now empty debris-littered wastelands. In all cases the valuable scrap-rails, sleepers and machinery were removed to leave the actual building isolated and ready for potential use, but all were subsequently flattened.

In many cases the buildings, sometimes with all their facilities, water columns, and so on, were left intact for a number of years. Stafford, a splendid brick-built industrial site, stands empty and mouldering after more than twelve years, a vandals' playground. Warrington, Aintree and Bell Vue, Manchester, provide other examples. The splendid roundhouse at Croes Newydd, near Wrexham, survived intact from closure in 1968 until demolition, for no apparent reason, in 1975. The depot was an industrial *Marie Celeste*, being absolutely untouched, apart from broken windows, from the day the last engines and men left the shed. All facilities were present, and even the various

Above *Inverness; entrance to the former roundhouse*
Left *Highbridge; former Somerset and Dorset Railway locomotive shed*

cast iron notices around the yards for the guidance of staff still remained. Could *no* use have been found for this building?

The pattern of demolition and disposal is certainly inexplicable. In many cases it seems almost to have been simply a desire to erase all reminders of the old order; to remove all trace of a system that was quickly disappearing – far too quickly for good economic sense, it has since been argued.

Some of the buildings happily were disposed of properly. The shed at Sutton Oak, St Helen's, was converted simply and cheaply for use by an industrial concern, with the yard providing a good-sized car park. The tiny shed at Sidmouth is now the only attractive building on a busy industrial estate, and Mansfield, Bangor and Skipton among others have found industrial or commercial use.

Some sites have been given over to leisure pursuits. The roundhouse National Railway Museum at York and the Camden Roundhouse theatre have already been mentioned (and for a more detailed discussion of Camden's reuse see page 217). Private railway preservation societies have set up shop at

a number of locations. The best known, perhaps, are at Didcot and Carnforth, where steam engines and various historical railway items are restored and available at frequent intervals for viewing by the public.

Other such sites exist at Southport, Radstock, Ashford (Kent) and, hopefully soon, at Swanage. In fact people have even been building replicas of engine sheds! A pure Victorian-style shed has been constructed to house the locomotives of the Cranmore Railway in Somerset and even British Rail operates one, at Aberystwyth, to house the

narrow gauge engines working the scenic line to Devil's Bridge.

A lot of time has been wasted, though. Many of the buildings noted by the authors in a partial survey of the country in the early 'seventies have since suffered demolition, seldom to be replaced. The real waste occurred in the 'sixties when shed and works closures were at their height. Their location in Development Areas or position as sole local employers exacerbated the unemployment problem. The little town of Woodford Halse, an isolated country junction, virtually died overnight

Far left *Acklington, Northumberland; Gothic engine shed*
Left *Christon Bank, Northumberland; Gothic engine shed*

when its local, fairly large depot closed. A further use could and should have been found to maintain some kind of continuity of employment.

Although the whole question is now rapidly becoming one of industrial archaeology, the closure and disappearance of these unique buildings deserves at least to be remembered when consideration is given to any present or future similar industrial upheaval.

RAILWAY TOWNS
SOPHIE ANDREAE

IN THE EARLY DAYS of the railway the many companies were principally concerned with the construction of lines and building of stations while they bought their rolling stock from independent manufacturers. These early steam engines were unreliable and needed regular servicing; furthermore, engines had to be changed at intervals on long runs in rather the same way as horses. It became apparent that if the railways were to run efficiently it would be essential for the companies to have their own repair shops and locomotive works.

Some of the railway companies founded their works in already established industrial towns such as Derby, Doncaster and Darlington. York was another large town which became a railway centre and Stratford in east London also had important railway works. Other companies founded entirely new settlements – Crewe, New Bradwell and Eastleigh are three such examples. In a third category were the small market towns which became railway centres and expanded rapidly. Swindon, for example, owed its sudden growth to its becoming the centre of the Great Western Railway repair and locomotive works. Other towns, while not actually manufacturing rolling stock and equipment, because of their positions as 'stages' on the railway network where engines were changed had a large percentage of railway workers among the population. Peterborough developed from a small cathedral city into a large town as a direct result of the railway. Rugby, a market town with its famous school, grew likewise.

The obvious advantage of setting up a company's works in an established industrial town was the ready availability of a skilled workforce. There was also not the need to build houses that there was at completely new settlements. While these towns expanded as a direct result of the railway the companies did not, on the whole, undertake to provide housing for their workers, preferring to leave the task to speculative builders. It was only in the new settlements like Crewe and the small towns which had to expand very rapidly, like Swindon, that the railway companies themselves built houses on any scale, and a large proportion of the houses even at these towns was provided by speculators. In the smaller railway establishments such as Wolverton, Ashford and Eastleigh speculative building accounted for almost all of the housing.

When a new town was to be set up a location at the centre of the particular company's railway network was almost invariably chosen. The fact that such sites were sometimes scarcely populated rural areas did not deter the railway companies and having chosen a site they wasted little time in importing a skilled workforce and making provision to house them.

Railway housing was nearly always well built and solid. However, the houses, which were almost invariably built as terraces, were architecturally modest. They were usually of brick with few decorative features. Some of the terraces at Crewe boast decorative bargeboards but on the whole the houses were very plain. The outstanding exception to this is Winton Square in Stoke-on-Trent. Stoke

Winton Square, Stoke-on-Trent, Staffordshire; 1850 by H. A. Hunt. The North Stafford Hotel faces the station across the square containing Jacobean buildings

was the centre of the North Staffordshire Railway and the company was responsible for laying out the square with the station and hotel at opposite ends flanked by two rows of cottages for the railway workers, all in an elaborate and decorative Jacobean style.

The first company to found its own works was the London and Birmingham Railway, which set up locomotive works at Wolverton shortly after the opening of the railway in 1838. At first the Company did not build any houses and expected its workers to commute from neighbouring towns like Stony Stratford and Newport Pagnell, but this soon proved impractical. At Crewe and Swindon, both of which were developed at the beginning of the 1840s, the houses were built at more or less the same time as the works. Locomotive works were set up in Ashford in 1845, while Eastleigh was comparatively late on the scene, for the works were not opened until 1891. In building their own rolling stock the English railway companies differed markedly from those elsewhere, for comparatively few Continental or American railways went in for this. Indeed Crewe eventually became the greatest works owned by a single railway company anywhere in the world.

In 1841 the population of Crewe was 203. At that time the site of the present town lay in the small rural parish of Monks Coppenhall. The name Crewe was derived from Crewe Hall, the local manor. The railway which ran near to this then unimportant spot was opened in 1837. The story of Crewe began in 1840 on 20 June and 1 July when the Grand Junction Board ordered the purchase of land in the parish of Monks Coppenhall, having decided that this was a much better location for their works than the cramped and remote premises at Edge Hill. By 1842 Crewe was at the junction of four major lines, those from Birmingham, Manchester, Liverpool and Chester. These were to be joined by lines from Shrewsbury, Preston and Stoke-on-Trent. Despite the fact that there was no local coal or iron ore the central position of Crewe

Normanton, Yorkshire; railway cottages, now demolished

on the railway network was of paramount importance. Joseph Locke, the Grand Junction's engineer, was commissioned to lay out the town and the works and to draw up 'plans, drawings and estimates for an establishment at Crewe which shall include shops required for the building and repairs of carriages and wagons as well as engines'.

In 1842 the Grand Junction appointed John Cunningham, an architect, 'to superintend the whole of the buildings ... the drainage also, and every other matter connected with the proper completion of the building, cottages and other erections at Crewe'. He held his post at a salary of £300 a year until 1850. Building went apace and by the end of 1842 thirty-two new cottages were occupied. In 1843 the building of further cottages was placed under the supervision of the resident engineers, R. S. Norris, and by 1844 a total of 217 cottages were occupied.

The railway estate was centred around Moss Square and Prince Albert Street. About thirty acres were laid out with cottages and the cost of the new colony was estimated to be in the region of £110,000. This included the cost of the gasworks which were opened in 1843. The great move from Edge Hill took place in 1845 when the mechanics arrived in Crewe; 750–900 people coming from various parts of Liverpool were involved in the move. In December that year the new colony and the works were more or less complete and to celebrate the Grand Junction arranged for a 'grand dinner, tea and ball' for 'superintendents, clerks and workmen'. On 18 December that year the new church of Christ Church was consecrated. It cost £6,000 of which £1,000 had been contributed by the Grand Junction shareholders, who also made small grants to the Nonconformists and Catholics. In 1845 the Public Baths were also opened and about the same time the Company provided an Assembly Room, a Magistrates' Room and schools. By 1851, the year of the next census, Crewe's population had risen to 4,571.

Normanton, Yorkshire; detail of window illustrating the sad neglect that has befallen much railway housing

Contemporary accounts provide valuable information on the types of houses being built by the Company. A description dating from 1846 runs as follows:

> The dwelling-houses arrange themselves in four classes: first the villa-style lodges of the superior officers: next a kind of ornamented Gothic constitutes the houses of the next in authority: the engineers domiciled in detached mansions, which accommodate four families, with gardens and separate entrances: and last, the labourer delights in neat cottages of four apartments, the entrances with ancient porches.... The rooms are capacious; the ground floors are tiled, and, as the back and front are open, ventilation is perfect. Each house is supplied with gas: the water is always on at present in the street, but is to be immediately introduced into the houses. The engineers ... pay 3s. 6d. per week, the labourers 2s. For water there is no charge, but for gas they pay in winter 2d. per week for each burner. The fittings cost them nothing.

Another description of Crewe dating from 1850 comments that:

> The general appearance of Crewe is very pleasing. The streets are wide and well-paved; the houses neat and commodious, usually of two storeys, built of bricks, but with the bricks concealed by rough cast plaster, with porches, lattice windows, and a little piece of garden ground before the door.... The accommodation is good, and it would be difficult to find such houses at such low rents even in the suburbs of a large town.

Crewe continued to grow at a steady pace for the rest of the century. There was an acute shortage of housing in the early 1850s after the establishment of a rail-rolling mill which caused a new influx of workers. The census of 1881 showed that there was a total of 4,864 houses in Crewe of which about 845 had been built by the Grand Junction Company. Much has been demolished in the centre of Crewe in this century to make way for shops and the present commercial area, but there are still a few terraces left of the early railway housing.

Before the railway arrived in Swindon, it was a small market town. In 1831 its population was 1,742, which was considerably lower than the populations of some other Wiltshire towns: Marlborough, for instance had 3,426 and Warminster 6,115. However, by the end of the century Swindon was the largest town in Wiltshire, larger even than Salisbury, with a population of over 40,000.

The town had grown up as a route centre and staging post. In 1801 the opening of the Wiltshire and Berkshire Canal had linked Swindon to the national canal system and thus to the rest of the country. The railway network, however, was to be of far greater significance. On 16 December 1840 the line to Swindon was officially opened. As Swindon was situated on the edge of what is known as the Wootton Bassett incline it was clear from the beginning that a stock of engines would have to be kept there to enable the London to Bristol trains to get up the slope, which was too steep for the engines usually used on that run. Furthermore, in 1841 the Great Western Railway, which owned the line, agreed to use their own rolling stock on the Gloucester branch line (then independently

owned) and also on the Bristol to Exeter line. This necessitated the building of railway workshops, and Swindon, lying as it did almost midway between London and Bristol, was an obvious choice. In ten years the population of Swindon rose to 2,459 and according to the 1851 census 500 of the men were railway navvies.

In 1843 the GWR workshops were opened with a workforce of just over 400 men. A few of these were local, but many had come from the declining textile areas around Bristol. A number also came either from London or from the big industrial towns of the Midlands and north. It was clear that accommodation had to be provided, for the works were located alongside the railway about a mile from the old town. In 1842 the first estate of about 300 cottages was laid out, on the southern side of the railway. Messrs J. and C. Rigby of London were commissioned to undertake the building. Rents were then payable to the builders, and the GWR, to compensate the Rigbys for the capital cost of building the houses, gave them a ninety-nine year lease of the station refreshment room from Christmas 1842 at 1*d*. per year. This proved

Above and left *Crewe, Cheshire; a street of railway houses. Though very plain, the houses are given character by the projecting gables*

to be extremely profitable for right up until 1895 every train had to stop for at least ten minutes at Swindon, and this was the only long stop between London and Bristol. The Rigbys immediately sublet the refreshment business to S. J. Griffiths of the Queen's Hotel, Cheltenham, for seven years at £1,000 per year and £6,000 premium. In August 1848 the lease was sold outright to J. R. Phillips for £20,000, and in 1875 it was resold for £45,000.

The houses that were built by the Rigbys are thought to have been designed by Sir Matthew Digby Wyatt. The layout was symmetrical round a central square called Emlyn Square from which four streets ran off on each side parallel with the railway. The streets, appropriately enough, were named after stations on the line: those on the west side were Bristol, Bath (later changed to Bathampton), Exeter and Taunton and those on the east side were London, Oxford, Reading and Farringdon.

The railway village soon became known as New Swindon. The terraces were built of local limestone and were mostly one- or two-bedroomed. Each house had a small yard behind containing the wash-house and privy. Professor Pevsner describes New Swindon as 'one of the few planned Victorian estates, small and modest and laid out without ingenuity but planned all the same, and architecturally as orderly as the design of the street'. By 1843 a total of 136 houses had been completed, most of them in Bath Street and Exeter Street and a few in Bristol Street and Taunton Street. Eleven years later only a further 109 houses had been built and the shortage of housing was causing considerable overcrowding. A survey undertaken by the GWR in 1843 showed an average of five persons per house; by 1847 the population had more than doubled and there was an average of seven persons per house.

By the 1850s congestion in New Swindon had worsened and the Company, in an enterprising attempt to ease the problem of overcrowding, decided to build a large three-storeyed building to house single men. The idea was to provide single rooms with a shared entrance and communal kitchen; day and night porters were provided by the Company. However, the scheme was not the success that had been anticipated and soon the building earned itself the name of 'The Barracks'. Despite the overcrowding, the men preferred to live in the village, where there were fewer restrictions. The building was eventually converted into flats and these were occupied largely by workers from South Wales who came in considerable numbers after the rail-rolling mills were opened in Swindon in 1861. Each family had three rooms and shared communal washing facilities. However, even this did not work and from the Company records it appears that the families were unsettled and the wives constantly quarrelling with each other. The Barracks was converted into a Wesleyan church in 1869, and is now the home of the Great Western Railway Museum.

After the mid-century the GWR ceased to build houses and the task of providing accommodation was taken over by private speculative builders. The first extensive area of working-class housing provided by these builders was in Westcott Place and Westcott Street. Very often these speculative builders formed themselves into building societies; Thomas Ellis, the manager of the rolling mills, was one of the first to do this; he founded a society in the early 1860s and in 1864 built near the works two rows of cottages called Cambria Place. It was almost entirely inhabited by Welsh families and a small Welsh Methodist church was erected in 1866. Other societies were formed, among them the Swindon Permanent Benefit Building and Investment Society, the Oxford and the Reading Societies.

The works were enlarged in 1853 to serve the new GWR line to Birmingham and by 1855 their number of workers had risen to over 1,000. The works were extended further in 1864 after GWR's acquisition of many new lines in the west and south-west. In 1868 the GWR carriage workshops were transferred from Paddington to Swindon and the repair works previously carried out at Worcester, Saltney and Newton Abbot were also moved to Swindon. As small independent lines were taken over their workshops were closed so that all repair work, maintenance and building was concentrated at Swindon. As the works expanded so did the labour force; the population increased by 1,478 between 1851 and 1861, an increase of 67 per cent. New Swindon had grown to be almost twice the size of Old Swindon, having a population of 7,628 as compared to 4,092. None the less, a considerable number of railway workers lived in the old town, and outlying villages soon became dormitories to the railway town. By 1881 Swindon had become the largest town in Wiltshire, with a combined population of 17,678. At this time the new town had four times the population of the old town, but although there were several pubs the trek still had to be made to the old town for shopping.

A GWR director, G. H. Gibbs, left £500 towards a church and school when he died in 1842. A church called St Mark's, costing £6,000, was duly built to the designs of George Gilbert Scott who, incidentally, also designed the parish church of Old Swindon, Christ Church, in 1851. The other important building in Swindon was the Mechanics' Institution, which was established in 1844. It was the centre of the social and cultural life of the new town for nearly a hundred years. It was intended for 'disseminating useful knowledge and encouraging rational amusement amongst all classes of people employed by the Company at Swindon'. To begin with there was no building, and meetings, classes and entertainments had to take place either in the school or at the works. In 1855 the Institution moved to its new premises. The GWR provided the capital and it was built by a specially formed company called the New Swindon Improvement Company, which later undertook the construction of the 'Bath, Reading, Lecture and Refreshment Rooms, and Market and Shops', as well as some housing.

As at Crewe, the town was completely railway oriented until the beginning of the last quarter of the nineteenth century. It was not until 1875 that a clothing manufacturer moved from London and set up in Swindon. This followed the signing of a contract with the GWR for the firm to supply the Railway with uniforms. Other clothing factories followed in 1901 and 1918, a tobacco factory opened in 1915 and a gramophone works in 1919. The main advantage of this gradual diversification was that it provided employment for the women

of Swindon, who previously had had no opportunities of work.

Old and New Swindon were gradually drawn together as building filled in the land dividing the two settlements. In 1864 two local Boards of Health had been set up, but they were joined as a Municipal Borough in 1901. The railway village was acquired in 1966 by the Borough Council, who applied for permission to demolish the houses. Wiltshire County Council refused, and the Borough Council to their credit decided to repair the cottages and modernize them.

Wolverton was merely a village, and its choice as a railway centre may, at first, seem an unlikely one. It was not at a route centre, but it did lie almost half-way between the terminal points of the very important London to Birmingham line, which was opened in 1838. It was also near to the Grand Junction Canal at the strategic point where the canal crossed the Great Ouse. Although the opening of the canal in 1805 did not immediately affect Wolverton, its proximity was undoubtedly an important consideration when the London and Birmingham Railway made their decision to locate their works there.

An estate of some 200 houses was begun to the south of the works in 1845, and this layout included the building of a church and schools. However, further expansion was somewhat curtailed by the refusal of the Radcliffe Trustees, who owned the surrounding land, to sell any more land for development. To overcome this problem a new settlement was established in 1854 at New Bradwell, a little way to the south of the old village of Bradwell. It consisted of a grid of red brick terraces, 187 houses in all, with the unusual architectural feature that the end houses of each terrace were one storey taller than the rest. There were seventeen of these larger houses, which were intended for the foremen. Sadly, most of the houses were demolished quite recently and only one street now remains. Despite the local authority's desire to demolish this too, it was saved following a public inquiry.

In the 1860s, as Crewe was becoming the main centre for locomotive building, Wolverton had to

186

adapt and began to concentrate on carriage and waggon building. The Wolverton works were expanded when those at Euston and Saltley (Birmingham) were closed. Wolverton again was entirely railway oriented; it was the town's sole industry until 1876 when a printing works was set up. Like the light industries of Swindon this was a very welcome development, for it provided much-needed employment for the women of the town. The factory was sponsored by the London and North-Western Railway and was employing over 500 women by 1900. By 1901 the population of Wolverton had reached 5,200 and including the railway suburb of New Bradwell the total population was 9,200. Sixty years before the population had been merely a few hundred.

Ashford was a market town which served the eastern end of the Weald. It was at a bridging point on the River Stour and on the main London to Dover road. The railway followed the same route as the road along the valley but on the other side of the river. This was where the railway settlement grew up, at a distance from the old town.

In 1845 the South-Eastern Railway decided to move its locomotive works there. Formerly the SER had had its works at New Cross where it shared premises with the London and Brighton Railway. The works were completed by 1847 on a site south-east of Ashford on the east side of the Stour. Construction of locomotives began in 1850. About 600 men were employed initially and by 1861 this number had risen to 950. By 1847 a nucleus of twelve houses had been built and more were added in the 1850s, together with a chapel, school and shops. The new town, separated as it was from the old town by both the railway line and the river, became known as New Ashford. After 1870 Willesborough and South Ashford also became areas of railway housing. By 1901 the population of Ashford (including the old town) and Willesborough was more than 16,400. It was at about this time that further expansion took place, for in 1899 the SER agreed to let the London, Chatham and

Wolverton, Buckinghamshire; Bridge Street, late nineteenth century railway housing

Dover Railway move its locomotive works from Battersea where they were situated to Ashford. An interesting aspect of railway housing at Ashford was that much of the accommodation was built in the form of tenement flats rather than of terraced houses, as at the other railway towns, but many of them have since been demolished.

Eastleigh was a comparatively late railway town, not becoming a major centre until the end of the last century. The site was chosen for its location on the London to Southampton route at the junction of the important lines to Fareham (opened 1842) and Salisbury (opened 1847). The settlement was originally named after the village of Bishopstoke on the River Itchen, but, possibly because of confusion with Basingstoke, it became known as Eastleigh.

The London and South Western Railway provided a small group of houses near the junction in the late 1840s, but no major developments took place until the Company took the decision to move its locomotive works, which were located at Battersea, to Hampshire. The reason for the move was that more space was required for the handling of freight in London. The new works were opened in 1891 and most of the workers moved from London to the new location. The task of providing housing was left mainly to speculative contractors who were responsible for a series of terraces to the west of the works. However, the L & SWR did build a few houses at Bishopstoke. These cottages must have been intended to be something of a showpiece, as they were felt to warrant a full description and illustrations in *The Builder* of 1890. The architect was Ralph Nevill, and the drawings had been exhibited at the Royal Academy the previous year.

This group was to consist of one hundred cottages in all, arranged in 'one irregular and one complete quadrangle enclosing village greens'. Each had a small garden and provision was made for each to have an allotment as well. They were to be sturdily built of 'red brick in Selenitic mortar, with tiles for the roofs, and the windows are to be of imperial stone, all wood and paint thus being avoided'. The cost was not to exceed £200 per cottage, which did not include the cost of the gravel

(for concrete) which was to be 'dug on the spot'. The illustration shows them as pleasant terraced houses with tile-hung gables and decorative dormers. Each consisted of a parlour in front and kitchen behind, with a small scullery opening on to a verandah off which the coal shed was located. On the first floor were three small bedrooms.

The construction of planned towns to house the workforce of particular industries was nothing new in the mid-nineteenth century. By 1840 a number of such towns had been built, some dating from the eighteenth century: Cromford and New Lanark were both textile towns; Stourport and Ellesmere Port had become canal towns. In addition a number of towns grew up round the centres of the iron industry, like Winlaton, which dates from the early eighteenth century and Blaenavon and Dowlais, which were later. However, what characterizes the building of railway towns in particular was the sheer scale of the operation and its extent. In 1841 a mere 2,000 men were employed to run the railways, but by 1851 this had mushroomed to 25,230. Furthermore, though on the whole fairly simple in design, railway housing was almost invariably well built and considerably in advance of housing being provided at the same time by other industries.

Wolverton, Buckinghamshire; Spencer Street. Plain housing in the Georgian tradition with three-storey buildings for emphasis at the ends

HALF STEAM AHEAD
British Rail's Attitude Today
DAVID PEARCE

HUNDREDS OF STATIONS have been demolished since the Beeching Report and countless more declared redundant. The word 'countless' is appropriate, because no thorough record has been kept of the fate of the many buildings which have passed into the hands of local authorities, industry or private individuals.

In SAVE's booklet *Off the Rails* Gillian Darley discussed what she dubbed 'a despised heritage':

> ... even a small sample of lost buildings indicates the enormous diversity of architectural styles and scale ... from city termini (Euston, Birmingham New Street), large town stations (Birkenhead Woodside and Bradford Exchange, for example), small rural halts in regional style (Malmesbury, Shrivenham) ... There are hotels, examples of those demolished include the Great Western, Birmingham and the Station Hotel, Stafford, warehouses (Halifax) and workshops (Crewe), stables (Lincoln), railway monuments (Euston Arch), cottages (Normanton and Wolverhampton) and toll houses (those along the Cromer-Norwich line), pumping stations, viaducts (Crumlin) as well as bridges, engine houses and properties which, though not built for or by the railway companies, had become railway property (Deepdene).

Even listed building status has often provided only delay rather than protection. Neath and Bridgend, both stations by Brunel, are being mutilated in the cause of modernization. Port Talbot is waiting for this treatment. Another fate is eventual demolition after a long period of uncertainty and decay. Birmingham Snow Hill and Lytham Railhead are examples of this.

The toll of solid, serviceable and dignified buildings, often in basically sound condition, continues. At Walsall and Ware, Dorking, Elstree and Radlett at least partial demolition has been proposed. Many other stations, like Oundle, are abandoned to weather and vandals, while others still in use continue to be neglected – Frome (again by Britain's greatest engineer, Brunel) and Exeter St David's. The most serious case in Scotland is the early and handsome classical Edinburgh Haymarket.

There is a gulf of misunderstanding between conservationists and British Rail. Gillian Darley again: 'A sense of history is not incompatible with practicality or imagination; the loss and waste of good buildings, the dispersal and destruction of important monuments of engineering, such as the engines at the Sudbrook pumping station, Monmouth, or the breaking up of archival material, is all depressing proof of irresponsibility.' Historians take a different view of responsibility from railway managers. Julian Orbach and Dan Cruickshank write, in the same booklet, of the three-quarters of stations still predominantly nineteenth-century: 'They survive to show how a completely new

building type was evolved using current architectural forms together with structures that had no real precedent, the iron sheds and the platform canopies.' The historian is concerned that consistency be retained: 'the minor fixtures and fittings have a special value that too often is only appreciated after removal and replacement with standardised items of banal design'.

The purpose of this chapter is to attempt to understand the rather different attitude of British

Birmingham, Snow Hill; demolished 1977

Rail and to show that it is moving, albeit slowly and unevenly, nearer that of the conservationists. At its most sympathetic the new face of British Rail was seen in the 1977 exhibition train, showing that there is a recognition at British Rail headquarters that public opinion has changed. Here is part of British Rail's storyline:

> The destruction of the Euston Arch in order to make way for the new Euston station marked a turning point in attitudes and thinking concerning conservation of our industrial building heritage. If the arch could have been dismantled and stored or re-erected ... the British Transport Commission was not empowered to provide the necessary money and the government was not prepared to help. The significance of this event is in the fact that it drew attention to the increasing interest in heritage and conservation. Many people had felt deeply for some time that it was of fundamental importance to conserve for posterity the best examples of our industrial building heritage and because of the controversy aroused, additional support came from the general public as well as the architectural profession and learned bodies.

British Rail recognizes this interest and actively fosters conservation within the constraints of a continually changing modern transport system with limited finance.

But this recognition is not found in all regions and at all levels. The idea that modernity and a care for history are antagonistic has become strongly embedded in the last fifteen years. In the 1960s the modernizing zeal of the managers of British Rail had no patience with conservationist attitudes. Dr Beeching was busy cutting the whole system down to what was considered an economic size. While there was some regret at the loss of services, especially the wholesale closure of rural branch lines, there was a positive pleasure in the opportunity to change the image of the rail system from a predominantly nineteenth-century one to a late-twentieth-century 'white heat of technology' version. To many of those working on British Rail it seemed a great opportunity to streamline, to un-

load much of the massive weight of Victorian buildings which the railways had to maintain to their cost. The picture in their minds was of passengers in clean, air-conditioned comfort being hurtled smoothly and silently at 130 mph in bullet-nosed, blue and yellow electric or diesel monsters between efficiently integrated transport interchanges. Nostalgia did not come into it.

Indeed, some aspects of modernization cannot be gainsaid. The steam engine, for all its romantic associations, had to go. Track improvements to make journeys safer and smoother, as well as faster, are necessary. If such improvements, together perhaps with electrification, mean that some platform

Above *Oundle, Northamptonshire; 1845 by J. W. Livock –* 'left to rot'
Right *Sudbrook, Gwent; the engine house at the Monmouthshire end of the Severn tunnel*

canopies *have* to be cut back slightly further to give extra clearance – then so be it. But even this should be critically examined. British Rail's factors of safety often exceed international standards, as do many British engineering practices – unnecessarily. In any case the valance can be replaced or reproduced. Some of the changes have been genuinely functional, such as the increase in lighting levels on platforms to compete with the much brighter illumination in trains. Others, however, are the product of a desire to impose a corporate image: for example, many modern station signs seem to be actually smaller than the ones they replaced. There is no reason why lettering and lighting should be identical in Scotland and Cornwall.

However, simple platform and 'bus shelter' stations are undoubtedly easy to staff and supervise. Unions and management are in agreement over this. Staff have a legitimate aversion to working in old buildings and they have co-operated in a huge reduction in numbers – mostly by natural wastage – on the clear understanding that the new, computerized age would provide those who remained with incomparably better pay and conditions of work. They still have to be convinced that a thoroughly refurbished old station can be as efficient and comfortable a place to work in as a new one. The breakthrough will come when a few Victorian stations have been carefully restored and include first-class staff facilities. British Rail is slow to do this in most of its regions because, on the basis of some Dutch research and some monitoring of traffic on the Southern Region, it is still convinced that 'when we demolish and rebuild with prefabricated stations, there is an increase in traffic'. When a whole line of stations is reorganized and restored, as has recently begun in parts of the Liverpool commuter system currently being electrified, there may well be a similar increase.

In the majority of medium-sized stations buildings were traditionally strung out along the platforms: ticket office, waiting rooms, lavatories, bookstalls, stationmaster's room, other offices, bar, cafeteria, staff mess room and stores. Platforms were very long and mostly covered by awnings. Such an arrangement is expensive to staff and hideously costly to maintain. Roof canopies of cast iron, wood and glass can require, in the case of large engine sheds, a maintenance staff constantly at work, and in all instances need cleaning, painting and replacement on a regular basis.

Nowadays it is preferred to group the passenger facilities around one square space, the station entrance, which includes travel centre, buffet, bookstall, lavatories and left luggage. There is access to the platform at one central point with, it is claimed, only a short canopy needed because most trains now have corridors. This all sounds functional until

Above *St Botolphs; a modernized booking hall, convenient but characterless*
Right *Brierfield, Lancashire; evocative of the age of steam*

one remembers the reality of getting on a busy train from a crowded platform, with people stringing themselves out along the length of a platform in order to secure a seat. The removal of canopies on small, but at times busy, suburban stations then appears indefensible. Why should we stand in the rain, when our forebears did not? 'Modernization', a desire to sweep away what is seen as the junk of the past, has in such cases become a justification itself.

However, even at the height of the enthusiasm for streamlining, British Rail saw justification in keeping some old stations in repair. There was a modest long-term programme for station restoration. The Minor Stations Improvement Scheme started in 1961. A number of small stations like Taplow and medium-sized ones like Cambridge have been at least partly refurbished under one programme or another. Today some fine stations show signs of having been cared for both immaculately and imaginatively.

The hope is that these exceptional cases may gradually come to be the norm. At the top of British Rail the enthusiasm for the heritage is real.

Peter Parker, appointed Chairman in 1976, is a well-known conservationist and a trustee of the Civic Trust. The appointment of a new Director-Environment in the person of a former chief architect and property development director, Bernard Kaukas, was a welcome move. Mr Kaukas's tasks include: the review and encouragement of proposals for the improvement and refurbishing of stations and other railway buildings used by the public; preparing an annual programme for British Rail's listed buildings, whether for conservation, adaptation or sale; and reviewing standards of cleanliness in buildings and rolling stock. His powers to initiate change received a further stimulus from the creation of an Environmental Panel with a number of distinguished outside members – Sir Hugh Casson, Lord Esher, Michael Middleton and Sir Paul Reilly. Perhaps the translation of promises into deeds is necessarily slow.

Apart from genuine concern, there are various other factors which have influenced the change in British Rail's attitude. Public opinion has swung away from the redevelopment of the familiar and 'we claim to be at least up with public opinion', as a senior architect at Board Headquarters says. There is no longer a thriving property development industry willing, together with financial institutions and even local authorities, to enter into consortia for redevelopment. British Rail's efforts at profitable office block development largely failed. For example, the bureaucrats of British Rail and the bureaucrats of the GLC and central government spent so long arguing about office blocks over the rebuilt Euston that every possible profit-making opportunity was lost. Now the only complete modern terminus in London, which is impressive in a cool horizontal way, will be completely masked by office towers in front of it, instead of on its roof.

Historic buildings are now better protected by listing, by grants – from the Historic Buildings Council as at St Pancras, from local authorities in a small but increasing number of cases and from other bodies such as tourist boards – and by public concern expressed in local amenity groups, civic trusts and building preservation trusts. There is, fin-

ally, general official encouragement to reuse old buildings, and it is now clear that British Rail will not be able to sweep away many more of the historic termini, though its efforts continue. St Pancras is safe because those with a taste for nineteenth-century architecture have a stronger voice than they had at the time of the destruction of the Euston Arch. Nevertheless, progress towards a caring attitude remains patchy. For example, the demolition programme continues on Southern Region, the busiest rail network in the world. (It is surprising that British Rail should claim that in Sussex, Surrey and Kent, where the conservation movement is at its strongest in Britain, the taste for historic buildings hardly exists.) Tatty ten-year-old prefabricated buildings, such as those on Southern Region, are hardly proving maintenance-free. They will need replacement several times during the lifetime of a well kept conversion of an old, solidly built structure. Even when buildings are restored, the architect's hand is seldom a light one, as the restorations of Cambridge and Drayton Park attest.

From wishing it could rid itself of most of its termini, and indeed setting out to do so fifteen years ago, British Rail can now evince enthusiasm about parts of St Pancras, Waverley, Charing Cross and Paddington. But it is only parts. Having exposed the justly admired and monumentally simple façade of King's Cross, it cannot resist cluttering up the huge arched entrance with one of its precious travel centres.

Little store is set by consistency or completeness. Apart from travel centres, there are bright, shiny and new stainless steel and laminated plastic indicators, barriers, signs, catering facilities and other fittings to go in to show that the railways are in the twentieth century. At whatever cost in maltreatment there is a determination to impose the British Rail house style on buildings of whatever age or quality.

In order to indicate the progress that has been

Left *Cambridge Station*; above *before modernization, a crude canopy but nice glazing to arches*. Below *stripped down and given a horizontal emphasis to accommodate British Rail's corporate image*

made, and the direction in which British Rail should continue to go, a series of case studies follows. These illustrate station restoration or reuse on both large and small scales.

The façade of St Pancras station and the hotel is perhaps the most evocative monument to Victorian entrepreneurial confidence and craftsmanship. It is constructed in red brick and stone with marble dressing. There is splendid ironwork, though some was unfortunately removed in the Second World War. Otherwise the station survives virtually intact.

Intact but empty. Some of the hotel building is used as offices, but most has been unused for many years, 'because of fire hazard and inadequate means of escape', says British Rail. It is difficult to imagine a commercial company leaving so many floors of prime London space empty for so long; fire escapes could have been improved before now at far less than today's cost.

British Rail had hoped to redevelop, of course; indeed only in 1976 a grant of £50,000 from the Historic Buildings Council towards repairs was turned down. The following year agreement was

reached on a five year £200,000 programme to which the HBC will contribute 50 per cent. The GLC Historic Buildings Committee has embarked on the cleaning of the brickwork and stonework of all the ground-floor arches and the redecoration of external joinery and ironwork. This is being carried out by Community Industry under the aegis of the Manpower Services Commission. Community Industry specializes in giving conservation opportunities to young people from disadvantaged backgrounds; in this case six schoolleavers work under a skilled foreman. It is hoped

Above *Drayton Park, London in London Transport's hands, modest but with a sense of occasion*
Left *The same station showing the ruthless application of the British Rail house style*

that this scheme can be repeated elsewhere, such as at the Italianate station at North Woolwich.

At the other end of the scale, Cressington station, after being closed for five years, has now been reopened after electrification of the line from Liverpool Central to Garston. The station was built in 1871 by the Cheshire Lines Committee to serve the private estate of Cressington Park. The latter has now been designated an Outstanding Conservation Area. Thus an HBC grant (£8,000) has been forthcoming; this together with £1,000 from the Liverpool Heritage Bureau has encouraged British Rail to carry out works to restore the original external appearance of the building. Local volunteers collected funds to provide suitable gas lamps.

Liverpool Edge Hill, opened in 1836, is probably the oldest working station in the world. The two engine houses and accumulator house originally contained the fixed engines which worked the 'Liverpool Incline'. The canopies of a later date have been demolished, as has a later brick skin to much of the building. When external and internal renovation have been completed it is hoped that suitable tenants will be found for all these buildings. An interpretation centre on a heritage trail is a possibility, and one engine shed is already being used as a rehearsal room by the Edge Hill railway brass band. There is intense local interest in steamage heritage buildings.

Work on that part of the station to be used by British Rail continues. The cost of restoration was estimated to be lower than that of a new station with minimal buildings. The problems of maintenance will be eased by the replacement of the early valances by GRP (glass reinforced plastic) replicas – hardly a solution for purists, but surely preferable to no valances. In this context it is important to note that the actual valance should be reproduced – if replacement is necessary – as variety is essential. The Southern Region alone can show some 200 different patterns of timber valancing along awnings.

Winchelsea in Sussex is a cosy mid-Victorian red brick station building on the flat lands formed by the withdrawal of the sea away from the now hilltop town, once a Cinque Port, founded by Edward I in 1290. There is quite a busy pay train service from the platform, but the stationmaster's house, ticket office and waiting room were no longer required by British Rail some five years ago. The building was on the books of a local estate agent for a year before he had the bright idea of advertising it in the *Daily Telegraph*. Two hundred people applied. Pamela Nash and Ernest Collyer were late in the queue. They had just lost their home and pottery studio when the GLC bought them from their landlord for a housing development. They left their names with the agent and forgot about it. Several months later they heard that, because the local authority preferred their proposed new use – a pottery – over other more industrial uses, the station was theirs for £4,000. They borrowed the money from a friend and moved into the booking hall the day after the last tickets were

sold. There is an hourly pay train service from the platforms and the potter's wheel turns in the old waiting room.

The saving of Heckington station in Lincolnshire and its associated buildings, a unique group, has been a triumph for voluntary effort in co-operation with British Rail and a local authority. Heckington, one of the few surviving Great Northern branch line stations, with the original signal box (still working), across the road a rare eight-sailed windmill and, in the station yard, a Lincolnshire pea-picking shed, another monument to the 'industrial past' – all these have been converted into a community asset by the Heckington Village Trust. Meanwhile the railway line remains in constant use; the advent of pay trains has made only some of the station buildings superfluous.

The Trust had been working on a plan for the group of buildings when it was disconcerted to learn that British Rail had sold the sidings and buildings to the District Council, retaining only the waiting room and ticket office on the north platform and intending to demolish the station and shelter on the south side, replacing them with open concrete boxes. The Trust approached British Rail to save the buildings (undecorated, unrepaired and in some cases boarded up after vandalism) and, with a joint effort, repair and maintain them for village purposes. Agreement was reached and the South Lincolnshire Archaeological Unit, in co-operation with British Rail, has converted the larger waiting room and ticket office to a meeting hall, offices and a museum. The smaller waiting room was rehabilitated for use by the public.

As a result of much voluntary effort, the total cost was kept down to £3,000. Four hundred people took part in fund-raising; money also came from the County Arts Association, the parish council and British Rail, modest sums, but enough.

Several points emerge from this brief selection of cases. It is clear that British Rail is prepared to 'do the right thing' – but only selectively. Constructive conservation work depends on support from the top in the case of major buildings, and local initiatives in the case of small stations of interest. The fate of particular buildings is influenced by

Above *Wickham, Hampshire; yet another crude attack on architectural character*
Right *St Pancras, London; 1863–73 by George Gilbert Scott. Complete apart from the railings melted down in the Second World War*

which region they are in and even which district civil engineer is responsible.

It is still largely a question of attitudes. Ten years ago much old housing was said to be unsuitable for modernization. Now, after more decay, it is being rehabilitated. Many railway district civil engineers will look at bridges and viaducts of solid but literally incalculable Victorian brickwork with a jaundiced eye. Responsible as they are for passenger safety, they may often prefer a modern replacement in steel and/or concrete – with a living consultant engineer to share responsibility. The ability to save and reuse an old structure depends as much on inclination as on facts. A discussion of the same 'facts' by people with a different attitude towards them is at the nub of many inquiries into proposed demolitions.

The scale of the responsibility British Rail is being asked to shoulder is immense. Although 5,000 miles of line have been closed since 1964, and 71,000 acres of land sold, the system still has over 11,000 miles of track and 2,800 stations. There are 476 listed buildings, 128 buildings in Conservation Areas and 41 ancient monuments on railway land.

HALF STEAM AHEAD

The principle adopted by British Rail appears to be that the maintenance and restoration of our heritage from the railway age is a shared responsibility for society at large, not just another burden for the nationalized industry to carry alone. It is apparently prepared to regard twelve or fourteen stations as outstanding and, given grants from local or central government, to restore and maintain them as such. There are indications that it is prepared to extend this approach, at least partially, to much of the Victorian Society's list of sixty principal railway buildings which survive (eight have been demolished in

Top *Liverpool, Mersey Road; brick and barge-boarded station on the same line*
Above *Liverpool, Edge Hill; 1836. Later accretions are being removed as the earliest working station in the country is restored*
Left *Liverpool, Cressington, on the Liverpool–Manchester line; sympathetically refurbished by London Midland Region*

the last decade). There are also the new Director-Environment's plans to do *something* about the listed stations, and to 'top-up' here and there the redecoration budgets for various stations so that historical features may be more thoughtfully treated. On top of this a small but increasing number of modest stations in certain regions, particularly Western, are being restored, and a budget of £1,500,000 was allocated in 1978–9 for cleaning stonework.

Modern equipment has to be installed for ticket issuing and indeed automatic ticket collection, but

it does not have to be contained in space capsules inserted into marble halls. It is unnecessary to tear down all the ironwork platform barriers – they could be coated with gold-leaf for the price of their stainless steel replacements.

In the Railway Architecture train of 1977 the British Rail architects point out that at Cressing 'the canopy valance was replaced by a Great Eastern valance when the canopy had to be set back for electrification' and 'one of the original smaller windows (from Hull Paragon) was saved and a new use was found at Cressing'. Clearly *ad hoc* arrangements are made to salvage and reuse fittings. It is sad that these arrangements should have to depend entirely on the foresight and enthusiasm of particular engineers and architects.

It should surely be possible for British Rail to set up national or, better still, regional salvage centres for station fittings and furniture, lighting equipment and even some signs. Cast iron columns and canopy supports could well be reused. Already some of the smaller items of 'recovered materials', like waiting room furniture, lamps and signs, are preserved for sale in Collectors' Corner at Euston. A handful of outstanding items go to museums such as those at York, Darlington and Swindon. The best fate of all would be reuse in future station restorations.

But sale to enthusiasts is preferable to destruction. The same applies to redundant stations on closed lines. There are many cases where a more energetic effort by British Rail to find a buyer in good time would have saved a would-be restorer the additional difficulties caused by damage from vandalism or sheer decay.

The tide is clearly turning at British Rail as elsewhere, and historic buildings are being seen as a precious heritage rather than a liability. When the work at Cressington, Edge Hill and some other small stations is completed, when St Pancras is glowing in all its former glory, perhaps then everyone – including their owners – will be converted to the intricate charm on the one hand and breathtaking grandeur on the other of these documents of Britain's engineering and even architectural preeminence.

Above *Dorking, Surrey; arches and windows blocked up but building preserved for future revitalization*
Left *London, Waterloo; 1848. The Waterloo buffet in all its former glory*

REUSING RAILWAY BUILDINGS
MARCUS BINNEY

RAILWAY BUILDINGS, whether termini, stations, depots, train sheds or construction works, are archetypal examples of the functional building, tailor-made for a single purpose: for this reason it is all the more remarkable that they have been adapted to such a wide range of new uses. Conversions include houses, offices, restaurants, pubs, clubs, factories, workshops, museums, art galleries, shops and markets, field centres and even a sports hall. These conversions were not the result of any official or even conscious national programme to save redundant railway buildings – far from it. Rather they are a response from commercial interests, local authority initiative and enterprising voluntary groups and charitable organizations.

A full survey of railway conversions in Britain has never been carried out. However a Parliamentary question on 11 November 1976 elicited the fact that 'since publication in 1963 of the report "The Reshaping of British Rail", 3,539 railways stations have been closed to traffic, of which 1,570 have been sold'. British Rail has no record of the uses to which they have been put, but a questionnaire sent to county planning officers in 1969 by Dr J. H. Appleton produced useful information about planning permissions granted for change of use of railway buildings (though these were not necessarily carried out). The findings, published in his report *Disused Railways* (Countryside Commission, 1970), showed that 'Residential buildings (38% of successful applications in the sample) emerged as the most common category, followed by warehousing (21%), education (14%) and manufacturing industry (12%). Other recurring uses included machinery depots and workshops, office and catering businesses. A 9 bedroom hotel and a bank illustrate the range of potential uses.

One of the obstacles to such schemes – and the reason why so many redundant stations remained unsold – has been British Rail's obdurate attitude towards potential buyers. The former Richmond Borough Council, for example, indicated to British Rail some years before the station closed in 1969 that it wished to buy it as a garden centre. Yet despite intensive negotiations, according to the

Council, completion did not take place until September 1972, 'by which time the buildings at Richmond had been seriously vandalized and considerable deterioration had resulted from lack of maintenance. . . . A great deal of money could have been saved if British Rail had been able to bring negotiations to an earlier conclusion.' British Rail, wrote Dr R. I. Youell of Leeds, 'have in fact priced these stations out of the market. Local examples are Sledmere and Fimber and Burdale stations, which would easily have been sold to local people as homes or farm annexes but an abnormally high price demand resulted in their remaining unsold and vandalized until no one will buy them.' In January 1977 the Peak Park Planning Board claimed that neglect by British Rail had run up a £500,000 repair bill on an eleven mile stretch of disused line in only eight years. The Board had begun negotiating for stretches of the Buxton–Matlock line in 1968 immediately after it had closed, intending to use it as a leisure trail. In 1972 British Rail claimed that bridges, viaducts and tunnels were in good order. Five years later the

Cocking, Sussex; converted into a house. The platform now doubles as a ha-ha

Board was told by civil engineers that urgently needed repairs on these structures would cost £222,000, while cleaning up eight years' mess could take seven years, raising the total to £500,000. Originally the Board had been willing to pay British Rail £54,000 for the line, now it would only take it for free, on the understanding that British Rail would contribute towards repair. By a simple process of procrastination British Rail had turned an asset into a liability. Just how often this has happened is evident from the photographs in this book. The folly of this approach is all the

more amazing in view of the range of uses to which redundant stations have been put.

Numerous stations have been converted into houses – both stations on disused lines and stations on lines that are still in use which have been closed. Many smaller stations were designed in a picturesque vernacular resembling cottages, so conversion has involved virtually no external alterations. In Yorkshire, at Bartlow, Booking Hall is not some ancient ancestral seat but a converted station. In Devon, Thorverton station is a house called Beeching's Way and the station at Tavistock, with

evident feeling, has been renamed Beeching's Folly by a former railway employee. At Privett, in Hampshire, the owner of the former station has created a swimming pool in the track bed, using the platforms as retaining walls. Many former stations are in fact hardly recognizable as such, platforms have disappeared or track beds been filled in – an example is the pretty station in the form of a *cottage orné* at Piercebridge on the borders of Durham and Yorkshire. Similarly, awnings have often been removed: at Loddiswell in Devon however, the station, now a house, is one of the few single-storey Great Western Railway buildings which retains its awning.

A small number of former stations have become hotels and restaurants: examples are St Kew Highway in Cornwall, now a hotel, Great Chesterford in Cambridgeshire and Hedgeley in Northumberland, both now restaurants, and Holmsley station in the New Forest and Grindleford, Derbyshire, both of which are tea-rooms. Finally there is the delightful station at Alton, Staffordshire, run by the Landmark Trust and available, like the Trust's other buildings, for renting as a holiday house.

Some stations have survived through conversion to offices – though this is obviously dependent on the willingness of the local authority to grant a change of use. This has been the solution to the remarkable Greek revival station at Ashby-de-la-Zouch in Leicestershire, which stood empty and deteriorating for several years. In November 1976 Amber Estates was granted planning permission for an office and a flat in the station building and for five houses in the old station yard – a trading in planning permissions which covered the expensive restoration involved. The station is now occupied by an insurance broker, and the conversion has preserved the exceptional exterior intact. At the time of writing British Rail is converting Sir William Tite's handsome Italianate terminus in Southampton to offices for its own use. York old station has also been used for some years by British Rail. In Wales, the handsome old Cambrian station at Llanidloes is occupied by the John Mills Foundry Company, which has a drawing office on the first floor. This building was threatened by a proposal

Above *Great Chesterford, Essex; station converted into a restaurant and wine bar*
Left *Warkworth, Northumberland; redundant station, now a house, on a line still in use*

for a by-pass along the old railway line but it was saved following a public inquiry.

Industrial uses of railway buildings are manifold. Laura Ashley, the fabric manufacturers, have been using the railway buildings at Carno, Breconshire (now Powys), for the last fifteen years. One of their most modern pieces of equipment, a steamer, which bakes the cloth after it has been printed, is housed in the old shunting shed. A praiseworthy example of local authority initiative in this field is the conversion of an old goods shed at Ross-on-Wye by South Herefordshire District Council for

two large train sheds. Other commercial uses include an agricultural merchant's in the station at Alnwick, Northumberland, a builder's yard at Gilesgate, County Durham, a timber merchant's in the pretty red and white brick station at Hadleigh in Suffolk, a crash repair shop at Mildmay in London, and a fisherman's store at Llandago, Monmouthshire (now Gwent). Sometimes such uses leave much to be desired in terms of appearances but at least they preserve the building against better days and demonstrate that station buildings can be put to economically viable uses.

rental to a Midlands plastics firm. The old engine shed, which the Council also owns, is leased to a haulage contractor as a heavy vehicle garage and workshop. Both of these have a special historical interest as they are among the few surviving buildings made for GWR broad gauge rolling stock, and it is interesting that the local authority found tenants for them so promptly – as promptly as could be hoped with a new building.

In Devon the publishers David and Charles, well known specialists in railway books, operated in part of the station at Newton Abbot for a number of years, but have recently moved into a range of former South Devon Railway buildings, including

Above *Ashby-de-la-Zouch, Leicestershire; transformed into offices*
Right *Maldon, Essex; turned into a pub*

Some of the most interesting new uses are in the fields of recreation and tourism. These can be divided into those undertaken by public bodies and local authorities and those initiated by voluntary groups – including of course the flourishing railway preservation societies. Quite a number of disused railway lines have become linear parks or long distance country walks in this way. In the Peak District National Park, three lengths of railway have been closed since the Second World War, and two have been bought by the National Park Board for use as trails: the Cromford–High Peak Line, closed

in 1967, is now the High Peak trail (the southern section is owned by Derbyshire County Council) while the Buxton–Ashbourne line is now known as the Tissington trail. Together they form twenty-five miles of continuous paths for walkers, cyclists and riders, linked to the peak by a pathfinder bus service. The Tissington trail was supported by 75 per cent grants from the Countryside Commission. At Hartington the signal box survived in such good condition that it proved possible to put it into working order: a voluntary group of British Rail staff restored the lever frame. At Box the station

Above *Burton-on-Trent, Staffordshire; railway warehouse converted to industrial use*
Left *Alnwick, Northumberland; adapted and renovated for industrial use*
Overleaf *Hadlow Road, Cheshire; restored, now part of Wirral Country Park*

serves as a rangers' briefing centre and information point. Two full-time rangers are employed: one lives at Hartington in a former railway house, the other in a former railway cottage at Parsley Hay.

The Wirral Country Park outside Birkenhead is centred on a railway line some twelve miles long that ran from the town of West Kirby to Hooton. This has been developed by Cheshire County Council and the Countryside Commission as a place to walk, ride, picnic, camp and fish. At Thurstaston there is a visitor centre with a permanent slide show and exhibition. At Hadlow Road the station has been restored to look as it might have done on a normal working day in 1952. Whitegate station has been renovated as a house for a countryside ranger. The park is open all the year round and from July to September there are guided walks and talks at the visitor centre.

Redundant stations are finding a role as educational and interpretative centres. Tyne and Wear County Council has converted the tiny but derelict station at Felling, Gateshead, into an urban studies centre. The station at Tintern, Monmouthshire (now Gwent), was bought by the County Council

216

in 1969 and is now a visitor centre with a permanent exhibition on the Wye Valley line – one of the most scenic in the country. The closure of the Ashby-de-la-Zouch–Nuneaton railway helped pave the way towards opening the site of the battle of Bosworth Field to the public. Leicestershire County Council acquired the disused Shenton station, sited almost exactly in the centre of the battlefield, and three-quarters of a mile of track bed. At the same time a nearby farm, made redundant through amalgamation, was purchased and has become the battlefield interpretation centre. The scheme has re-

Above and left *Richmond, North Yorkshire; station, before and after conversion into a garden centre by the local authority*

ceived grants from the Countryside Commission. In Scotland, on the line between Achterneed and the Highland spa of Strathpeffer the local authority has created a country walk under the Job Creation Programme. Currently it is drawing up plans for the reuse of Strathpeffer station. The Council wants the buildings to be used to provide a number of craft workshops, an interpretation centre and a tearoom and is considering proposals from the Scottish Development Agency and two private developers. At Kerne Bridge station in the Wye Valley the National Association of Boys' Clubs has an Adventure and Training Centre.

Two stations in England have become transport museums. At Darlington a specially formed charitable trust has transformed part of the oldest passenger station still in use into a splendid railway museum. The work was done with grants from the Historic Buildings Council for England, the English Tourist Board (which can give grants to projects promoting tourism in Development Areas) and from local industry. The museum now contains several hundred exhibits including Locomotion No. 1, the first (George Stephenson) locomotive ever used on a public railway line. Between August 1975 and August 1976 the museum had 20,000 visitors.

The handsome Greek revival station at Monkwearmouth built in 1848 by Thomas Moore has become a highly successful museum of transport. The station was bought by the former Sunderland Corporation in December 1971 and reopened as a museum just eighteen months later, in May 1973, by the Duke of Edinburgh. By the end of 1976 it had had more than 300,000 visitors. In November 1975 it was transferred to the museum service of Tyne and Wear County Council, which has begun negotiations to take over the former goods warehouse as a store for its collection of land transport vehicles.

One of the best known conversions of a railway building is the Roundhouse theatre in Camden in north London. This was a magnificent circular engine shed, 160 feet in diameter, built in 1846 by Robert Stephenson and R. B. Dockray. By the 1860s however engines had become too long and after serving a few years as a goods shed it became in 1869 a liquor store for W. and A. Gilbey. Its present use was born out of Centre 42, the arts project inspired by the Trades Union Congress of 1960. In 1964 Arnold Wesker and George Hopkins launched an appeal for £590,000 to subsidize, equip and convert the first centre, but after a lively beginning the appeal failed, leaving debts of £50,000. The project was saved from collapse by the donation of a sixteen year lease on the Roundhouse by Louis Mintz and after that the freehold was acquired for £27,500 from British Rail, a

generous sale in view of a valuation of £100,000 placed on it. The Historic Buildings Council gave a grant of 50 per cent (£2,000) towards reslating the roof and the building was licensed by the Greater London Council as a theatre, cinema and concert hall. Despite the high hopes of the organizers the Arts Council did not contribute at this stage. The first year saw a series of headline-catching events including all-night pop concerts, which eventually ceased after protests from local residents, when the building took on the principal role of a theatre.

Perhaps the most intriguing of all new uses in this

country is the conversion of the disused station at Pocklington in Yorkshire (now Humberside), built in 1845 by G. T. Andrews, into a gymnasium for the next door school. The station had a continuous iron roof across the tracks and by filling in the space between the platforms and closing the ends the school has created an indoor sports hall (divisible into two) measuring 200 by 44 feet. The former waiting rooms now serve as changing rooms with showers attached, while the booking hall is a spectators' gallery. The total cost of the work was £52,000, aided by a grant of £20,000 from the

Left and below *Darlington North Road, County Durham; 1842. The terminus of the Stockton–Darlington railway, now a museum*

Sports Council, considerably less than the cost of a new hall of the same dimensions. During the evenings the hall is used by some twenty local clubs, while residential courses are held in school holidays.

Two other unusual and ingenious conversions are the station at Little Walsingham in Norfolk, which has become a Greek Orthodox church, capped by a delightful cupola, and the old station at Leigh-on-Sea in Essex, which for some years has been a sailing club. The men's bar is in the ticket office, the saloon in the waiting room and the ladies' changing room in the stationmaster's office.

So far, station conversions in Britain have been confined to small or medium-sized stations: no really large station or railway complex has yet been tackled. Instead, like St Enoch's station, Glasgow, or Snow Hill in Birmingham, they have been demolished despite imaginative and potentially viable suggestions for their reuse, or, like Manchester Central station, they have just been left to rot. To find examples of really major city termini

Below and right Pocklington, Humberside; 1847. *The station before and after conversion into a sports hall*

converted to new uses one has to go abroad. The most ambitious adaptation of all is under way in Paris at the Gare D'Orsay, the colossal station on the left bank of the Seine next to the Invalides, which has been left virtually disused for many years. The station, built in 1898–1900 by V. Laloux, is famous for its superb iron and glass train shed. Attached to the station is a large hotel, also disused, consisting of two basement stories and five floors above ground level, a grand *salle des fêtes*, a restaurant, six salons and 270 bedrooms. All this is in the process of becoming a major new museum, fill-ing the gap between the old masters in the Louvre and the twentieth-century art in the new Centre Nationale Pompidou and the Musée de L'Art Moderne. It is to be devoted to the period between 1860 and 1905 when Paris was the art capital of the world and will bring together the works of the pre-Impressionists, the Impressionists and post-Impressionists, the Symbolists and the Pointillistes with those of the Academicians of the Salons whose work has been so long deprecated and consigned in embarrassment to the vaults of the Louvre. For many years, of course, some of the best works of

the period have been on display in the Jeu de Paume but the number of visitors has so increased that conditions are no longer satisfactory in terms of security and conservation. In the train shed extra floors will be inserted for the galleries but part of the area under the great arched roof will be transformed into a vast interior garden with a display of sculpture and architectural works. The hotel is to be used for offices for the administration and technical services of the Direction des Musées de France and the Réunion des Musées Nationaux. In all the Gare d'Orsay will provide some 54,000

two volume report, *Reusing Railroad Stations* (1974). Further fascinating material on the subject is to be found in Walter C. Kidney's *Working Places: the adaptive use of industrial buildings* (1976, Ober Park Associates, Pittsburgh, sponsored by the Society for Industrial Archaeology.)

One of the most interesting aspects of the conversions in the United States is the high level of financial initiative and involvement of commercial interests and chambers of commerce. The former terminal at Chattanooga, Tennessee, has been transformed into a giant holiday centre by a con-

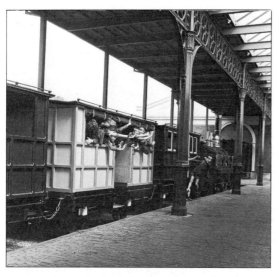

square metres of floor space and jobs for 725 people.

Another Continental conversion which could serve as a model in this country is the adaptation of the S-Bahn station at Knollendorfplatz in West Berlin as a flourishing antiques market, with bars and restaurants and numerous small cubicles for dealers in antiques, coins, stamps and every kind of bric-à-brac. The stalls are in the railway coaches.

The most enterprising and successful new uses for stations are to be found in the United States. A massive research project on the subject of recycling railway stations was undertaken by Educational Facilities Laboratories of New York, with finance from the National Endowment for the Arts – culminating in a well documented and illustrated

Above *Oberlin Station, Ohio, USA, now a nursery school*
Left *Old coaches preserved at Maliebaan station*
Far left *Maliebaan station near Utrecht, Holland; 1874. Converted in 1950–54 to a railway museum run jointly by the Ministry of Culture, the Province, the City and Netherlands Railways*

sortium of local businessmen. The main concourse is now a restaurant seating up to 450 people while the train sheds have become a modern-day caravanserai with guests staying not in bedrooms but in sleeping cars on the railway tracks.

In Indiana the huge Richardsonian Union station, built in 1888 and remodelled in 1916, was under threat for many years as the railway service contracted. A preservation group kept interest alive by holding New Year's Eve Parties there and in 1971 the Metropolitan Development Corporation acquired an option to purchase with a view to find-

ing a development company to adapt the building. It settled on a consortium called Union Station Associates, consisting of a local property developer and twenty other limited partners. The station has been transformed into an indoor shopping centre, with a rentable area of some 45,000 square feet.

Below Chattanooga, Tennessee, USA; turned into a holiday centre where visitors can sleep in Pullman cars. The former station concourse is now a restaurant
Right Pittsburg, Pennsylvania, USA; the station hall is now a flourishing restaurant

Rents at between $5 and $9 per square foot are considerably below the Indianapolis average of $13.

A combination of commercial and charitable interests is transforming the station at Pittsburgh, Pennsylvania, built in 1901. Here the Pittsburgh History and Landmarks Foundation, one of the largest and most successful city preservation societies in America, is undertaking a $30 million conversion, financed partly by the construction of a new 250-room hotel tower by the station, with Pullman cars on the tracks providing extra beds.

In Washington itself the massive Beaux-Arts Union station, built in 1903–8 by Daniel H. Burnham and modelled on the Baths of Diocletian, has become the National Visitor Centre and train services have been removed to an adjacent site. The centre opened on 4 July 1976 and contains information stalls staffed by the National Parks Service, answering questions on lodging, eating and travel, a remarkable eighty-screen audio-visual programme on the beauties of the nation's capital and stalls for the different states grouped under nine regions. The upper concourse has become an exhibition gallery used for touring exhibitions while below there is a large fast food centre.

In Baltimore the large Mount Royal station, built in 1894–6 by Baldwin and Pennington, closed in 1961, has been acquired and brilliantly transformed by Maryland College of Art. The building, with $3\frac{3}{4}$ acres, was acquired for $250,000 including the air rights over the tracks and the college raised $1 million in a very successful appeal. The baggage platforms have been transformed into a sculpture school for graduates, with space for heavy equipment including a two ton overhead crane. Around the central working area each of the school's twelve students has a private studio, facilities unsurpassed anywhere in the United States. By inserting additional floors into the huge barrel-vaulted concourse the college has more than doubled the available floor space – the cost of the conversion finished in 1967 worked out at $18 per

Right Baltimore, Maryland, USA Mount Royal Station; now an art college. The baggage platforms have become a graduate school of sculpture

square foot, compared to $25 per square foot for a new building.

Among conversions of medium-sized stations one of the most interesting is in Savanna. Here a visitor centre set up by the local Chamber of Commerce in the Cotton Exchange on the waterfront was proving too small. Just at this time the Central of Georgia station, built in 1860, was closed and according to the terms of the lease reverted to the City. The station was then offered to the Chamber of Commerce, on condition that the money for the conversion could be raised in six months. An appeal was launched, and the conversion was complete in 1974. Visitors enter through the train shed where two steam engines form the embryo of a railway museum; upstairs the Chamber of Commerce has its offices. There are plans to use the area of the disused tracks beyond the train shed as a cattle market.

At North Barrington in Vermont a smaller station has been transformed into offices. Here a local citizen put up the money to buy and repair the station on the condition that the village would then take over responsibility. The original plan was to let the building commercially but the village decided to retain the ground floor for community offices and the architect of the conversion took over the first floor for his offices. Union station in Connecticut, designed in 1885 by H. H. Richardson, was threatened with demolition until a firm of Boston planners and architects persuaded the authority in charge of urban renewal to allow them to convert the building into offices, with Amtrak facilities on the ground floor and a museum below.

At Lincoln in Nebraska a small whistle-stop station – Rock Island Depot – has been taken over by a branch of the City National Bank. Conversion cost $75,000, much less than a new building, and inside the station has been furnished with old railroad and bank furniture. At Brattleboro in Vermont a group of local people saved the former station from demolition and have converted it into an art gallery and concert hall. Most of the initial work was carried out by volunteers.

What conclusions can be drawn from this experience? First, that there is a solution for railway buildings of almost every type in almost any place

providing time is allowed and the railway company is willing to be flexible over price and not hold out for the highest possible sums while the building deteriorates for lack of maintenance, a process that is self-defeating. Second, that the central position of many railway buildings in cities, towns and villages makes them ideal for many public, commercial and charitable uses. Third, that many successful new uses, particularly of larger buildings, are the result of a partnership between the public sector, commercial interests and voluntary or charitable effort. Sometimes just two of these elements are involved, occasionally all three. The result however is more than just the preservation of fine and interesting buildings: in many cases conversion has been genuinely creative, providing facilities and opportunities for employment, recreation and enlightenment.

Lincoln, Nebraska, USA; converted for use as a bank

APPENDIX

Notes on Selected Stations and Associated Buildings
MATTHEW SAUNDERS

THE FOLLOWING LIST covers the main historic stations and a limited number of secondary ones. It is not comprehensive and is to be regarded as a basis for further research and reading. Inclusion is not to be taken as a guarantee that the station survives either unaltered or at all although where a station is known to have been changed or lost, this is stated. Similarly if the building is known to be closed. Not all former stations or existing stations within a particular town or city are necessarily included.

Alnwick, Northumberland. The former railway terminus of 1887 (a rebuilding probably by William Bell) survives in Wagonway Road. It was specially built 'to be worthy of a ducal town'.

Alton Towers, Staffordshire. 1849. Broad-eaved Italianate. Formerly, and incorrectly, attributed to A. W. N. Pugin (architect of the mansion), the arch castigator of stylistic pastiche in railway architecture. Now a holiday home.

Ambergate, Derbyshire. By Francis Thompson, c. 1840. One of the very best of the picturesque Jacobean designs. Later altered and re-erected in modified form. Demolished, 1972.

Apsley, Hertfordshire. By W. H. Hamlyn, London and Midland architect, 1938. 'One of the first reinforced concrete stations' (Harry Holland).

Ashby-de-la-Zouch, Leicestershire. 1849. One of the finest of the neoclassical designs. Credited to Robert Chaplin by J. Mordant Crook. Closed but not demolished. Converted to offices.

Ashford, Kent. Station by Samuel Beazley built in connection with railway town of 1847–51. Present station 1963–7.

Atherstone, Warwickshire. By J. W. Livock. 1847. Building disused.

Audley End, Essex. By Francis Thompson, 1845. Originally called Wenden. The large *porte-cochère* was for carriages from the mansion.

Bagworth, Leicestershire. Unusual design shaped like a tollhouse.

Bakewell, Derbyshire. By Edward Walters, the Manchester architect, 1860. Closed.

Banbury, Oxfordshire. By I. K. Brunel, 1850. Demolished and rebuilt 1959.

Barking, Essex (now Greater London). By H. H. Powell, 1961. Striking 14-bay booking hall.

Barnes, Surrey (now Greater London). By William Tite, 1846. 'Old English' style. Altered 1881.

Basingstoke, Hampshire. Originally by William Tite, 1839. Reconstructed *c.* 1903.

Bath, Somerset (now Avon).

a Great Western, now Bath Spa. By I. K. Brunel, 1840. Form of façade, with single quadrant, predates that of St Pancras. Original roof demolished.

b Midland, Green Park, also known as Queen Square. By J. C. Crossley, 1870. Fine Palladian forebuilding. Roof of train shed by Andrew Handyside and Co. of Derby and London. Closed; train shed to be subject of public inquiry on possible new uses, January 1979. The contemporary Midland Goods Station in Sydenham Field adjoining the station was designed by Messrs Allport and Wilson, engineers, and Mr Saunders, architect (*The Builder*, 1870, p. 264).

Battle, Sussex. By William Tress (cf. Wadhurst, etc.), 1852. In style of Gothic school. Canopy later.

Bedford Midland Road. By C. H. Driver, 1859. Enlarged 1868. Replaced by new station 1978.

Belvedere, Kent. By W. G. and E. Habershon, who built parish church in 1853–61 (*The Builder*, 1858, p. 585). Rebuilt 1968.

Berwick-upon-Tweed, Northumberland. 1844–6. Rebuilt in conservative style 1924.

Beverley, Yorkshire (now Humberside). Probably by G. T. Andrews, late 1840s. Roof renewed and entrance altered later in century (Ivan and Elisabeth Hall, *Historic Beverley*).

Bingley, Yorkshire (now West Yorkshire). *The Builder*, 1849, p. 547 spared no punches in describing the original building as a 'wooden station of wretched description'. The offending station was rebuilt to the designs of Charles Trubshaw, the Midland Company architect, in 1892, a goods warehouse occupying the immediate site of the first station.

Birkenhead, Cheshire (now Merseyside).

a Hamilton Square. By G. E. Grayson (architect of blitzed James Street station in Liverpool), 1886. Tall campanile for hydraulic lift.

b Town. By R. E. Johnston, 1890s. Demolished.

c Woodside. By R. E. Johnston, 1878. Roof by E. W. Ives, who also did the roof at Liverpool Lime St Station (*The Builder*, 1879, p. 550). Dem. 1969.

Birmingham.

a Curzon Street. By Philip Hardwick, 1838. Terminus of London–Birmingham Railway. Converted in 1854 into a goods station. The Ionic Propylaeum (which answered the Doric arch at Euston, the other terminus) contained the booking hall and other rooms. Hitchcock points out that this was the first station to have public refreshment rooms. There is a three-storey annexe of 1853 (to be demolished). The train shed was demolished in the early 1960s. Property is being offered for sale by British Rail Property Board.

b International. 1977.

c New Street (Central). Completed 1854. Station and hotel (70 rooms) designed by William Livock. Messrs Branson and Gwyther were the contractors. The roof, made by Fox and Henderson, was designed by E. A. Cowper and William Baker, engineers. It had a span of 212 ft and a length of 1,080 ft and *The Times* claimed it was the largest in the world at the time. Chance's 'fluted glass' was used in the roof (*The Builder*, 1853, p. 77). *The Architect* (1853, p. 518) reported that some 200 workmen were employed on the site as the station was nearing completion. The latest rebuilding of New Street began in 1964.

d Snow Hill. By W. G. Owen, opened 1852. Rebuilt 1909–14 and demolished 1976.

Bolton, Lancashire (now Greater Manchester). *The Builder* (1874, p. 827) reported the opening of the L&NWR station in Great Moor Street, built at a cost of £40,000. General contractor Messrs Knight and Pilling. Ironwork supplied by Messrs DeBurgh and Co. of Manchester. 'Carriage shed' 320 ft long and 100 ft wide.

Bournemouth, Hampshire (now Dorset). Central. By William Jacomb, 1885. Relentless 22-bay facade.

Bow, Greater London. By E. H. Horne, 1870. In form of large medieval hall. Cost the impressive sum of £25,000 (*The Builder*, 1870, p. 264). Demolished. Similar station by Horne at High-

bury, also demolished, cost £17,000.

Box Hill, Surrey. By C. H. Driver, 1877. Good little turret over waiting room.

Bradford, Yorkshire (now West Yorkshire).
a Exchange. By Eli Milne, 1886. Demolished and rebuilt 1973–4. *The Builder*, 1975, p. 879, reported that the Great Northern Company intended to spend £40,000 in converting 'the old passenger station and engine shed' into a goods depot.
b Interchange. 1977.

Bradford-on-Avon, Wiltshire. By I. K. Brunel, 1858.

Bridgend, Glamorgan (now Dyfed). By I. K. Brunel, 1850. Extended 1877. Some demolition work to begin soon but main Brunel building to stay.

Brighton, Sussex (now E. Sussex). By David Mocatta, pupil of Soane, 1841. J. U. Rastrick designed the roof. In the year of Mocatta's death, 1882, this, his largest station, was substantially altered by the addition of a new *porte-cochère* and the construction of a new train shed. The designer was H. E. Wallis of Westminster and it cost over £100,000. *The Builder* (1884, p. 79) stated that the roof contained 110,000 sq. ft of rolled plate glass $\frac{1}{4}$ in. thick applied without putty by Mr T. W. Helliwell of Brighouse, Yorkshire, on his patented plan. Proposal to redevelop in late 1960s not executed but some rebuilding still intended.

Bristol Temple Meads (now Avon). Brunel section of 1840–41, Tudor Gothic in frontage, has a wooden hammerbeam roof of a span 4 ft wider than that of Westminster Hall. Now used as car park. Former office building of Bristol and Exeter Railway by S. C. Fripp, 1852, to the south. Present station built by Matthew Digby Wyatt in 1865–78 and in 1930–35 by P. E. Culverhouse. Former Great Western Hotel in St George's Road, by R. S. Pope, 1839, has been converted to offices (and called 'Brunel House').

Bury St Edmunds, Suffolk. Northgate. 1847. Has been credited to Frederick Barnes but Pevsner quotes the *Bury and Norwich Post's* ascription to Sancton Wood. Jacobean with two baroque turrets.

Buxton, Derbyshire. *c.* 1862. Matching façades

233

for L&NWR and Midland with large semicircular windows. Joseph Paxton said to have advised on the design. Only L&NWR section survives in part.

Cambridge. Opened 1847. For long ascribed to Sancton Wood but now established as the work of Francis Thompson. One 400 ft platform. Elegant quattrocento façade of tall arcading, now partly glazed. College arms on each bay.

Canterbury, Kent.

a East. 1860.

b West. 1846. Baseless Greek Doric columns *in antis* as porch.

Cardiff, Glamorgan (now South Glamorgan).

a. Bute Street. 1841. Simple classical. New station in Clarence Road, Bute Docks, proposed by J. C. Inglis, GWR engineer-in-chief (*Building News* 1884, II, p. 233).

b. Queen Street. 1887. Old train sheds demolished.

Carlisle, Cumberland (now Cumbria). By William Tite, 1848. Greatly extended in 1873. Very impressive 30 ft retaining walls with pointed and blind arcading.

Castle Howard, Yorkshire (now N. Yorkshire). By G. T. Andrews, 1845. Italianate. Now a house.

Chapel-en-le-Frith, Derbyshire. By Edward Walters, the Manchester architect, 1867. Altered.

Charlbury, Oxfordshire. By I. K. Brunel, 1853. In wood. Original nameboard on up platform survives (and is listed).

Cheltenham Lansdown, Gloucestershire. 1840. Baseless Doric *porte-cochère* now demolished. *Building News*, 1894, II, p. 377 announced opening of GWR station in St James's Square 'designed by Company architect' at a cost inclusive of ground of £50,000.

Chepstow, Monmouthshire (now Gwent). By I. K. Brunel, 1850. *The Builder*, 1879, p. 723, reported that 'some time ago' the station was jacked up 2 ft to allow easier passenger access into trains. The Brunel building survives although unstaffed and let.

Chertsey, Surrey. By William Tite, 1868. Italianate.

Chester. By Francis Thompson, completed 1848. Thompson's greatest surviving work. Described by *The Builder* (1859, p. 579) as 'the best for the convenience of plan and appropriateness of decorative character that we are acquainted with in that part of England'. It attributed the design in that article to 'the late C. H. Wild and Mr Thompson acting under Robert Stephenson'. Long Italianate design broken by pavilions. Later office extension has been gutted by fire.

Chichester, Sussex (now W. Sussex). Original station remodelled 1881 by Mr Myre, architect, of Westminster (who also designed new stations at Cocking, Singleton, Midhurst and Lavant). Rebuilt 1961.

Chippenham, Wiltshire. 1841 I. K. Brunel block survives (as does his viaduct of 1839–40, which is listed 11★). Considerable remodelling in 1856 by Rowland Brotherhood.

Christs Hospital, Sussex (now W. Sussex). 1899–1902. Mostly demolished.

Cirencester, Gloucestershire. By I. K. Brunel, 1841. Carved scrolls on main building as at Temple Meads. Now used as offices for bus depot. Cotswold Council applied to demolish it in November 1977. Application refused November 1978.

Colchester, Essex. Original station of 1843 rebuilt in 1896. (by 'Mr Wilson, Chief Engineer of the Great Eastern') and again recently in part. The railway hotel, built in 1843 by Lewis Cubitt, and illustrated in *The Builder*, 1843, p. 350, does survive as part of a hospital.

Coventry, Warwickshire (now W. Midlands). Rebuilt 1962.

Crewe, Cheshire. Mixed building. Mention is made in *The Builder* of a rebuilding in 1865–7 to the designs of J. B. Stansby, assistant engineer under William Baker, chief engineer to the company. Total length 300 ft and cost £36,000. The former joiners' shop and railway workshops at Eaton Street are listed.

Cromford, Derbyshire. *c.* 1860. Ascribed to G. H. Stokes, Joseph Paxton's assistant and son-in-law.

Crystal Palace, Surrey (now Greater London).

a High Level. LB&SCR. Opened 1876 (*The Builder*, p. 540). Joint design of Mr Banister, Company engineer and Mr Gough, architect. Messrs

Dove were the builders. Minton encaustic tiles in booking hall. Demolished.

b Low Level. 1854. Lofty booking hall with brick arches. Demolished.

Darlington, County Durham.
a Bank Top. 1884, probably by William Bell. Very fine. Three great naves on slight curve. On rising land so clock tower commands view up Victoria Road.
b North Road. 1842. The initial purpose-built terminus of the Stockton–Darlington railway, 'the world's first'. Portico. Timber roof. Now a museum.

Denmark Hill, Surrey (now Greater London). 1866. Italianate. Glazed stairs to platforms.

Derby Trijunct. Originally operated by three companies. Complicated iron-tied roof by Robert Stephenson and long façade by Francis Thompson, 1839–41. Little survives. Adjoining Midland Hotel is by Thompson, 1840; very early (cf. York).

Dorchester, Dorset.
a South. 1847. Altered.
b West. By I. K. Brunel, 1857.

Dover Kent. Station with imposing tower by Lewis Cubitt (cf. Colchester). Demolished. Lord Warden Railway Hotel of 1850–53 by Samuel Beazley.

Downham Market, Norfolk. 1846. Good example of use of local materials, in this case brown carstone.

Dulwich North, Greater London. By Charles Barry the younger, 'Jacobethan'.

Dundee, Angus (now Tayside). *The Builder* (1876, p. 1279) talks of a new station being erected in 1876 – Mr Bouch, engineer to the North British Railway Company designing it. Ironwork by Messrs Wright Young and Co. of Edinburgh. Station was 1,100 ft long.

Earlestown, Lancashire (now Merseyside). *c.* 1845. Interesting Gothic-cum-Tudor waiting room.

Eastbourne, Sussex (now E. Sussex). 1884. (*The Builder*, p. 607) Top-lit booking hall.

Edinburgh.
a Haymarket. By John Miller, 1842. To be demolished.

b Waverley. *The Builder*, 1874, p. 712, reported the new station about to open. Roof constructed on lattice girder principle with no columns. By Mr Bell, engineer of North British Railway company. Rebuilt 1896–9 – Messrs Cunningham, Blyth and Westland, engineers. Station is façade-less.

Exeter, Devon.
a St David's. 1862–4 rebuilding. Mr Fox, engineer. Architect was Mr Henry Lloyd of Park Street, Bristol, who also designed the Town Hall, Tiverton. Cost was £50–60,000 including the clearance of the old station. G. Spiller of Taunton contracted for £18,000 for the mason's work, glazing, decoration, etc., and Mr Kerslake of Exeter for the roof (*The Builder*, 1864, p. 452).
b St Thomas. By I. K. Brunel, 1844–6. Roof demolished.

Fareham, Hampshire. Original station by William Tite survives in part.

Farnham, Surrey. By William Tite, 1849.

Felixstowe Town, Suffolk. By W. N. Ashbee, 1898.

Frome, Somerset. By I. K. Brunel, *c.* 1847. Built solely in wood. Application by British Rail to demolish except for over-all roof refused.

Gainsborough, Lincolnshire. 1849. By Weightman and Hadfield, according to John Harris and Professor Welsh.

Glasgow.
a Central. By Sir Rowand Anderson (who also designed Hotel), opened 1879.
b St Enoch. By Sir John Fowler and James Blair, engineer of City Union Railway, 1875–9. The buildings and hotel were designed by James Willson [sic] of Hampstead assisted by Miles S. Gibson of Glasgow. Ground plan of station in *The Builder*, 1880, II, p. 440. Large additions 1901. Both train shed and hotel demolished 1976–8.
c Queen Street. By James Carswell, district engineer to the North British Railway, 1878–80.

Gloucester Central. Rebuilt by Lancaster Owen, 1887–9. £20,000 contract. Present station 1977.

Gobowen, Salop. By T. K. Penson, 1846. Semi-circular booking hall and waiting room.

Gosport, Hampshire. By William Tite, 1841–2. 14-bay Tuscan colonnade. To be a museum.

Right, above *Downham Market, Norfolk; 1846. A good example of use of local stone*
Right, below *Felixstowe Town, Suffolk; 1898 by W. N. Ashbee*

Gravesend, Kent.
a Central. By Samuel Beazley, 1849.
b West. 1883–4. Charles Douglas Fox, engineer; Messrs Kirk and Randall, builders. Demolished.
Greenwich, Kent (now Greater London). First built by George Smith, 1836. Reconstructed 1878. Imposing design.
Haltwhistle, Northumberland. 1835–7. Later station built alongside. Wooden waiting room.
Harrow and Wealdstone, Middlesex (now Greater London). First built 1837. Rebuilt by Gerald Horsley (cf. Hatch End) in 1911.
Hatch End, Middlesex (now Greater London). By Gerald Horsley (pupil of Shaw), 1912. 'Wrenaissance' box.
Haywards Heath, Sussex (now E. Sussex). The original station, like several others in the county, was by David Mocatta (cf. Brighton). Rebuilt 1932.
Hellifield, Yorkshire (now N. Yorkshire). 1880. Important canopies. BR wish to demolish.
Hereford Barrs Court. By R. E. Johnston of Birkenhead, 1855. New station begun 1879 at a cost of £50–60,000.
Herne Bay, Kent. 1861, by John Newton?
Hertford East. 1888.
Holywell Junction, Flint (now Clwyd). By Francis Thompson, 1848. Italianate with four freestanding pavilions. Closed. Now a house.
Huddersfield, Yorkshire (now W. Yorkshire). By James Pritchett the Elder, 1847–50. Mighty hexastyle Corinthian portico. Listed Grade I.
Hull Paragon, Yorkshire (now Humberside). By G. T. Andrews, 1846–8. Andrews's fine façade survives. Train shed reconstructed by William Bell in 1903–8. The Italianate hotel of 1847–50 is by Andrews 'under the superintendence of Mr Botterill' (*The Builder*, 1850, p. 107). Its two wings and attic date from 1936.
Ingatestone, Essex. 1846. Picturesque Tudor.
Ipswich, Suffolk. By Robert Sinclair, engineer to Eastern Counties Railway, 1858–60. Island platform canopy is later. Good footbridge on Corinthian columns.
Kendal, Westmorland (now Cumbria). Pevsner dates it to 1847. *The Builder* reports con-

struction work there in 1860.

Kettering, Northamptonshire. By C. H. Driver (cf. Bedford), 1857. Fine canopies.

Kidderminster, Worcestershire (now Hereford and Worcester). 1863. Unusual half-timbered design. Demolished.

Lancaster.

a Castle. 1846.

b Green Ayre. 1848. Closed.

Leatherhead, Surrey. By C. H. Driver, 1867. Gothic.

Leeds, Yorkshire (now W. Yorkshire). Original station designed by Thomas Prosser of Newcastle, architect to NER, opened in 1869. Messrs Butler and Pitts of Stanningley executed the roof, the rest of the station building being by George Thompson and Co. The contemporary railway hotel was designed by M. E. Hadfield, the Sheffield architect, and the figures carved by Theodore Phyffers of London. The present station, an amalgamation of the terminus and the through station, dates from 1937 (the booking hall, by W. H. Hamlyn) and the 1960s.

Leicester.

a Central. 1899. Closed.

b London Road. By Charles Trubshaw, 1892. Terracotta frontage to very large *porte-cochère*.

Lincoln.

a Central. Great Northern. By Joseph Cubitt, 1848. Neo-Tudor.

b St Marks. Midland. 1846. Neoclassical.

Liverpool.

a Central. By John Fowler and Brydone of Victoria Street, 1874. Contract was for £100,000. Roof composed of 7 elliptical spans. Demolished.

b Edge Hill. Originally by John Cunningham, 1836. Terminus of Liverpool and Manchester. To be restored.

c Exchange. Tithebarn Street. Rebuilt 1884–6 by Henry Shelmerdine who also designed the hotel. 1850 station by John Hawkshaw. Both station and hotel now closed – shed to be demolished.

d Goods station in Waterloo Road. Opened 1849. Covered 5 acres and on site of 150 homes. Described in *The Builder* as possibly the largest goods station in England at the time.

e Lime Street. The first station was built in 1836 to the designs of John Cunningham, the imposing classical screen being by John Foster, the Corporation architect (and partly paid for by his employers). The second station dated from 1846–51, the offices (illustrated in *The Builder* 1849, p. 79) being designed by Sir William Tite in a symmetrical Italianate style. John Jay of London Wall was the contractor (for £30,000); Mr J. Locke MP was the engineer and Sir William Fairbairn and Richard Turner of Dublin were responsible for the roof. Quentin Hughes points out that this was the first shed in which iron was used throughout. The third Lime Street was built in 1867. William Baker and F. Stevenson of Dartford were the engineers and like that of Lime Street II this shed (200 ft wide) was claimed at the time as the biggest in span in the world. At the same time Waterhouse designed a large hotel (now disused) for the site of Foster's screen. The shed was extended to the south in 1874–9 (E. W. Ives was responsible for the roof).

f Midland Railway goods offices, Crosshall Street. Built *c.* 1850. Impressive sweep.

g James Street Underground station. Rebuilt after the Second World War (cf. Birkenhead).

Llandudno Junction, Caernarvonshire (now Gwynedd). New station opened 1862. (*The Builder*, p. 474.) 'Mixed Gothic' in style and faced in Penmaenmaur stone. Two ornamental gables and hexagonal chimneys. Architect Mr Mellard Reade of Liverpool in conjunction with Company engineer, Mr Hedworth Lee. George Glaister of Liverpool did mason's work and Edward Geflowski the carving.

Llanidloes, Montgomeryshire (now Powys). 1864. Converted to offices.

London (For full details see Alan Jackson's *London's Termini*, Sir John Betjeman's *London's Historic Railway Stations* and the booklet by LISSCA on *The London Stations*.)

a Blackfriars. The 1886 station by J. Wolfe Barry, H. M. Brunel and Mills, the main elevation decorated with the incised names of destination points, has been demolished and the site redeveloped at a cost of £11m as a new station (in which the incised panels are displayed) and offices. This development, designed by Richard Seifert, was opened in 1977. The only original building to survive is the bomb-damaged entrance and former restaurant facing Unilever House. This, originally 80 ft high, was designed by F. J. Ward in 1873 in the 'Oriental style'.

b Broad Street. By William Baker, engineer, 1865–6. Imposing French Renaissance symmetrical front elevation partly obscured by 1913 additions. Intricate train shed roof survives. BR application to redevelop in conjunction with Liverpool Street, decision from DoE awaited.

c Camden Town. Roundhouse. An exceptional engine shed now converted to a theatre. Described in *The Builder*, 1849, p. 135, as being 160 ft in diameter and built for 24 engines with a 41 ft central turntable. The architect was Robert Dockray.

d Cannon Street. 1864–6. By John Hawkshaw, engineer (and E. M. Barry). Roof demolished 1958 after war damage and hotel (by E. M. Barry) redeveloped 1960s with offices designed by J. G. L. Poulson. The roof was described in *The Builder*, 1866, p. 629, as 'wider in single span and longer than any roof of any other building in London'. The fine twin cupolas facing the Thames and the flanking walls remain.

e Charing Cross. By John Hawkshaw, engineer, 1863–5. Hotel of same date by E. M. Barry (except for upper floors, rebuilt in tame Lutyens classical as a result of bomb damage). Roof of train shed rebuilt from 1905 after partial collapse.

f Euston. The station was rebuilt in 1962–6 by R. L. Moorcroft. Some of the statuary, carved by John Thomas, and the listed 1870 lodges survive. The mighty Doric Arch (1836) and the Great Hall and other buildings (1846–9) were both designed by Philip Hardwick (assisted in the latter case by his son, P. C. Hardwick). The builders of the Great Hall were William Cubitt and Co. The train shed was built 1835–9 by Robert Stephenson. The Great Hall, which was a double cube, was designed to contain a large refreshment counter in the centre. The Hall was redecorated in 1916 by Lutyens.

g Fenchurch Street. By George Berkeley, 1854. Enlarged 1881. Application was made in 1978 to build offices behind the façade.

h Holborn Viaduct. 1873. When the station opened, the columns were painted cream, the capitals and girders pale blue and red, the woodwork of the roof white and the rafters yellow or primrose. Hotel designed by Lewis Isaacs, opened 1877. Substantial rebuilding 1961. Hotel replaced by offices.

i King's Cross. By Lewis Cubitt, 1851–2. Engineers William and Joseph Cubitt. John Jay was the contractor. Justly famous 'functional' façade taken together with the Crystal Palace as the most proto-modern Victorian building by apologists of the Modern Movement. Each shed is 800 ft long, 105 ft wide and 71 ft high. The clock on the bell tower was exhibited in the Great Exhibition. Listed Grade I. Great Northern Hotel was opened 1854.

j Liverpool Street. 1875 by Edward Wilson and 1894 by John Wilson and, as architect, W. N. Ashbee. Cathedralesque train shed (cf. Paddington). Builders of 1875 section were Lucas Bros. (ironwork by Fairbairn Engineering of Manchester). Great Eastern Hotel by C. E. Barry and R. W. Edis, 1884–1906. Decision awaited on BR application to demolish the station.

k London Bridge. Very complicated building history. First station designed by George Smith in 1836 (earliest in London). 1844 station by Henry Roberts (to whom George Gilbert Scott was articled) with additions in 1850–51 designed by Samuel Beazley. Present train shed dates from 1866. The Terminus Hotel was built in 1861 and designed by Henry Currey (builders Lucas Bros.). In 1880 a signal box with 280 levers and designed by the firm of Saxby and Farmer was built at the station. Substantial redevelopment is now being carried out.

l Marylebone. By Sir Douglas and Francis Fox, 1899. H. W. Braddock was architect for detailing. Hotel by R. W. Edis. 222 Marylebone Road, the former Great Central Hotel, is now BR HQ.

m Paddington. By I. K. Brunel and Matthew Digby Wyatt, 1854. Interior originally painted red and grey. Glorious roof, with 189 wrought iron elliptical ribs, was executed by Fox, Henderson and Co. A library of 1,000 volumes was planned as one of the added attractions for travellers. Station extended 1909–16. Listed Grade I.

240

n St Pancras. Train shed by W. H. Barlow and R. Ordish, 1865–8. Hotel by George Gilbert Scott, 1868–76, (partly converted to offices 1935). The roof (700 ft long, 100 ft high and 240 ft wide) described in *The Builder*, 1868, p. 744, 'as regards length, breadth and height, the greatest in the world'. It was credited with the widest span of any in existence and moreover one which was 'unbroken by ties or braces'. 690 cast iron columns support the floor. The ironwork was originally painted dark chocolate in colour and the station was lit by 60 small sun burners. Listed Grade I. Hotel to be cleaned soon.

o Victoria. Originally built 1860 (Robert Jacomb Hood, engineer) and 1862 (by John Fowler). The simple Italianate façade and platforms (1–8) of the original buildings survive. Roof renewed by H. E. Wallis, engineer. Baroque façade by Arthur Blomfield, 1908 (remaining façade 1898). Grosvenor Hotel 1860–61 by J. T. Knowles. Cleaned 1978.

p Waterloo. Originally constructed 1848 in succession to Nine Elms, Joseph Locke being the engineer. 1874–5 extensions by Mr Jacomb. 1900–1902 work by J. W. Jacomb Hood and A. W. Szlumper. Largely rebuilt 1907–22. Rich baroque entrance by J. R. Scott.

Lostwithiel, Cornwall. By I. K. Brunel, 1859. Former carriage works also listed.

Louth, Lincolnshire. By Weightman and Hadfield of Sheffield, 1854. Freight only.

Maidenhead, Berkshire. Predecessor to present station was by Brunel and the contemporary and surviving viaduct of 1837–8 was the inspiration for Turner's *Rain, Steam and Speed*.

Maldon, Essex. 1846. Neo-Jacobean. Closed (till recently in use as restaurant).

Malvern, Great, Worcestershire (now Hereford and Worcester). By E. W. Elmslie, 1863. Builders, Messrs Wood of Worcester. Famous set of capitals by W. Forsyth, 'who has cleverly introduced the foliage of the plants of the neighbourhood' (*The Builder*, 1863, p. 16). Walls in Malvern Hill stone and dressings in Bath stone. Style is 'Gothic of the period of Charles VI of France'. The wooden tower over the entrance which rose to 50 ft (from the ground) has been demolished.

Left, above *Ipswich Town, Suffolk; 1858–60 by Robert Sinclair, engineer to the Eastern Counties Railway*
Left, below *Birkenhead Woodside, Cheshire; 1878 by R. E. Johnston. Roof by E. W. Ives, who designed the roof of Liverpool Lime Street station*

Manchester.

a Central. By Fowler and Sacré, Johnson and Johnstone, 1876–9. Total span of shed 210 ft (240 ft according to Cecil Stewart). Hotel directly in front unbuilt. Nearby Midland Hotel by Charles Trubshaw, 1898. Station closed 1969 – in use as car park.

b Liverpool Road. Probably by John Foster the younger. Terminus of original Liverpool–Manchester Railway. Listed Grade I. Converted to goods depot and closed 1972. To be restored.

c Oxford Road. By W. R. Headley, 1960. One of the best post-war stations. Conoid shell roof.

d Piccadilly. Formerly known as London Road. Begun 1862 and largely rebuilt 1959–66. Office block by Richard Seifert, 1968. Architects for 1862 station were Mills and Murgatroyd of Manchester.

e Victoria. Earliest sections by George Stephenson, 1844. His roof described at time as 'largest in the kingdom' – 700 ft long and covering 80,000 sq. ft. Offices of Lancashire and Yorkshire Railway planned at station 1884. New front 1909.

Margate, Kent. By John Newton, 1864. Rebuilt in cinema classical 1926.

Market Harborough, Leicestershire. Present forebuilding 1885 – pleasant 'Wrenaissance'. All platform buildings demolished 1976–7.

Matlock, Derbyshire. Joseph Paxton said to have been involved in design of station house.

Matlock Bath, Derbyshire. *c.* 1885. Swiss Chalet style.

Micheldever, Hampshire. By William Tite, 1839–40.

Middlesbrough, Durham (now Cleveland). Rebuilding by Cudworth, engineer, and William Peachey of Darlington, architect, 1873–7. Final cost £80,000. Remarkable roof destroyed in Second World War.

Millbrook, Bedfordshire. *c.* 1846. Listed July 1977.

Mitcham, Surrey (now Greater London). A house of *c.* 1800 probably converted to the station in 1855. (Stations were not always purpose-built – from 1849 till 1872 a converted seventeenth century schoolhouse served as the station at Enfield, Middx and at Bourne, Cambridgeshire, the large Tudor Red House was similarly used until 1959.)

Monkwearmouth, County Durham (now Tyne and Wear). By Thomas Moore (not Dobson), 1848. Proud classical design. Now converted to a museum. Stationmaster's house on first floor. Footbridge of 1879. The imposing design was chosen because George Hudson, the Railway King, was MP for nearby Sunderland.

Needham Market, Suffolk. By Frederick Barnes, 1846. Delightful Jacobean. *The Builder*, p. 476, said the tender accepted was for £3,150. Unstaffed and partly let.

Netley, Hampshire. 1867. In Tite L&SWR tradition.

Newark, Nottinghamshire.

a Castle. 1846. Classical.

b Northgate. Good iron spandrels. Big clock by Potts and Sons of Leeds.

Newcastle-upon-Tyne, Northumberland (now Tyne and Wear). By John Dobson, 1848–50. (Finally completed by Thomas Prosser 1865.) Superb classical station. Original drawings for station rediscovered recently. The style adopted is 'Roman Doric' and *The Builder*, 1847, p. 258, says that it suspects Dobson's prototype to have been the 'antique building' at Albanoeer. It also states, that the famous central portico was to be 180 ft long, 68 ft deep and 55 ft high internally. The total external length was then envisaged to be 584 ft, with the clock tower and 'contemplated' hotel (Dobson's hotel being greatly enlarged by Thomas Prosser in the 1860s), making the total length 770 ft (in fact the great portico intended by Dobson was built only later in modified form by Prosser). The building is in Prudhoe stone. The magnificent 3-span roof is 700 ft long. When the station was being completed in 1850 some 600 men were working on it. Interestingly, a model of the projected station was displayed on site in 1847. Sections of the *portecochère* rebuilt 1978.

Newmarket, Suffolk. Striking baroque design of 1848. Derelict. 1902 station now in commercial use.

Northampton.

a Bridge Street. By J. W. Livock, 1845. Demolished.

b Castle. 1883. Contractor, J. Hartley of Birmingham. Cost nearly £40,000. Rebuilt by R. L. Moorcroft, 1963–4.

c St John's. By Alexander Milne, 1872. Demolished.

Norwich Thorpe, Norfolk. Rebuilt 1884–6. At the time the largest GER station after Liverpool Street. *The Builder*, 1884,ii, p. 443, describes it as being in 'freely-treated Renaissance'. Domical mansard roof over booking office with zinc scales. Queen post truss roofs. Chief engineer, John Wilson (son of Edward). J. A. Radley, assistant engineer. W. N. Ashbee also involved.

Nottingham.

a Midland. By A. E. Lambert, 1904.

b Victoria. 1898–1900.

Oldham, Lancashire (now Greater Manchester). Railway warehouses in Park Road/Woodstock Road listed.

Oundle, Northamptonshire. By J. W. Livock, 1845. Disused.

Oxford. The original 1851–2 Midland station was by Fox and Henderson. It used prefabricated parts in its construction and had a particularly large canopy at the entrance. Closed and in commercial use. The present station dates from 1972.

Par, Cornwall. Engine sheds in St Blazey Road listed.

Perth (now Tayside). *Building News*, 1884, ii, p. 483, reports on the enlargement of the station at a cost of £100,000. New total length 1,750 ft. Blyth and Cunningham of Edinburgh, engineers. Later in 1893 there were alterations for £9,000.

Peterborough, Huntingdonshire (now Cambridgeshire). GER and GNR both had stations in the city. Peterborough East, attributed by Biddle to J. W. Livock, 1845, has been demolished. In 1869 the GNR church for the locomotive establishment a mile north of Peterborough station was opened. It was 104 ft long with a low central tower. Mr Teale of Doncaster was the architect (*The Architect*, 1869, p. 310). In 1893 a new station was begun for the city although the 'present booking offices' stayed. Two platforms of 800 ft length were planned. The cost was estimated at £100,000. Present Peterborough station being demolished. Great Northern Hotel remains.

Petersfield, Hampshire. 1859. Design of interest for tall attached stationmaster's house.

Pickering, Yorkshire (now N. Yorkshire). *c.* 1848, possibly by G. T. Andrews. Being reopened.

Plymouth, Devon. Originally by Brunel, 1849. Present station built 1958–62.

Pocklington, Yorkshire (now Humberside). By G. T. Andrews, 1845–7. Converted to gymnasium.

Polegate, Sussex. First built 1846. New station opened 1881 and described in *The Builder*, 1881, ii, p. 415, as 'an imposing new pile'. It was faced in cement 'to withstand the saline breezes'. Mr Myers of Westminster, architect, F. D. Banister, engineer in chief. Now largely demolished.

Portsmouth and Southsea, Hampshire. 1866. Deuxième Empire. First station on site 1847.

Ramsgate, Kent. Proud design of 1926. (cf. other resort stations such as Clacton and Newton Abbot, 1927.)

Reading, Berkshire. Originally by I. K. Brunel, 1840. Substantially rebuilt 1867. Mr Lane, engineer. Contractor, Henry Lovatt of Wolverhampton. 1899 extensions. The Great Western Hotel, now converted to offices, could be the oldest surviving railway hotel building in the world (*c.* 1844). (See York and Derby, however.)

Richmond, Yorkshire (now N. Yorkshire). By G. T. Andrews, 1848. The most renowned station in monastic Gothic. Now a garden centre.

Rochdale, Lancashire (now Greater Manchester). Plans for new station announced 1887 (*The Builder*, ii, p. 414).

Rowsley, Derbyshire. Original station, 2 houses and 4 cottages by Joseph Paxton, 1849. Station building now in goods yard. New station, demolished, by Edward Walters, 1860.

Roydon, Essex. 1841, perhaps by Francis Thompson. Coupled columns supported bow-fronted canopy. BR application to demolish refused. Now for sale.

Salisbury, Wiltshire. Original Brunel GWR goods shed survives in Fisherton Street. Present station largely 1900.

Saltburn-by-the-Sea, Yorkshire (now Cleveland). *c.* 1860–61, probably by Thomas Prosser or

William Peachey. Centrepiece of new town.

Scarborough, Yorkshire (now N. Yorkshire). Earliest section by G. T. Andrews, 1844–5. Clock tower built in Hayburn Wyke stone 1884.

Sheffield, Yorkshire (now S. Yorkshire). Reconstructed by Charles Trubshaw, 1904–1905.

Sherborne, Dorset, 1860.

Shrewsbury, Salop. Originally by T. K. Penson, 1848. Substantially rebuilt, in part-facsimile, 1903. Listed railway warehouses in Howard Street built in 1835 by Fallowes and Hart of Birmingham with iron columns, openwork roof and neoclassical façade (originally built as canal warehouses).

Slough, Berkshire. First built by I. K. Brunel, 1840. Rebuilt 1879 in French *château* style.

Southampton, Hampshire. By William Tite 1838–40. Tite's original terminus survives, one of his best works. Nearby former South-Western Hotel extended by J. Norton.

Southend Victoria, Essex. By W. N. Ashbee, 1887–9.

Southport, Lancashire (now Merseyside). By Charles Driver, 1882–4.

South Shields, County Durham (now Tyne and Wear). Station built 1875 at a cost of £30,000 (*The Builder*, p. 306). Large plate tracery rose window on façade.

Stafford. 1843 and 1862. Built by Mr Parnell of Rugby to a tender of £20,990. Designed by the 'L&NWR Company architect' (*The Builder*, 1862, p. 332). Livock not named in latter article. *The Builder* complained that the black bricks used gave a 'gloomy aspect'. Station rebuilt 1961–2.

Stamford, Lincolnshire.
a East. By William Hurst, 1856. Closed.
b Town. By Sancton Wood, 1848.

Starcross, Devon. Pumping station by I. K. Brunel (associated with his atmospheric railway).

Stockport, Lancashire (now Greater Manchester). £22,000 plans to rebuild announced 1861 (*The Builder*, p. 777). The former L&NWR goods warehouse and engine house in Wellington Road listed.

Stockton-on-Tees, Durham (now Cleveland). One of the termini of the world's first railway, 1825. Present station on different site by

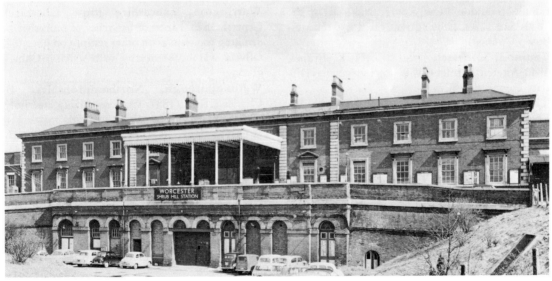

William Bell, 1893. The original Stockton and Darlington Railway booking office survives at 48 Bridge Road. BR wish to demolish roof (1978).

Stoke-on-Trent, Staffordshire. By H. A. Hunt, 1850, as part of Winton Square development. A Jacobean country house in an urban setting. Train shed is later.

Stone, Staffordshire. By H. A. Hunt (cf. Stoke-on-Trent), 1848. Crossing keeper's lodge, Whitebridge Lane, is listed.

Stowmarket, Suffolk. By Frederick Barnes, 1849. *The Builder*, 1846, p. 569, says the station has been 'founded' (i.e., foundations laid) by Mr Revett, builder of Stowmarket, who had obtained the contract for the station in 'the Elizabethan style' (Barnes not being mentioned). Platform was to be 230 ft long. A new street with a bridge over the river was opened in connection with the station. A fine building largely unaltered.

Sunderland, County Durham (now Tyne and Wear). William Bell and William Peachey designed the station of 1879. Bombed 1940 and rebuilt 1965.

Surbiton, Surrey (now Greater London). By J. R. Scott, 1937. A starkly 'functional' contrast to his baroque Waterloo entrance.

Swindon, Wiltshire. Originally by I. K. Brunel, 1841–2. Enlarged 1875 for £11,000. Now largely rebuilt. Swindon New Town, laid out in the 1840s and 1850s, is being renovated by Thamesdown Council.

Taunton, Somerset. Original by I. K. Brunel, 1842. Altered. Former GWR hotel survives as District Engineer's offices.

Thrapston, Northamptonshire. By J. W. Livock, 1845. Demolished.

Thurgarton, Nottinghamshire. Picturesque Tudor.

Thurston, Suffolk. By Frederick Barnes. *The Builder*, 1846, p. 476, says winning tender was for £3,753.

Torquay, Devon. New station reported finished September 1879 (*The Builder*, p. 161).

Trentham, Staffordshire. Charles Barry reportedly involved. Broad-eaved Italianate. Demolished.

Truro Newham, Cornwall. Original by I. K. Brunel, 1855. Rebuilt 1876.

Tunbridge Wells, Kent.
a Central. By Sancton Wood, 1845. Reginald Blomfield probably involved in 1912 section.
b West. 1882. Clock tower.

Tynemouth, Northumberland (now Tyne and Wear). First station, probably by Benjamin Green, reported as being greatly enlarged and improved in 1862 (*The Builder*, p. 416). Present station, probably by William Bell, dates from 1882. Important roof. Application in 1978 to demolish west side for new Metro.

Ulverston, Lancashire (now Cumbria). 1873. Italianate. Credited to Paley and Austin. Application in 1978 to demolish canopies.

Wakefield, Yorkshire (now W. Yorkshire). Westgate. By J. B. Fraser, architect, of Leeds. Total cost £60,000. Archibald Neill of Bradford contractor. Clock tower. Wooden coffered ceiling to booking office (*The Builder*, 1867, p. 355).

Wallsend, Northumberland (now Tyne and Wear). New station by William Bell, 1893 (*The Builder*, 1893, I, p. 200).

Walsall, Staffordshire (now W. Midlands). Original station 1849. 1922 replacement (by W. J. Davis) with fine booking hall. To be demolished.

Wareham, Dorset. 1866. Elaborate Flemish.

Warrington, Lancashire (now Cheshire). Central. 1873. Motif of bas-relief of bulrushes on drinking fountain as on other stations on line. 1873 railway warehouse nearby with striking Chinese glazing.

Wellingborough, Northamptonshire. By Charles Driver, 1857. Chinese glazing and polychrome brick. To be rebuilt in 1978.

Wemyss Bay, Renfrewshire (now Strathclyde). Partly circular.

Weymouth, Dorset. By I. K. Brunel, 1855–7. *The Builder* reported (1855, p. 407) that 'the station house' was to cost £20,000.

Whitby, Yorkshire (now W. Yorkshire). 1846 contract of £10,000 for new station (*The Builder*, p. 413). Probably by G. T. Andrews. New station 1884 (Building News, 1884, II, p. 884), at West Cliff. Closed.

Whitchurch, Salop. Foundation stone laid 1858 (*The Builder*, p. 238).

Whitley Bay, Northumberland (now Tyne and Wear). 1910. Seaside Jacobean.

Windsor, Berkshire.

a Riverside. By William Tite, 1850–51. Tudor-cum-Gothic. Contains royal waiting rooms.

b Windsor and Eton. 1897. Large *porte-cochère*.

Wingfield, Derbyshire. By Francis Thompson, 1840. Delightful broad-eaved and ashlar-faced neo-classical design. Closed and for sale.

Woburn Sands, Buckinghamshire. 1846. Timber-framed.

Wolverhampton, Staffordshire (now W. Midlands). 1849 ticket office in Horseley Fields survives and is to be restored by West Midlands County Council. Symmetrical Italianate design with two attached Doric orders. Present station by R. L. Moorcroft, 1964–7.

Worcester Shrub Hill. 1865, probably by Edward Wilson. Unusual black facing.

Worthing, Sussex. Original 1845 station in Railway Approach converted into two cottages in 1859. Earliest example of a new non-railway use for a redundant station?

Wylam on Tyne, Northumberland. 1835–7. Platform wing probably added 1840s. Due to age is listed II★. The mid-eighteenth-century cottage where George Stephenson was born in 1781 belongs to the National Trust (not open to the public). Typical of the toy-like stations, many of which are now boarded up, on the line from Carlisle to Newcastle.

York. By G. T. Andrews, 1841–2. Engineer, Thomas Cabrey. According to Pevsner and Hitchcock, this was the first station to have a hotel (by Andrews as well, completed 1853; still survives). The Andrews station is largely preserved, but the present station is mostly the work of Thomas Prosser in 1874–7, William Peachey being responsible for the roof. Famous 800 ft long curved train shed. Builders, Messrs Keswick of York. *The Builder*, 1876, p. 671, described the station as the largest in the world, and said it contained 171,951 sq. ft of platform space. Royal Station Hotel by Prosser 1877, with 1896 addition.

BIBLIOGRAPHY

APPLETON, J. H., *Disused Railways*, Countryside Commission, London, 1970.

BARMAN, Christian, *Introduction to Railway Architecture*, London Art and Technics, London, 1950.

BETJEMAN, John and John Gay, *London's Historic Railway Stations*, John Murray, London, 1972.

BIDDLE, Gordon, *Victorian Stations*, David and Charles, Newton Abbot, 1973.

BIDDLE, Gordon and Jeoffry Spence, *The British Railway Station*, David and Charles, Newton Abbot, 1977.

BOWERS, Michael, *Railway Styles in Building*, Almark, London, 1975.

CHALONER, W. H., *Social and Economic Development of Crewe*, Manchester University Press, Manchester, 1950.

COCKMAN, F. G., *Railway Architecture*, Shire Publications, Aylesbury, 1976.

CRITTALL, Elizabeth, K. H. Rogers and Colin Shrimpton, 'Swindon', in R. B. Pugh and Elizabeth Crittall (eds.), *Victoria History of the Counties of England: Wiltshire*, vol. IX, Oxford University Press, London, 1970.

DENTON, J. Horsley, *British Railway Stations*, London, 1965.

ELLIS, C. Hamilton, *British Railway History*, Allen and Unwin, London, 1954, and Macmillan, New York, 1955.

HITCHCOCK, H. R., *Early Victorian Architecture in Britain*, Yale University Press, New Haven, Conn., 1954.

HOLLAND, Harry, *Traveller's Architecture*, Harrap, London, 1971.

HUDSON, Kenneth, 'The Early Years of the Railway Community in Swindon', *Journal of Transport History*, vol. 1, no. 2, 1968.

JACKSON, Alan, *London's Termini*, David and Charles, Newton Abbot, 1971.

KIDNEY, Walter C., *Working Places: The Adaptive Use of Industrial Buildings*, Ober Park Associates, Pittsburgh, Penn., 1976.

LISSCA (Liverpool Street Station Campaign), *The London Stations*, LISSCA, London, 1977.

LLOYD, David, *Steam Horse, Iron Road*, BBC Publications, London, 1972.

LLOYD, David and Donald Insall, *Railway Station Architecture*, David and Charles, Newton Abbot, 1966, repr. 1978.

LLOYD, Roger, 'The Railway Towns', in *The Railwayman's Gallery*, Allen and Unwin, London, 1953.

MARSHALL, John, *Biographical Dictionary of British Engineers*, David and Charles, Newton Abbot, 1978.

PEVSNER, Sir Nikolaus (ed.), *The Buildings of England* series, 46 vols., Penguin, London, 1951–74.

SAVE (ed. D. Pearce and M. Binney), *Off the Rails*, SAVE Britain's Heritage, London, 1977.

SIMMONS, Jack, *St Pancras Station*, Allen and Unwin, London, 1968.

TURTON, B. J., 'The Railway Towns of Southern England', *Journal of Transport History*, vol. 2, no. 2, July 1969.

WELLS, H. B., 'Swindon in the 19th and 20th Centuries', in L. V. Grinsell and others (eds.), *Studies in the History of Swindon*, 1950.

Contemporary volumes of *The Builder*, *The Architect*, *Building News*, *Illustrated London News* and *Civil Engineers' Journal* are extremely informative. *The Builder*, 1857, p. 381, contains a very interesting account of the early history of railways.

BIOGRAPHICAL NOTES
ON CONTRIBUTORS

SOPHIE ANDREAE read History of Art at Cambridge. She is secretary of SAVE Britain's Heritage.

DAVID ATWELL is an architectural historian, an expert in nineteenth and twentieth century buildings of commerce and entertainment. He is author of *Battle of Styles*. He works as the Information Officer in the architects' department of the Greater London Council.

MARCUS BINNEY is chairman of SAVE Britain's Heritage. He is architectural editor of *Country Life*, joint organizer of 'The Destruction of the Country House' and 'Change and Decay' exhibitions and co-author of the companion books, joint author with Peter Burman of *Chapels and Churches: Who Cares?* and a spokesman at international conferences on conservation.

PETER BURMAN is an architectural historian and secretary of the Council for Places of Worship and of the Cathedrals Advisory Committee. He was joint organizer of 'Change and Decay' at the Victoria and Albert Museum and co-author of the companion book covering the peril of church buildings. He is also joint author, with Marcus Binney, of *Chapels and Churches: Who Cares?*

CHRIS HAWKINS is a laboratory technician at Birkbeck College, London. He is joint author with George Reeve of *Southern Railway Engine Sheds*.

RICHARD HUGHES is a qualified geologist and industrial archaeologist who has carried out research into the industrial history of major railway monuments including St Pancras, London and Snow Hill, Birmingham. He has also been involved in the practical side of conservation with civil engineers Ove Arup and Partners.

DAVID LLOYD is a town-planner, lecturer and writer with an encyclopaedic knowledge of railway architecture in England. He is joint author of *Save the City* (of London) and of volumes in Sir Nikolaus Pevsner's *The Buildings of England* series published by Penguin. He is a keen committee member of both the Society for the Protection of Ancient Buildings and the Victorian Society.

CHRISTOPHER MONKHOUSE is an art historian and Curator of Decorative Arts at the Museum of Art, Providence, Rhode Island. He has spent several years researching into hotel buildings and has written a book on the subject entitled *Grand Hotel*.

DAVID PEARCE is vice-chairman of SAVE Britain's Heritage. As a freelance writer he is a frequent contributor to architectural magazines. He was the editor of *Built Environment* and is now secretary to the Society for the Protection of Ancient Buildings.

GEORGE REEVE is a cartographer at the University of London and joint author with Chris Hawkins of *Southern Railway Engine Sheds*.

MATTHEW SAUNDERS is an architectural historian. He was previously secretary of SAVE Britain's Heritage and is now secretary of the Ancient Monuments Society.

ALAN YOUNG is a school teacher and railway enthusiast who has systematically recorded thousands of lesser railway stations in Britain.

PICTURE ACKNOWLEDGMENTS

We are indebted to the following for permission to reproduce the photographs on the pages listed:

Ove Arup/Alfie Wood 191; David Atwell 53; O. Banell 81 (top); British Railways Board 13, 17 (bottom), 20, 29, 52, 63, 65 (bottom), 66, 70, 71, 76, 83, 84, 98, 105, 116 (bottom), 134, 170, 171, 194, 195, 196, 198, 199, 200, 202, 203, 204, 236, 245 (bottom); British Transport Hotels 125, 126, 138, 139; Country Life 34, 122; George Cserna 227; Christopher Dalton 8, 12, 14 (bottom), 21, 22, 49, 51, 56 (top), 59 (top), 60, 62, 65 (top), 73, 77, 78 (top), 79, 80, 81 (bottom), 82, 85 (top), 89 (bottom), 92–93, 94, 95, 96, 97, 99, 100–101, 102, 106, 107, 108, 109, 112, 113, 115, 117, 159, 166, 174, 175, 192, 205, 207, 208, 209, 211, 212–213, 218, 233 (bottom), 241 (top); Educational Facilities Laboratories, Inc. 224, 229; John Garner 136; Jonathan M. Gibson 122; Greater London Council 9, 26, 28, 31, 69, 86, 116 (top), 127, 156, 161, 245; Guildhall Library, London 119, 130 (bottom); Angelo Hornak (jacket front); A. F. Kersting 27, 45, 141, 142–143, 144 (top), 149, 150, 151, 153, 154, 157, 201; Randolph Langenbach 15 (top); Duncan McNeill 16, 103; Christopher Monkhouse 123, 124; Napper Errington Collerton Partnership 216, 217; National Library of Wales 90–91; National Monuments Record 19, 23, 32–33, 36, 38, 39, 40, 41, 44, 46, 47, 55 (top), 58, 59 (bottom), 61, 67, 78 (bottom), 130 (top), 132, 163, 177, 182–183, 186, 188–189, 210, 241 (bottom); National Railway Museum 74, 110–111, 148, 155; North Road Station Museum, Darlington 219; Photomatic 167, 168, 169, 173; Photomatic/John H. Meredith 172; Pittsburgh History and Landmarks Foundation 225; Arthur Quarmby & Associates 55 (bottom), 220, 221; Royal Commission on the Ancient & Historical Monuments of Scotland 42, of Wales 193; RIBA Drawings Collection 128–9, 135; Jack Simmons 56 (bottom), 85 (bottom); D. Simpson 43; City of Southampton Planning Dept 50; Spoorweg Museum, Utrecht, 222, 223 (left); Terry Sutton 14 (top), 37, 178–179, 180; Victorian Society 64; Rex Wailes 25; Robin Ward 7, 10, 11, 15 (bottom), 17 (top), 104, 145; Western Mail & Echo 146–147; Wirral Country Park 214–215; William A. Wynne 223 (right); Yorkshire Steam 38.

INDEX

All references are to stations, unless otherwise indicated.

Page references to illustrations are in italics.

Aberdeen 42
Aberdovey 87
Aboyne 116
Acklington 96
  engine shed *173*
Aintree, engine shed 173
Allen, George 118
Allom, Thomas 133
Alnmouth *85*
Alnwick *213*
Alton Towers 115; *101*
Anderson, Sir Robert 6, 42
Andrews, George Townsend 6, 38, 49, 57, 74, 82, 114, 126, 219
Appleby *110*
Ardgay 114
Ashbeen, W. N. 6, 35
Ashby-de-la-Zouch 7; *210*
  conversion of station 209
Ashford (Kent), development as railway town 187
  engine shed 174
  locomotive works 171
  railway housing 177, 179
Askham 105, 115
Audley End 68, 82
Ashwell and Morden 112
Avon Bridge 30
Aylesbury 30
Aylesford 82; *101*
Aylsham South 110

Baker, William 26, 44, 145
Balcombe Viaduct *143*
Ballochmyle Viaduct 144
Baltimore, Md., USA, development of Mount Royal Station 226; *227*
Banbury 30
Bangor, engine shed 174

Barcombe 103, 106
Barlow, William Henry 35, 153
Barmouth 87
Barnes, Frederick 59, 82
Barry, C. E. 35
Barry, E. M. 28, 34, 132
Barry, locomotive works 169
Barry Railway 145
Bartlow, conversion of station 208
Bath, Green Park 24, 65
  Spa 30, 49, 54
Battle 8, 72; *73*
Beazley, Samuel 28, 127
Bedford 60
Bell, William 43, 63
Belton and Burgh 107
Benton 93
Berkeley, George 28
Berwick-on-Tweed, Royal Border Bridge 152; *150*
Betchworth *14*
Betjeman, Sir John 28
Biddle, Gordon 21
Birkenhead Joint Railway 96
Birkenhead, Woodside 12, 24; *61*
Birmingham, Central 120
  Curzon Street 44; *42*
  Curzon Street, Queen's Hotel 120
  Great Western Hotel 44
  New Street 24, 44
  New Street engine shed 12
  Saltley locomotive works 187
  Snow Hill 37, 44, 190; *37*, *191*
Bishopstone 100
Bishop's Stortford 82
Blair, James 25
Blake Hall 108
Blomfield, Sir Arthur 34
Blore, Edward 66
Bodorgan 98
Bolton, engine shed 171
Bouch, Thomas 153
Bournemouth 67
Bow (Devon) 100
Bow, R. H. 145
Box, tunnel 30

Box Hill and West Humble 115; *115*
Braddock, H. W. 29
Bradford, Exchange 12, 37
  Manningham, engine shed 158
Bradford-on-Avon 75; *78*
Bramhope Tunnel *19*
Brentnor 101
Bridgend 190
Bridlington 84
Brierfield *194*
Brighton 46, *47*
  engine shed 158
  locomotive works 169
  London Road Viaduct *144*
Brinscombe 78
Bristol, Temple Meads, 30, 37, 54; *19*, *38*
Bristol and Exeter Railway 37
Britannia Tubular Bridge 151, 152; *150*
Brocklesby 94, 115
Bruce Grove 105
Brundall Gardens 94
Brunel, H. M. 26
Brunel, Isambard Kingdom 6, 11, 12, 24, 30, 37, 49, 54, 57, 74, 75, 78, 79, 80, 105, 114, 121, 129, 131, 140, 149, 152, 190
Bucknell *103*
Burges, William 72
Burghclere 114
Burley, Benjamin 38
Burntisland *81*
Burton, Decimus 121
Burton-on-Trent, warehouse conversion 10; *213*
Bury St Edmunds 59; *59*
Butterfield, William 72
Butterley Iron Company 35
Buxton 60; *61*
Buxton Lamas 110

Caerphilly, locomotive works 169
Caledonian Railway 42
Cambridge 57, 68, 69, 82, 195,

197; *56, 197*
Carcroft and Adwick-le-Street 116
Carlisle 25, 49, 52, 60, 66; *52, 65*
 engine shed 162
Carnforth, engine shed 174
Carno 210
Carrbridge 104
Carrington Viaduct 144
Carswell, James 42
Castle Howard 115
Cemmes Road 95
Charlbury *93*
Chathill 95; *95*
Chattanooga, Tenn., USA,
 development of station 223; *224*
Cheddleton 96
Cheltenham 54
Chepstow 78
 bridge 152
Chertsey 97
Chessington 100
Chester 25, 49, 57; *56*
Chester and Holyhead Railway 82
Chirk Viaduct 150; *144*
Christon Bank, engine shed *175*
Churchward 164
Clacton *82*
Clapham (Yorks) 95
Clare 110
Cleland 88
Clenchwarton 114
Cocking 98; *207*
Colchester, Victoria Station Hotel
 121
Collingham 98
Colwick, engine shed 173
Connel Ferry 117
Corbridge *21*
Corfe Castle 101
County School 101
Cowlairs, locomotive works 171
Cowper, E. A. 24
Cressing 105; *105*
Crewe 26
 development as railway town
 179–189
 engine shed 10, 162, 165
 locomotive works 12, 171, 176
 railway housing 177, 179; *183*
Croes Newydd, engine shed 173
Cromford 116
Cromford and High Peak Railway
 158

Cross Inn 103
Crudgington 114
Crumlin Viaduct 12, 145, 152; *145*
Cubitt, Lewis 6, 30, 127
 Joseph 30
 Sir William 30
Culham 78, 114
Cullompton, bridge 158
Cumwhinton 110
Cunningham, John 44, 181

Darley Dale 117
Darlington, Bank Top 43
 locomotive works 169, 179
 North Road 43, 217; *219*
Darsham 107
Dawes, William 44
Deadwater 100
Dean 162
Deepdale Viaduct 145
Derby, locomotive works 176
 Midland Hotel 121
 Trijunct 57
Derry Ormond 105
Dersingham 105
Didcot, engine shed 174
Dilton Marsh 95
Dinting Vale Viaduct 150
Ditchingham 107
Dobson, John 6, 24, 38, 40
Dockray, Robert 120, 217
Doncaster, locomotive works 171,
 176
Dorchester, West 80
Dorking 205
Dorn, Marion 138
Dove Viaduct 149
Dover, Lord Warden Hotel 127
Draycott 114
Drayton Park *199*
Drybridge 105
Dundee, West 42
Dunkeld 117
Dunrobin Castle 115
Durham 69; *219*
Dyce 105
Dyos, Professor James 21

Earlestown Viaduct 144
East Barkwith 103
Eastbourne 62, 87

Eastern Countries Railway 57
Eastern Railway 121
Eastleigh 51
 development as railway town 187
 locomotive works 176
 railway housing 177, 179
East Norfolk Railway 110
Ebberston 114
Edinburgh, Caledonian Hotel 8
 Haymarket 42, 190; *42*
 North British Hotel 8, 42
 Princes Street Station 42
 Waverley 41, 197; *40*
Edinburgh and Glasgow Railway
 42
Edis, Robert 30, 35
Elmslie, E. W. 72
Elstree 105
Eltham Park *93*
Ely 82
Emerson Park 94
Eridge *109*
Etchingham *89*
Etherow Viaduct 150
Exeter 52, 54
 St David's 54, 190
 St Thomas 54

Fawley 114
Felsted 108
Fenny Stratford 8, 95; *93*
Ferry, Benjamin 72
Filey 84
Fleet 114
Fleetwood, North Euston Hotel
 120, 121; *122*
Flitwick 112
Flixton 106, 112
Folkestone, Pavilion Hotel 120
Forth Railway Bridge 11, 153; *152*
Fort William 94; *14*
Foster, John 44
Fowler, Sir John 6, 25, 31, 34, 44
Fox, Sir Douglas 29
 Sir Francis 29
Fripp, S. C. 37
Frome 79, 190
Furness Railway 105, 114

Gara Bridge 114
Geldeston 107

Georgemas Junction 100
Giggleswick 95
Gilberdyke 114
Gill, Eric 138
Gillingham, engine shed 160
Glasgow, Central 66
  Maxwell Park *105*
  Queen Street 42; *10, 42*
  railway workshops *171*
  St Enoch 6, 24, 25, 42, 44; *8, 17*
  St Enoch Hotel 25
  St Enoch engine shed 12
Glen Belah Viaduct 145
Glenfinnan Viaduct 144
Glendon and Rushton 8, 106, 110;
  107, 109
Gleneagles Hotel 125; *125*
Gobowen 60; *81*
Golspie 116
Goonbell 93
Gorton, locomotive works 169
Gosport 51, 52; *50*
Grand Junction Company 179–181
Great Central Railway 29, 94, 112
Great Chesterford 82, 97, 107, 209;
  209
Great Eastern Railway 35, 66, 93,
  105, 107, 108, 109, 133
Great Malvern 7, 72; *71*
Great Northern Railway 10, 30,
  59, 80, 112, 127, 162
Great Western Railway 30, 37, 52,
  66, 72, 74, 93, 114, 121, 127,
  162, 164, 183, 184; *165*
Green, Benjamin 96, 149

Habrough 112
Halifax *14*
Hampton Court 115
Hanwell Viaduct *144*
Hardwick, Philip senior 6, 26, 44
  Philip junior 6, 26, 30, 127, 129
Hasland, engine shed 167; *169*
Hatch End 116; *116*
Hawkshaw, Sir John 28, 34
Hayward, Charles 133
Headcorn 104
Heckington 200
Heisby 95
Hellifield 105; *107*
Hertford East 87
Hertingfordbury 112

Heyford 114
Highbridge, engine shed *167*
  locomotive works 169
Highland Railway 114
Hill, Oliver 125, 138
Hindolveston 114
Hodnet 114
Holme Moor 114
Holyhead Railway 57, 82
Holywell Junction, 82
Hood, J. W. J. 36
  R. J. 31
Horseshoe Curve Viaduct 145
Horwich, locomotive works 171
Hove, tunnel *17*
Hoylake 100
Huddersfield 7, 25, 49, 50, 54, 58;
  55
  Colne viaduct 11
  George Hotel 127
Huddersfield Railway Company
  127
Hudson, George 38, 54, 57
Hull, Dairycoates engine shed
  165
  Paragon 25, 49, 50, 57, 63; *55*
  Paragon Station Hotel 126
  Royal Station Hotel 127
Hull and Barnsley Railway 114
Humphrey, John 118
Hunt, H. A. 57, 66, 127
Hunts Cross 116
Hurst, William 81

Insch 106
Inverness, engine shed 158; *167*
Inverurie, locomotive works 171
Ipswich and Bury Railway 82
Irchester 88
Ivybridge Viaduct 149

Johnston, R. E. 24

Kemble 68
Kennard, Thomas 145
Kettering 60; *76*
Kingham, engine shed 162
Kirkby-in-Ashfield, engine shed
  162
Knowles, James 34, 131

Laing, David 50
Lairg 98
Lakenheath 82
Lancashire and Yorkshire Railway
  125, 164; *165*
Lavant 98
Lavenham 110
Lealholm 114
Leamside Viaduct 143
Leeds, Central canal bridge *158*
  Central wagon-drop *167*
Leicester, engine shed 160
  London Road 67
Leigh-on-Sea, conversion of station
  220
Leith, Central 42
Lewes 63, 87
Lincoln, Neb., USA, conversion of
  station 226
Little Walsingham, conversion of
  station 220
Litchfield (Hants) 114
Little Weighton 114
Liverpool, Adelphi Hotel 8, 137;
  138
  Albert Dock 10
  Bank Hall, engine shed 173
  Central 44
  Cressington 199; *203*
  Edge Hill 44, 199; *203*
  Edge Hill, engine shed 173
  Lime Street 44
  Lime Street Hotel 44; *132*
  Mersey Road *203*
  Speke Junction, engine shed 173
Liverpool and Manchester Railway
  44
Livock, J. W. 6, 8, 58, 120
Llanbradach Viaduct 145
Lochearnhead Viaduct 144
Locke, Joseph 35, 140, 181
Loddiswell, conversion of station
  209
Lodge Hill 114
London, Arnos Grove (London
  Transport) 100
  Battersea Park 116; *116*
  Battersea Park, engine shed 167
  Blackfriars 26
  Blackfriars, bridge *12*
  Bow, locomotive works 171
  Broad Street 26
  Camden, engine shed 10, 160,

161, 174, 217
Cannon Street 28; *28*
Cannon Street, City Terminus
 Hotel 28, 133
Charing Cross 28, 34, 197
Charing Cross Hotel 8, 34, 132;
 131
Clapham Junction 26
Cricklewood, engine shed 162
Crystal Palace 87; *85*
Denmark Hill 87
Ealing 75
Euston 12, 25, 26, 120, 192, 197;
 8, 26, 44
Euston, Victoria Hotel 12, 120
Fenchurch Street 28
Greenwich *69*
Highgate 100
Hornsey, engine shed 172, 162
Holborn Viaduct 26
Kentish Town, engine shed 162,
 167
Kew Bridge *156*
King's Cross 30, 197; *28*
King's Cross, Great Northern
 Hotel 127; *127*
Liverpool Street 26, 35, 48; *34*
Liverpool Street, Great Eastern
 Hotel 8, 35
London Bridge 28, 118
London Bridge, Bridge House
 Hotel 118; *119*
Lower Edmonton 105
Marylebone 26, 29
Marylebone, Great Central Hotel
 29
Marylebone, turntable *161*
Nine Elms, engine shed 35, 161
North Woolwich 96, 197
Paddington 30, 35, 38, 48, 197; *31*
Paddington, Great Western Hotel
 30, 127–131; *127, 129*
St Katherine's Dock 10
St Pancras 24, 30, 35, 37, 42, 44,
 48, 197, 198; *31, 200*
St Pancras, Midland Grand Hotel
 8, 25, 35, 120, 133–137
Stewarts Lane, engine shed 161
Tooting 95
Victoria 31
Victoria Grosvenor Hotel 8, 34,
 129; *131*
Waterloo 28, 35, 66; *205*

Westbourne Park, engine shed 162
London and Blackwall Railway 28
London and Birmingham Railway
 26, 44, 119, 120, 179, 185
London, Brighton and South Coast
 Railway 31, 50, 60, 87, 104, 116,
 158, 169, 187
London, Chatham and Dover
 Railway 26, 31, 160, 187
London and Greenwich Railway
 28, 118
London, Midland and Scottish
 Railway 125, 167
London and North-Western
 Railway 26, 60, 87, 104, 120,
 125, 127, 162, 164, 187; *165*
London and Southampton
 Railway 35
London and South-Eastern
 Railway 127
London and South-Western
 Railway 35, 50, 52, 60, 66, 67,
 97, 103, 162, 187
London, Tilbury and Southend
 Railway 94
Long Melford 110
Lostwithiel 79
Louth 80
Lowdham 96
Lowry, L. S. 10
Lune River Viaduct 150
Lutyens, Sir Edwin 138
Lytham Railhead, demolition of
 190

Maidenhead 75
Malden Manor 100
Maldon *210*
Maldon East 80
Maliebaan, Holland, station
 conversion *223*
Malton 84
Malvern Link 72
Manchester, Agecroft, engine shed
 171
 Belle Vue, engine shed 173
 Central 6, 44; *47*
 Edgeley, engine shed 173
 Heaton Mersey, engine shed 173
 Liverpool Road 44
 Midland Hotel 137; *137*
 Patricroft, engine shed 173

 Piccadilly 44
 South Junction Viaduct 143
 Victoria 44
Manchester, Sheffield and
 Lincolnshire Railway 112
Mansfield, engine shed 174
Maple, Sir Blundell 30
March 76
Market Harborough 87; *85*
Market Weighton *81*
Marlesford 107
Matlock Bath 87; *98*
Melksham 78
Melton 107
Menai Straits Bridge 11; *98*
Micheldever 51, 101
Middlesborough 24, 65; *8, 65*
Midland Railway 10, 25, 35, 44,
 60, 67, 87, 95, 96, 105, 110, 133,
 134, 160, 162, 165; *165*
Midland and Great Northern Joint
 Railway 114
Millbrook 95
Miller, James 60
Miller, John 144
Mills 26
Mitcham 88; *89*
Mitchell, Arnold 125
Mocatta, David 6, 8, 46
Monkseaton 63
Monkwearmouth 25, 49, 54, 63,
 217; *49*
Monmouth, Sudbrook pumping
 station, 12, 191
Monsal Dale Viaduct *140*
Moorcraft, R. L. 26
Moore, Thomas 54, 217
Morecambe, Midland Hotel 125,
 138
Morton Road 112
Mortimer 105, 114
Moseley, A. 133
 W. 133
Mostyn 82
Moulton 114

Nailsworth 74; *76*
Neath 190
Needham Market 59, 82
Nevill, Ralph 187
New Bradwell, locomotive works
 176

railway housing 187
Newcastle, Central 24, 40, 48, 50;
40
engine shed 6
High Level Bridge 40, 152
Newcastle and Berwick Railway
93, 95, 114
Newcastle and Carlisle Railway 88
Newcastle and North Shields
Railway 149
New Cross, locomotive works 187
New Holland 117
Newmarket 69
Newport, Ebbw Junction 167
Transporter Bridge *156*
Newton Abbot, locomotive works
169, 184
Normanton 38
railway cottages *179, 181*
Norris, R. S. 181
Northampton, Bridge Street 58
North British Railway 41, 94
North-Eastern Railway 38, 43, 63,
112, 114, 126, 165
North London Railway 26
North Midland Railway 57, 96,
121
North Staffordshire Railway 57,
96, 115, 127, 177
North Tawton 100
Norton, John 133
Nottingham, engine shed 173
Midland 30, 67; *67*

Oakamoor 96
Oban *85*
Oberlin, Ohio, USA, conversion
of station *223*
Old Oak Common, engine shed
162
Oswestry, locomotive works 169
Oulton Broad South 107
Oundle *192*
Ouseburn Viaduct 149, 150
Overseal, engine shed *169*
Oxford 68, 70

Pampisford 108
Paris, Gare d'Orsay 222
Paxton, Sir Joseph 6, 60
Peachey 24, 38, 124

Pearson, J. L. 72
Pennine Tunnel 11
Penson 60
Pen-y-Groes 89
Perth 60
Peterborough 58, 59, 69
locomotive works 176
Petworth 104, 105; *103*
Pittsburgh, Pa., USA, development
of station 226; *224*
Plockton 104
Plymouth 52
Duke of Cornwall Hotel 122,
133; *122*
Pocklington 84
conversion of station 219; *220*
Pontdolgoch 95
Portsmouth 50, 52, 60
Harbour 62
Port Sunlight 116
Postland 112
Preston Park Hotel 125; *125*
Preston and Wyre Railway 121
Pritchett, J. P. 127
Privett 98, 209
Prosser, Thomas 38, 40
Pugin, A. W. N. 72

Radipole 93
Radlett 112
Radstock 105
engine shed 174
Rannoch 94
Reading 54
Great Western Hotel 54
Redhill, engine shed 162
Ribbleshead Viaduct 144
Richardsonian Union Station,
Indiana, USA, conversion of
224
Richmond (Yorks) 74, 206; *217*
Ridgemont 95
Riding Mill 88
Rippingdale 112
Ritz, César 137
Roberts, Henry 28
Ross-on-Wye 210
Rothley 94; *12*
Roxburgh and Melrose *23*
Roydon 106
Rugby 30
engine shed 162, 165

locomotive works 176
Runcorn-Widnes Viaduct 145
Rushton 96
Rye *82*

Saddleworth Viaduct 11; *14*
Salisbury 51, 67
engine shed 162
Saltash, Royal Albert Bridge 11,
152; *155*
Saltburn-by-the-Sea 87
Saltburn, Zetland Hotel 124
Saltney, locomotive works 184
Salvin, Anthony 66
Sandling 98
Sandon 96, 106, 115; *112*
Saughall 98
Scarborough, train shed 84
Scott, Sir George Gilbert 6, 35, 72,
122, 133, 185
Scott, J. R. 36
Seddon, J. P. 122
Seghill 94
Severn Beach 106
Shanklin 87
Sharpness, Severn Bridge 156
Shaw, R. N. 125
Shenton 103
Shrewsbury 50, 60; *59*
Sidmouth, engine shed 174
Silverdale 114
Skipton, engine shed 174
Slough 66; *67*
Royal Hotel 121
Smirke, Sir Robert 118
Smith, George 28
Soane, Sir John 46, 50
Somerleyton 115
Somerset and Dorset Railway 65,
169
Southall, engine shed 162
Southampton 50, 97, 209; *50*
South-Western Hotel 133
South Cave 114
South-Eastern Railway 28, 34, 120,
132, 187
South-Eastern and Chatham
Railway 34, 104
South Elmsall 116
Southern Railway 100
Southport, engine shed 174
Southsea 60

Sowerby Bridge, Calder Valley
　　Viaduct 11
Spooner Row 95
Stafford, engine shed 173
Stamford, East 81; *75*
　Town 74
Stamford Bridge (Yorks) 114
Stamford and Essendine Railway
　81
Standedge Tunnel 54
Starston 107
St Botolphs *194*
Stephenson, George 6, 44
　Robert 6, 10, 11, 26, 40, 57, 140,
　217
St Germains Viaduct 149
St Helens, Sutton Oak engine shed
　173
Stirling 60
St Neots 21
Stockport Viaduct 10, 140
Stockton 63
Stockton and Darlington Railway
　122
Stoke (Suffolk) 109
Stoke-on-Trent 25, 50, 57, 58, 66;
　56
　engine shed *160*
　North Stafford Hotel 7, 58, 127;
　177
　Winton Square 7, 177; *177*
Stone *78*
Stowmarket 59, 82
Stratford East, London *17*
Stratford-on-Avon *167*
Strawberry Hill 101
Street, G. E. 72
Sturmer 109
Sudbrook, engine shed *192*
Sunderland 50, 65
Swanage, engine shed 174
Swindon 12, 54
　development as a railway town
　182–185
　locomotive works 10, 171, 176,
　179
Swineshead 112
Szlumper, A. W. 36

Taffs Well Viaduct 145
Takeley 108
Tamar Bridge 30

Taplow 195
Taunton 54
Tay Bridge 152
Taynuilt 117
Tenby 87
Thompson, Francis 6, 48, 57, 69,
　82, 97, 98, 107
Thorverton 208
Thurgarton 96; *96*
Thurston 96; *96*
Tintern, conversion of station 216
Tisbury 103
Tite, Sir William 6, 35, 44, 49, 50,
　52, 57, 60, 66, 67, 72, 97, 209
Toddington *23*
Tonbridge 70
Toyle, William 137–138
Tress, William 72
Treviddo Viaduct 149; *144*
Trubshaw, Charles 6, 137
Turner, Richard 44
Tweedmouth *78*
Tynemouth 63, 66; *63, 65*

Union Railway 143

Vignoles, Charles 149

Wallen, William 127
Wanborough 103
Warkworth 209
Warrington, engine shed 173
Washington DC., USA,
　development of Union Station
　226
Waterbeach 82
Wateringbury 82
Watkin, Sir Edward 29
Waveney Valley Railway 107
Waverton 115
Weeley 107
Wellington, engine shed *169*
Wellow (Somerset) 105
Welsh Coast Railway 122
Welshpool 87
Welwyn Garden City, viaduct 143
Wemyss Bay 87
West Auckland 94
West Berlin, Knollendorfplatz 223
West End of London and Crystal

Palace Railway 31
West Highland Railway 144, 145
Westhouses, engine shed 162
West Jesmond 98
Whitby Town 84
Whitley Bay 63, 87; *82*
Whittlesea 82
Wickham *200*
Wigan, Springs Branch engine
　shed 172
Willington Viaduct 149
Wilson, Edward 35
　John 35
Wiltshire, Somerset and
　Weymouth Railway 79
Winchelsea, conversion of station
　199–200
Winchester 51
Windermere 71
Windsor, Riverside 52; *52*
Wingfield (Derbys) 98
Wissey Viaduct 150
Wivenhoe 107
Woburn Sands 95
Wolfe Barry, J. 26
Wolferton 115
Wolverhampton, locomotive
　works 169
Wolverton 12, 120
　development as railway town
　185–187
　railway housing 177; *187, 189*
　locomotive works 179
Wood, Sancton 6
Wood End 93
Woodford Halse, engine shed 175
Woodhall Junction 112
Woodhouse 112
Wooler *112*
Wootton Bassett 78
Worcester, locomotive works 169,
　184
Wyatt, Sir Matthew Digby 6, 30,
　37, 184
Wylam 88
Wylde Green 104

York 24, 38, 48, 63, 84; *26*
　engine shed 6, 162, 165, 174
　locomotive works 179
York and North Midland Railway
　38